W9-ARG-007

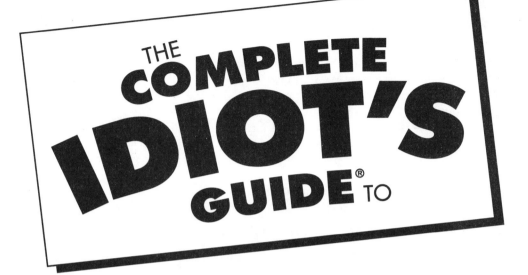

THE COMPLETE IDIOT'S GUIDE® TO

Online Investing

by Douglas Gerlach

que®

A Division of Macmillan Computer Publishing
201 W. 103rd Street, Indianapolis, IN 46290

Trademarks

Warning and Disclaimer

Executive Editor
Angela Wethington

Development Editor
Todd Unruh

Managing Editor
Thomas F. Hayes

Project Editor
Linda Seifert

Copy Editor
Keith Cline

Indexer
Larry Sweazy

Technical Editor
Bill Bruns

Illustrators
Judd Winick
Kevin Spear

Proofreader
Jeanne Clark

Layout Technician
Steve Geiselman

Contents at a Glance

Contents

Tell Us What You Think!

As the reader of this book, *you* are our most important critic and commentator. We value your opinion and want to know what we're doing right, what we could do better, what areas you'd like to see us publish in, and any other words of wisdom you're willing to pass our way.

As the Executive Editor for the General Desktop Applications team at Macmillan Computer Publishing, I welcome your comments. You can fax, email, or write me directly to let me know what you did or didn't like about this book—as well as what we can do to make our books stronger.

Please note that I cannot help you with technical problems related to the topic of this book, and that due to the high volume of mail I receive, I might not be able to reply to every message.

When you write, please be sure to include this book's title and author as well as your name and phone or fax number. I will carefully review your comments and share them with the author and editors who worked on the book.

Fax: 317-581-4663

Email: internet@mcp.com

Mail: Angela Wethington
          General Desktop Applications
          Macmillan Computer Publishing
          201 West 103rd Street
          Indianapolis, IN 46290 USA

Introduction

Everybody loves technology, right? After all, it's what makes our lives more productive. Technology offers conveniences of all sorts, saving us time and money, whether you're cooking a quick meal in the microwave or calling for roadside car service from your cell phone.

But you can't rely on technology to take the place of good, old-fashioned common sense. With just about any new technology, there's a learning curve that you need to master if you want to make good use of the tools at your fingertips. And there are significant problems that you might face if you get in over your head.

For instance, one newfangled gadget is finding its way into the hands of many adventure-minded people. "Global positioning system" (GPS) units interpret signals from military satellites and tell you exactly where you are on planet Earth. What's more, a GPS unit is small enough to fit into the palm of your hand, and can be accurate to within 100 yards.

Experienced hikers, sailors, backpackers, and other outdoors enthusiasts can readily put a GPS receiver to good use as part of their essential gear, to make sure they always know where they are, no matter how thick the fog may be, or how deep into the wilderness they go. Technology has provided a new tool for navigating the seas and forests (and highways, too!).

One unfortunate side effect of the increasing popularity of GPS systems is what happens when they fall into the hands of inexperienced users—individuals who don't take the time to learn how to use the devices before they venture into the woods. News stories are appearing regularly about "weekend warriors" who venture into the mountains, armed with a GPS device and a cell phone, who end up being the subject of a search and rescue operation. Why? Because the batteries ran out in their GPS, or their cell phone was out of range, or they learned that knowing where they *were* didn't help them know where they should be. In this case, users who didn't understand the technology and its limits ended up in life-threatening situations. Lulled by a false sense of security, these people often push themselves into dangerous circumstances because of their dependence on technology.

Like all technologies, the Internet can either help you to be more productive or present hazards to your financial well being.

Millions of people are getting online and looking for help with starting or building a portfolio. In fact, by the end of 2002, experts expect that a total of 14.4 million accounts will have been established at online brokerages, up from just 3.0 million at the end of 1997.

But just like with those GPS gadgets, if you don't take the time to learn how to use the Internet properly, you could very well end up getting lost. And where your finances are concerned, that could be an expensive proposition.

And that's where this book comes in. With *The Complete Idiot's Guide to Online Investing*, you can learn the basics of using the Web to research stocks and mutual funds. You'll find the sites that can teach you about the various approaches that you can use to build a portfolio. You'll discover online tools that you can use to search for the right funds and stocks for you.

What you won't find in this book is a way that you will "get rich overnight." Even in the fast-paced world of the Internet, the true path to wealth for most people are the slow-and-steady, tried-and-true methods of saving and investing.

How to Use This Book

The Complete Idiot's Guide to Online Investing is organized to help you get off the ground even if you know nothing about computers, the Internet, or investing! Like a great big lasagna, the book has a number of layers that all come together at the end to form a complete (if not delicious!) dish.

Part 1, "Getting Started on the Road to Successful Online Investing," lays out the basics of getting online, from turning on your computer to setting up an account with an Internet Service Provider. It also describes a few of the most important and most basic financial concepts—the knowledge you need before you start buying and selling stocks and mutual funds.

In Part 2, "Investing in Mutual Funds," you'll learn about the ever-popular mutual fund, including all the varieties from which to choose. You'll learn what to look for on a fund company's Web site, and where else you can research a particular fund.

Part 3, "Investing in Stocks," takes you into the world of the stock market. You'll learn that it's not enough to buy a stock just because you have a "hunch" that it might go up in price—you'll need a disciplined approach if you want to make money in the stock market. You'll uncover the best way to put together a balanced and diversified portfolio of stocks, and learn where to turn for advice. You'll also get a peek into the world of the online brokers—how to choose one and how to use one. Finally, you'll get the inside track on ways you can invest without using a broker at all.

Part 4, "Managing a Portfolio," describes how to use online tools to manage the stocks and funds that you own. You'll see how quote servers and portfolio trackers work on the Web, and other ways that you can keep up-to-date with all your holdings.

Part 5, "The Dark Side of the Web," is where you'll get the bad news that investing online isn't all sugar and spice. But you'll also be armed with knowledge that can help you protect your privacy and keep your financial information secure. You'll also get an inside peek at the seedy tactics that are sometimes used online to stir up interest in stocks.

Finally, Part 6 is "Putting It Together." This is where you'll take all the knowledge you've learned in this book and put it to work towards meeting your goals, no matter if you're trying to pay for college or retire a millionaire.

Extras

To pack as much information as possible into *The Complete Idiot's Guide to Online Investing*, you are presented with tips and advice as you read the book. These elements enhance your knowledge, or point out important pitfalls to avoid. Along the way, you'll find the following elements:

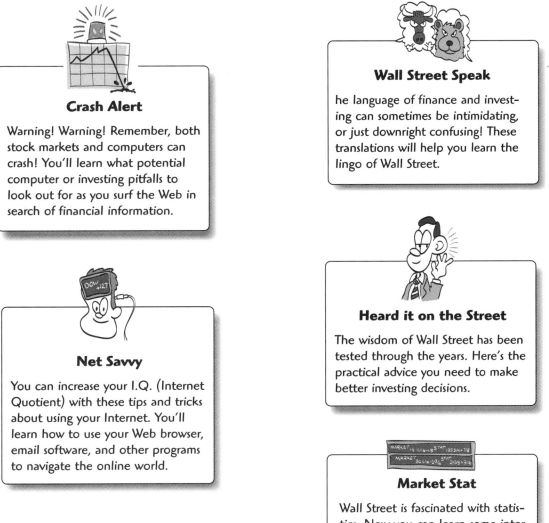

Crash Alert

Warning! Warning! Remember, both stock markets and computers can crash! You'll learn what potential computer or investing pitfalls to look out for as you surf the Web in search of financial information.

Wall Street Speak

he language of finance and investing can sometimes be intimidating, or just downright confusing! These translations will help you learn the lingo of Wall Street.

Net Savvy

You can increase your I.Q. (Internet Quotient) with these tips and tricks about using your Internet. You'll learn how to use your Web browser, email software, and other programs to navigate the online world.

Heard it on the Street

The wisdom of Wall Street has been tested through the years. Here's the practical advice you need to make better investing decisions.

Market Stat

Wall Street is fascinated with statistics. Now you can learn some interesting facts about the stock market and its history, often from a numbers perspective.

Acknowledgements

Along the way, there have been some people who deserve acknowledgement for their assistance and support in the creation of this book (whether they knew it or not!). First of all, thanks to Lewis Schiff and the staff of the Armchair Millionaire, and to the webops and sysops of NAIC Online.

Mary Ann Daszkiewicz could always be counted on for a dose of reality, when required (or even when not!). Special thanks goes to Joe Craig, Herb Barnett, Greg Elin, Don Danko, and Nancy Danko for their optimism and faith. Gary Wiebke was always available to set things straight, too.

Finally, this book is dedicated to Kathleen and Weston, who represent the best returns on investment in the author's own portfolio.

Part 1

Getting Started on the Road to Successful Online Investing

That computer over in the corner is ready to be used for something more than typing letters and playing games. It is your powerful investment tool—your personal research assistant that can bring you the best financial advice and resources that are available. However, it is no substitute for financial discipline and good sense.

Chapter 1

Using Your Computer and the Internet as Investing Tools

In This Chapter

➤ The basics of the Internet

➤ How to get your computer connected to the Net

➤ The advantages of online investing

That fairly substantial piece of hardware on your desk probably cost quite a bit more than the refrigerator or air conditioner or stove or dishwasher or any other major appliance you've got in your home. So it's only natural to wonder whether it's possible to do something useful on your computer, besides using it as an expensive typewriter.

Or perhaps you haven't even taken the plunge yet, and don't even own a computer. Before you make such a big-ticket purchase, you will want to make sure that you're getting the equipment you need to accomplish what you would like to accomplish.

And after you have the right computer, how do you go about getting online? What's the difference between an "online service," "the Web," and "the Internet," anyway?

Turning On, Tuning In, and Dialing Up

Although people often mean the "Internet" when they talk about "going online," they're really two separate things. Any two computers can communicate using telephone lines, as long as they're properly equipped. You could set up your computer to dial up a friend's house and "talk" to the computer on the other end, or send files back and forth. You would be online!

But the online world is more than just two computers talking to each other. Using the same sort of technology, computer systems were set up to enable a lot of users to communicate and share information. Known as "bulletin board systems" (BBSs), these computers acted as a central hub where users could dial up, log on, and communicate with each other. These networks were named after their capability for users to write and respond to messages in a public forum, similar to a cork bulletin board.

BBSs often featured libraries of files that users could "download" (transfer to their own computer from the main computer), and ranged from networks operated out of the basement of the sysop (system operator) to full-scale commercial operations. Although many BBSs were free, others required users to subscribe for a monthly fee. Although you can still find some BBSs around, these mini-networks really hit their heyday in the late 1980s and early 1990s.

Although BBSs were great ways for users to communicate, their reach was pretty much limited by geography—users generally aren't willing to make long-distance calls to connect to a particular BBS. And so another type of online computer service became popular, the "commercial online service." You will probably recognize the names of America Online, CompuServe, and Prodigy, three of the best-known computer networks. These networks were built to offer access to users all across the country—no matter where you were in the country, there was a good chance that you could reach a network with a local or regional phone call.

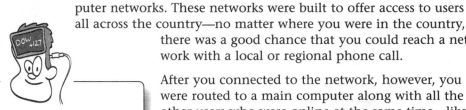

After you connected to the network, however, you were routed to a main computer along with all the other users who were online at the same time—like a giant BBS! On the main computer, you could have your choice of topics that you could discuss, or vast libraries of files that you could download. No matter what your interests, you could find someone online who was also engaged by the same topics. One big disadvantage of the commercial online services was the cost. Users paid by the hour for the privilege of connecting to the network.

Get a Complete History Lesson About the Internet

If you really want to dig into the history of the Internet, check out the various links collected by the Internet Society (http://www.isoc.org/internet/history). The Society is a not-for-profit group that works toward setting standards and guiding future development of the Internet.

"Going online" took on a completely new meaning in the early 1990s, as Internet fever began to sweep the United States. The Internet is truly a phenomenon of the 1990s, although its roots go all the way back to the 1960s. Just how popular is the Internet?

According to Relevant Knowledge, an estimated 57,037,000 people were using the World Wide Web in 1998, up from practically zero in 1993. In fact, the World Wide Web didn't really even exist before 1993!

Nowadays, you can't watch a television commercial, drive by a billboard on the highway, look at a magazine ad, or pay your telephone bill without seeing the addresses of Web sites! But what exactly is the Internet? And is the Internet the same thing as the World Wide Web? It's time for a primer on the Internet and how it works.

The Internet is a global communications network. No one "owns" the Internet, and no single authority governs the entire Internet. In fact, a number of private companies, government agencies, and other organizations all operate pieces of this giant, interconnected network. Standards have been established to make sure all the groups keep speaking the same computer language and to ensure that data can travel anywhere throughout the network.

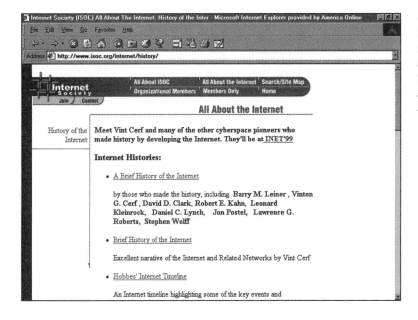

Get the full story behind the creation and development of the Internet directly from the people who created it, here at the Internet Society's Web site.

So who pays for the Internet? The Internet has a main "backbone" maintained by a handful of companies (including some familiar names such as MCI Worldcom and Sprint). These backbone providers sell access to the rest of the Internet via their high-capacity network to other companies, who sell to other companies, who sell to other companies (and so on), until, eventually, a company offers access to individual users. When you want access to the Internet, you will need to arrange it through one of the last companies in this network food chain, called an Internet service provider (ISP).

When you want to get on the Web, you will tell your computer to dial up and connect to your ISP's computer, using a small dialer program. After you're connected, however, your ISP's computer isn't your final destination. Your ISP is really just your gateway to thousands of other computers, all over the world, attached to the Internet.

Where does the World Wide Web fit into the Internet? The Web is actually nothing more than a way to send information across the global network of the Internet. In Internet-speak, the Web is a "protocol," just one of many ways that information can be delivered on the Net. If you have ever seen a Web site address, you've probably noticed that it begins with the letters *http*. This is an abbreviation for Hypertext Transfer Protocol, the exact name of the protocol for delivery of Web pages. Other protocols include email, for instance, and the File Transfer Protocol (FTP). The http protocol governs how text and images are sent from a Web *server*. This is a computer connected to the Internet that is devoted to delivering (or "serving") the pages of a particular Web site. These days, users think of the World Wide Web as being synonymous with the Internet, but they're not really the same.

Getting Online in Four Easy Steps

Although all this sounds complicated, you can get online in just four easy steps! And several of these steps couldn't be any easier. After you have taken care of these prerequisites, you can begin to explore the online world.

1. **Get a telephone.** You probably already have a phone that you can use to connect to the Internet, so this step is a cinch!

Call Waiting Can Disrupt Your Online Sessions!

If you have call waiting service on your telephone line, you will need to disable it before you call your online service provider. Otherwise, an incoming phone call will knock you off the line! To temporarily turn off call waiting, have your Internet dialer program dial "*70" (without the quotation marks) before the phone number of your online service provider.

If a regular telephone connection isn't fast enough for you, your phone company might offer a special telephone line called Integrated Services Digital Network (ISDN)—for a price, of course. An ISDN line can be many times faster than a regular connection, but can also carry hefty per-minute usage charges and requires some special equipment.

Another new technology called Asymmetric Digital Subscriber Line (ADSL) is also available from some telephone companies. ADSL works using your existing telephone lines, so you don't have to rewire your home!

For absolute beginners, WebTV is an option that can get you up and running in no time—without a computer! You will need to spend $150 or so on a WebTV console, which will plug into your telephone at one end and your television at the other. After you sign up for a monthly account ($25), you can surf the Web just by pointing a remote control at your TV! You can buy the WebTV equipment at just about any electronics store.

Although the telephone will probably be your conduit to the network of the Internet, other new technologies just arriving on the scene promise to be faster ways of connecting to the Net. New cable modems can provide a super-fast connection to the Internet, and satellite and wireless systems are also becoming available in some parts of the United States. These are reliable alternatives to telephone-based connections.

You Can't Use the Phone Line in Your Office to Connect to Your Computer

The snazzy telephone system you use at work is likely to be part of a digital network and incompatible with the hardware in your computer when it comes time to connect to an online service. In fact, you risk damaging your computer if you try to plug a phone line into this kind of phone system. You will have to ask your boss to have a special line installed that will let you connect to the outside world (just make sure you have a compelling business reason before you ask!).

2. **Get a computer.** This is another pretty easy step, right? At least if you already have a computer, that is! If you don't have a personal computer, you will probably be shopping for one, at least if you want to be a regular Internet visitor.

So what kind of computer should you look for? Basically, any new computer you purchase today comes with a pretty standard array of components that is sufficient to get you online, and many even include the software you will need to get connected.

When you shop for a new computer, you should follow this rule of thumb: Either buy the biggest, most powerful computer you can afford, or buy the absolute cheapest computer that will accomplish the tasks you want to accomplish. The rationale is that a well-equipped, state-of-the-art machine will last longer before it becomes obsolete, giving you years of service. The el cheapo version, on the other hand, will quickly become outdated; but what the heck, you didn't pay very much for it, and you can buy another!

When you shop for a computer, remember this: the bigger and faster, the better. The faster your computer's processor speed, the faster your computer will work. Having a lot of RAM can also help your computer work faster and let you do more tasks at the same time. While 14-inch and 15-inch monitors are standard, a 17-inch monitor might be easier on your eyes (if you find your eyesight isn't what it used to be).

3. **Get a modem.** A modem is a piece of equipment that translates the digital signals of your computer into analog signals that can be sent across a telephone line. At the other end of the line, a modem converts the signals back to digital so that the computer at that end can interpret them. The word *modem* actually comes from the description of how the equipment "modulates" the signal from one format to another; "modem" is a lot easier to say than "modulator/demodulator!"

A Noisy Telephone Line Can Cause Big Headaches

If you live in an older home or an older neighborhood, your phone lines might sound like someone's crumpling up cellophane on the other end of the line. This noise can interfere with the transmission of data when you're online, sometimes knocking you offline altogether. If this is a problem, ask your telephone company to test your phone lines for excessive noise, and see whether they can be repaired.

Nearly all new computers come with a modem, in either an "internal" version that lives inside your computer or an "external" version that connects to your machine via a cable. Modems are available in several speeds, rated by kilobits per second (Kbps). Currently, the most common standards are 28.8Kbps, 33.6Kbps, and 56.6Kbps (also known as 56K). The same rule of thumb applies here as with the rest of your computer setup: the faster, the better!

4. **Find an Internet service provider.** Now that your equipment is set up, there's one more step before you get online—set up an account with an online service provider. Companies that specialize in providing access to the Internet are known as Internet service providers (ISPs). Usually, you can set up an account that will provide you with unlimited access to the Internet for somewhere between $15 and $25 a month.

So, how do you find the right ISP for you? Finding an ISP can be tough if you don't know where to look! If you're already online, you can consult one of the directories of ISPs that are on the Web. The List (`http://thelist.internet.com`) and ISPs.com (`http://www.isps.com`) are two comprehensive databases of providers; just search by your telephone area code to find an ISP near you.

Sometimes Fast Is Too Fast!

Although the latest crop of modems can receive data at 56.6Kbps, current telephone lines can't handle speeds any faster than about 53Kbps. And when you send data from your computer to another, your uploads will be limited to about 33.3Kbps! Still, every bit of speed helps, so go for a 56K modem if you can.

Of course, if you don't have already have an ISP, telling you to search for one on the Web is a bit like asking you to drive to the auto dealer before you own a car! In that case, check for ads in the business section of your local newspaper or listings in the yellow pages, or ask for referrals from friends or at the nearest computer store.

Some national-based ISPs serve customers all across the country. Earthlink, Netcom, Mindspring, AT&T Worldnet, GTE.net, and MCI Worldcom are some of the best-known national and regional ISPs. You might notice a number of telecommunications companies in this list, and your local phone company might also be in the ISP business.

You might also consider one of the commercial online services, such as America Online, Prodigy, CompuServe, or MSN. Besides offering their own proprietary information, these services also provide access for their customers to the complete Internet. These services have local dial-up numbers all over the country, and even all over the world. If you travel outside the country frequently, an account with AOL or CompuServe can let you dial up from your laptop and check your email from thousands of places on the globe!

So after you've found a couple of ISPs in your area, how do you evaluate them? Here are a few things to consider.

Does the ISP have an access number that's a local telephone call for you? You might find an ISP advertising in your area, only to learn that it's a toll call every time you dial up.

Does the ISP offer flat rate monthly pricing for access to Internet? Is there a limit on how many hours you can use in a month?

Does the ISP offer a free trial? Many will let you try out their service for a week or two, or even a month. If they do, take advantage of this opportunity to test them! See whether you have any trouble connecting to their network, or if you constantly get busy signals when you try dialing up. If so, you might want to look elsewhere.

Can You Use Your Older Computer to Get Online?

Sure, you can log on to the Internet with a computer that's five or six years old—but you might not be happy with the lack of speed and other limitations. Unfortunately, as the prices of new computers fall, it might not be feasible to upgrade your computer—you just might be able to buy a new computer, one that's bigger, better, faster, and stronger, for less than the cost of upgrading! Before you use your old machine as a doorstop, you might consider handing it down to the kids or grandkids, or donating it to your local library or other organization.

Remember, you can always change providers if you need to; so don't give out your email address to hundreds of friends, relatives, and adoring fans until you're sure that you will be sticking with that provider!

Your ISP will probably provide you with all the software you need to get online, but here's a short list of what you might expect.

A *dialer* program does just what it sounds like: It dials your ISP and establishes a connection with your computer. Windows 95 and 98 include dialer programs, and that's all you will probably need. You will need a *Web browser*, probably Microsoft Internet Explorer or Netscape Navigator. Both can be freely downloaded from the Web from the Microsoft Web site (`http://www.microsoft.com/ie`) or Netscape site (`http://www.netscape.com/computing/download`).

Search The List's database of Internet service providers by entering your telephone area code. You will find all the companies who provide Net access in your region.

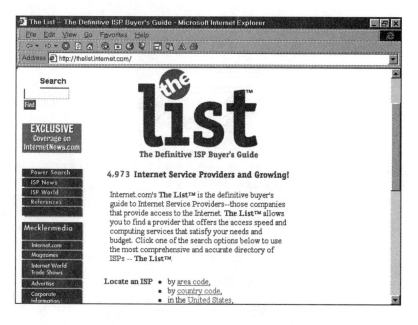

You Can't Beat the Price of Free Online Access!

In many communities across the country, organizations offer free Internet accounts to local citizens. Known as "free-nets," these groups provide an important public service to their communities. You can check a list of free-nets around the world at `http://www.lights.com/freenet`. Also check with your local library, because more and more libraries are providing free Internet access for research purposes. These tend to be popular, so try to schedule your visit at an off-peak hour. Finally, Juno is a national provider of free email services. Juno will give you the software you need to establish a free account with their service. Every time you check your email, however, you will see an advertisement—that's how they're paying for the service! To get your software, call Juno at 800-654-JUNO. (There's a small charge for shipping and handling.)

Internet Explorer and Navigator Aren't the Only Browsers in Town

Although Internet Explorer from Microsoft and Navigator from Netscape Communications are the most popular Web browsers, you do have other options for surfing the Web. A Norwegian firm named Opera Software makes a Web browser (called "Opera") that is small and fast. The installation file is about 1 megabyte in size (compared to more than 10 megabytes for the full packages of the other browsers), and Opera can run well on slower computers (such as older 386 and 486 PCs). In nearly all respects, you will get the same features as you will find in other Web browsers—and some you won't find anywhere but in Opera. You can download the browser to try it out at http://www.operasoftware.com; if you like it, there is a nominal fee to register the program.

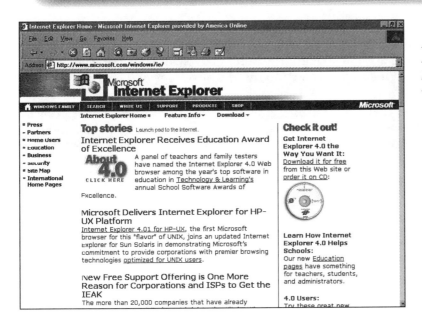

You can download Microsoft's Web browser, Internet Explorer, for free from the Microsoft Web site.

An *email program* is essential, and both Microsoft and Netscape include free email software with their full suite of Internet tools. Eudora is another popular email program, and a free version is available on the Web (http://www.eudora.com). A full-featured version of the program, Eudora Pro, can be purchased if you find yourself using email a lot and might be able to use some of the software's advanced capabilities.

Those are the essentials! You might also occasionally find a use for *FTP* (File Transfer Protocol) software, to upload and download files, or *Telnet* software, to connect directly to a remote computer, so those programs might be included in the software you get from your ISP.

All these new programs can take some time to really master, but the best way to learn them is to practice! Don't forget to make use of the Help file that comes with the program, too (and reading the manual is a good start!). Many developers of online software include their user manuals on their Web sites, so drop by there if you have unanswered questions.

Six Reasons Why Investing Online Is Good—and Good for You

Now that you're online, what about this investing business? One of the primary reasons that individuals are flocking to the Internet is because they want to use the many tools and sites related to personal finance and investing. And it's certainly true, as you will learn throughout this book, that there are some really terrific advantages to online investing. Here are a some advantages of the Internet when it comes to building a portfolio.

➤ **The Internet can save you time.** Before the Web, if you wanted to read the filings a company made with the SEC, you had to call the company and request that they send you a package of information. A couple of weeks later, an envelope would arrive. Today, you can go to the SEC's Web site and get the information in minutes.

➤ **The Internet is very convenient.** It's hard to beat the convenience of downloading a stock report from the Web, compared to driving to the public library to make a photocopy of that same report. And, the Internet never closes, so feel free to do your investment research in your bathrobe!

➤ **The Internet provides access to more information than you could get at your local library.** With tens of millions of pages on the Web, there's no way any library can stack up. And there's more information being published online every day! Much of the information that's online is only available in that medium—you won't find it anywhere else.

➤ **The Internet can save you money.** Brokerage commissions are at an all-time low, something that's made possible only by the low costs to firms of servicing customers on the Internet. It can cost less than $8 in commissions to buy or sell up to 5,000 shares of stock, if you're willing to place your orders online.

➤ **The Internet can offer you access to other investors who share your approach.** There are countless communities of investors on the Web, each one focused on a particular style or method of investing. Without the Web, you might never have the chance to meet and discuss potential investments with people who share your approach to the markets.

➤ **The Internet hosts a growing amount of educational investment resources.** If you don't know how to invest, you can learn from the many tutorials, glossaries, lessons, workshops, and seminars available online. You can learn how to start investing, how build a portfolio, or learn the lingo of Wall Street, all on the Web. And *The Complete Idiot's Guide to Online Investing* will show you how!

The Least You Need to Know

➤ The Internet is a vast network that connects users from all over the world. There are other online services as well, but the Internet and the World Wide Web have become synonymous with "getting online."

➤ All you need to get online is a telephone, computer, modem, and an Internet service provider. You will need to find the right provider for you, but you can often try out a company for a couple of weeks to get some first-hand experience.

➤ After you're online, you can look forward to enjoying the advantages of using the available tools to complete many of the tasks of investing.

Chapter 2

Understanding the Basics of Personal Finance

In This Chapter

➤ Understand that successful investing begins with saving

➤ Why you don't need to feel bad about not sticking to a budget

➤ Learn why it's so important to pay yourself first

➤ Discover the secret of compound returns

Now that you understand a bit about how your computer and the Internet works, you still need a few more lessons before you jump feet-first into the online world. It's time for an overview of some of the most important things you need to know as you begin a lifetime of investing.

You Gotta Learn to Swim Before You Surf

Whenever it comes to money, it's easy to feel intimidated. And with the millions of pages of information related to finance and investing out there on the Web, it's even easier to feel like you're in over your head.

Never fear! Even though you may have been taught to swim by being thrown into the deep end of the pool, most people start out in the shallow end doing the doggie-paddle, and gradually pick up the pace from there. In time, and with practice, you will be using the butterfly stroke or Australian crawl to swim lap after lap.

Before you start investing (and certainly before you start surfing the Web for answers to your financial questions), you need to know a few things about money.

It All Starts with Saving

How would you like to know the true secret to building wealth? The honest-to-goodness, surefire way to create your own million-dollar portfolio? Read carefully to learn how millionaires are made, in just two steps:

1. Spend less than you earn.

2. Invest the rest.

That's it!

Learning to be a good saver is the first part of any solid plan to accumulate wealth, whether you're looking forward to a comfortable retirement, an Ivy League education for your kids, or your dream home. But, finding the extra bit of money to fund your investing plan can be tough—at least until you finish this chapter!

The "B" Word—Budgeting (Yuck!)

Conventional wisdom says that you can find the money to invest just by preparing a household budget. Unfortunately, the mere mention of the word *budgeting* is enough to cause any reasonable person to turn and run in horror! So here's an idea that will throw most professional financial advisors into a frenzy: Forget about the "b" word entirely!

Most of the time, you probably have no trouble finding enough money to pay all your bills without going through the process of micromanaging your spending habits. It's likely you already have a pretty good idea of where your money goes each month—essentials such as rent, mortgage, utilities, auto expenses, and telephone bills; and nonessentials such as double mocha cappuccinos from your local coffee house or a newly remastered double-CD reissue of the hits of Ol' Blue Eyes (okay, well maybe that *is* an essential, but you get the point). You can probably trim plenty of fat from your monthly expenses.

If you aren't quite sure where you stand when it comes to your monthly income and expenses, check out FinanCenter. FinanCenter features a down and dirty calculator to let you figure out how much you're spending (http://www.financenter.com/budget.htm). Select the "How much am I spending?" ClickCalc from this page, and then enter how much you're spending each month on Utilities, Food, Auto Expenses, Entertainment, and so on. Then enter how much you would like to budget for each category, and how much you take home each month after taxes.

Throwing Out Your Budget Doesn't Mean You Can Spend Whatever You Like!

You don't need a degree in economics to understand this scientific concept: The amount of money you can spend each month is determined by the supply of money that you have access to, either money in the bank or money in your wallet. If you spend more than you have, month after month, you will be headed for just one place: bankruptcy court!

FinanCenter's spending calculator can tell you how much you're spending, how much you should be spending, and how much you can have saved in 10 years.

The calculator will add up all your expenses, your budgeted expenses, and your income, and then tell you how much you should have left over. Unfortunately, many people just can't find a way to actually end a month with anything left for their investing plan. But, there is a way to raise this money that you will need for investing.

Pay Yourself First—You're Worth It!

Who's the most important person to your financial plan? You are! So instead of trying to budget all the fun out of your life and *hoping* to end up with enough at the end of the month to put into a saving plan, tackle the problem from the other direction: Pay yourself first! Each month, before you pay the rest of your bills, write the first check to yourself and deposit it into a special account, either at a bank or brokerage firm or mutual fund company.

By putting your financial plan at the top of the priority list, you will never again give yourself the short end of the stick when it comes time to pay bills. And somehow, you will probably be able to find the money to meet the rest of your obligations each month.

So how much should you put away each month in a saving and investing plan? A good goal to shoot for is to save 10% of your paycheck, after all taxes and other deductions. If that sounds way too excessive for you, start with 5%. When you get your annual raise, increase the percentage a bit more. When you get a little extra cash from a freelance job or bonus, add that to the pot. Keep working toward your goal of setting aside 10% of your paycheck on a regular basis, and pretty soon you will be saving with the best of them!

What would you have to give up to be able to pay yourself 10% each month? The Armchair Millionaire features a fun calculator that will clue you in on just how easy it is to pay yourself first (http://www.armchairmillionaire.com/fivesteps/ step_2app.html). Just enter your monthly take-home pay, and the program will list a few ways you can keep that cash in your pocket. If your monthly paychecks totaled $1,000 after taxes, for instance, here's what you'd have to give up to save $100 a month:

$ 7.00	2 video rentals
$30.00	2 music CDs
$12.00	1 large pizza with the works, delivered
$ 3.00	1 fast food burger with fries
$ 3.00	1 pint of ice cream, the good stuff
$25.00	1 latest best-selling novel (hardcover)
$ 6.00	2 beers (at a bar)
$ 3.00	1 bag of Oreos
$ 4.00	2 muffins
$ 4.00	1 chips and dip
$ .50	1 candy bar
$ 2.00	1 cappuccino
$99.50	Total

```
Armchair Millionaire : Five Steps to Financial Freedom: Pay Yourself First: Test - Microsoft Internet E...
File  Edit  View  Go  Favorites  Help
Address  http://www.armchairmillionaire.com/cgi-bin/tabulator.cgi
```

armchair millionaire
Common Sense
Saving and Investing

The Five Steps to
Financial Freedom

aim Communities
● Getting Started
● Savvy Investing
● Fund-amentals
Register free @
Community HQ

Investor Center
with CharlesSchwab
Go to Investor
Center
What's Your Net
Worth?
Ask the Expert

aim Member Svcs

The Five Steps to Financial Freedom
What would you have to give up to "Pay Yourself First?"

5 Steps RELATED LINKS

10% of your monthly earnings is $100.00

```
$50.00   1 Newest shoot 'em up computer game(s) on CD-ROM
$36.00   3 Large pizza(s) with the works, delivered
$1.50    1 Espresso(s)
$4.00    2 Cappuccino(s)
$.75     1 Cup(s) of joe or tea
$3.00    1 Bag(s) of Oreos
$1.00    1 Chocolate chip cookie(s) from local bakery
$1.00    1 Beer(s) (at home)
$2.50    1 1 hour of AOL
--------
$99.75   Total
```

EMAIL THIS PAGE TO A FRIEND

The Armchair Millionaire can show you how easy it can be to pay yourself first with their simple calculator.

When you really start to look at where your money goes each month, and when you realize how far your money could go if it were invested for 25 or 30 years, you can be inspired to change your behavior.

Still, when it comes to writing that check each month, many people fall flat on their faces. Don't worry, there's another, even easier way to fund your savings plan. Nearly every financial institution offers a plan where they will electronically transfer money from an account at another firm at a specific date each month.

These automatic plans may be called "automated transfer programs," "moneylinks," or "automatic investment plans," but the concept is the same. You will have to fill out some forms (usually the company that's receiving the money will provide these) and specify the amount you would like to have transferred. Then all you have to do is remember to add the transaction to your checkbook register each month! Now, your "pay-yourself-first" plan will be taken care of each month!

Automatic Investing Plans Have Another Advantage

If you set up an automatic investing plan with a brokerage firm or mutual fund, you can often get around the minimum investment they might otherwise require all at once to open an account. By committing a certain amount of money to be invested each month, at least until you've reached the minimum account size, you will be paying yourself, without the need to come up with a minor fortune just to open an account.

Do You Appreciate Compound Interest?

After you've found the money to start your investing plan, you can proceed to step #2 of the secret of building wealth: putting the money to work! The key to success whenever you're saving and investing to meet any goal is to allow enough time for your money to *really* work for you. Time is the fundamental ingredient in the plan—without time, your money just can't work at its maximum potential for your benefit.

Why is time so essential? Because of the power of *compound interest*, referred to by some as the "eighth wonder of the world." The power of compound interest can cause your money to multiply to amounts that you might have thought impossible. Here's how it works.

Let's say you deposit $100 in a bank, and are able to earn 5% in interest a year. At the end of the year, you have $105 in the bank (5% of $100 is $5). Now, if you leave that $105 in the bank, how much will you have at the end of the second year, assuming you still earn 5% a year in interest? You will have $110.25. 5% of your original $100 is still $5, but the $5 you earned last year and left in the bank also earned you interest of $0.25, for a total of $110.25. This is compound interest, when you earn interest on your interest! Maybe this short example doesn't sound like much, but let's consider another story in which we let time work its magic. Two twins, Nelson and Nellie, are 18 years old. Nellie decides to start her saving and investing plan at this young age, so she invests $2,000 a year for the next four years. At the age of 21, she has invested $8,000.

Nelson is a bit slower when it comes to financial matters, so he doesn't invest anything until he's 30 years old. Then he puts away $2,000 a year, and keeps going until he's on the brink of retirement at age 64. Nelson is proud to have put $70,000 into his brokerage account.

Over the years, both Nelson and Nellie are able to earn an annual return of about 10% in their portfolios, the long-term average of the stock market (as you will learn later).

At age 65, Nelson smugly turns to Nellie and chastises her for neglecting her investments all those years. Nelson's account balance is $596,254, and he's feeling pretty good about it.

But Nellie produces her account statement, and Nelson's jaw drops. Her account is worth more than Nelson's—her original $8,000 has grown to a total of $615,000.

There's only one way to explain the difference in Nelson and Nellie's investing plans, and that's the power of compound returns. Nellie's account grew and grew, not necessarily because of her investing acumen. And it wasn't because she continued to put money in her account, either, but because she didn't take any money *out*! She left all the interest and profits she earned in her account, and that interest and those profits earned even more interest and profits, to the point where the biggest part of her portfolio by far comes from the compounding of returns.

Imagine where Nellie would be at age 65 if she had continued to invest $2,000 a year after age 21!

Time is your ally. Don't be a prisoner of time. Let it work for you and help you reach your financial goals. That means just one thing: start saving and investing *today*!

Setting Goals and Meeting Them

You've probably got a lot of dreams. We all do. You want things from life, whether it's your dream house or a worry-free retirement or a luxurious sailboat. So how are you going to make those dreams become reality? You're going to stretch to fulfill your desires with a saving and investing plan.

Articulating your goals is only part of what you will need to do in order to meet your objectives.

You also need to separate your long-term goals from your short-term goals. The reason for this is simple: If you expect to be paying for college in three or four years for that future doctor you've been raising, you don't want to invest your money in something that carries a lot of risk. If your investment didn't work out, you would be stuck without enough money to pay the bills!

On the other hand, if you have 25 years until you expect to retire, you might be able to maximize the returns on your investment if you don't need to worry so much about short-term changes (as long as you know that in the end you have a good chance of ending up with a solid portfolio.)

These two investors have vastly different goals, so they're likely to end up with two very different saving and investing plans to meet their objectives mainly due to their different time frames.

Overall, the Stock Market Goes in One Direction—Up!

Since 1928, the stock market (as represented by the Standard & Poor's 500 Index, a collection of the best-known companies from all industries) increased in 52 calendar years and declined in 20 years. However, the ups were much, much bigger than the downs. In 41 of those years, the market grew by more than 10%, but the market fell by 10% or more in only eight of the down years.

But how do you define "short-term" and "long-term?" Well, experts generally agree that five years is the dividing line. If you have a need for money in less than five years, you have a short-term goal. If you don't need the money for more than five years, you've got a long-term goal.

There are big differences between short-term and long-term goals and how you meet them. Remember the story about Nellie and her not-so-bright twin brother Nelson? If you have a long-term goal, the power of compounding plays a major role in helping you meet your objectives. If you have a short-term goal, however, the only way you will be able to build up your bank or brokerage account is by putting money into the account on a regular basis. Your contributions will be the most important part of your plan.

If you have long-term goals, you should probably be investing in the stock market. Over the long-term, the stock market has returned about 11% a year to investors. But over the short-term, the stock market fluctuates—and fluctuates a lot. In a single year, it's not unusual for stocks to decline 25%! This kind of unpredictable decline could wreak havoc on your financial plan, leaving you short by quite a few dollars just when you need the money the most.

Building Your Plan

Later in this book, you will learn how to put together a plan on the Internet that fits your personal situation. You will learn how to balance risk and return, and discover which investments are likely to be best for your own goals. And whether you're planning for retirement, or college, or some other aim, you can find the tools on the Internet to help you reach all your goals.

The Least You Need to Know

➤ No matter how rich or poor you are, the key to building your nest egg is learning to save regularly. Pay yourself first each month, and your savings will quickly begin to grow.

➤ It doesn't take much to begin your saving and investing plan, but every day you delay starting is one day less that your money could be working for you. The principle of "compound returns" is the key to building wealth, so let time work on your side and not against you.

➤ You need to separate your long–term and your short–term goals, and create a plan to help you achieve both. Different types of investments are appropriate for each goal, so make sure you're investing in the right place.

Chapter 3

"Debt Is Saving in Reverse"

In This Chapter

➤ Learn why it's so important to save, not spend

➤ Build a plan online to reduce your debt

➤ Get help from the pros if you need it

The legendary fund manager and author Peter Lynch once wrote that "debt is saving in reverse." This is an apt description of what happens when your debts pile up. Not only are the interest payments likely to drain your wallet faster than just about any force known to physical science, but you're severely crimping your ability to save. And the one thing you need *before* you invest is the money *to* invest!

It's time to get your debt load under control. You can start today by visiting some of the Web sites that offer tools and resources to help you get back on track.

They Don't Call It "Debt Burden" for Nothing

Yep, the phrase "debt burden" is really appropriate. It doesn't matter whether it's a car loan, mortgage, student loan, home equity loan, installment loan, or credit card debts—the interest you have to pay for the privilege of borrowing money can vary from 5% to 20%, and sometimes even more.

The Difference Between Interest and Principal

Interest is any payment you make for the use of borrowed money. *Principal* is the money you actually borrowed from a lender. Any debt payment you make is made up of interest, principal, or a combination of the two.

Sure, some of this debt might be unavoidable (or so you are convinced), but consider this: If you carry an unpaid balance on your credit card with an interest rate of 18%, paying off that debt is the same thing as getting a guaranteed effective 18% return on your investment. There's no other place on earth where you can get a guaranteed rate of return of 18% on an investment!

Here's an example. If your credit card carries an interest rate of 18%, and you have a $5,000 balance, it will take you five years to pay off the balance if you make monthly payments of $128 (a little bit more than the 2% minimum monthly payment required by most cards). Of course, you can't make any more charges on the card, either!

In those five years, you will have paid a total of $2,635 in interest! With that kind of return, it's no wonder the credit card companies are stuffing your mailbox with offers of pre-approved credit cards.

Not All Debt Is Evil

Of course, no one is saying that all debt is bad for you. A student loan with an interest rate of 6% might be a pretty good deal. And if you can get a better rate of return from a savings or investment account, say 9% or 10%, it might not make sense to pay off that loan early with other funds. You will get a better overall rate of return by making regular monthly payments on the loan and saving or investing the rest.

To put your savings plan in forward gear, you need to do three things:

1. Get your spending in check.
2. Start your saving and investing plan.
3. Reduce the amount you're paying in interest on existing debts.

For help, you need turn no further than the sites and tools described in the following sections.

Spend Not, Save Lot

Sometimes the best way to tackle your debt is to figure out how you got so deep in the hole in the first place—and then figure out how to modify your behavior so that you can avoid falling back in.

The Truth About "Frugal Living"

Although it may not seem very polite to refer to a person as a "cheapskate" or a "spendthrift," a lot of people embrace these descriptions! It's all part of a movement that some call "frugal living." It's not about being cheap, but about living well *and* living within your means. One important advantage of eliminating wasteful habits and reducing your spending is that you increase the amount you're saving and investing.

For many people, this means adjusting their lifestyle to enable them to live within their means. The idea is simple—don't spend more than you make! Putting it into practice can be a little more challenging. The folks at Cheapskate Monthly (http://www.cheapskatemonthly.com) are ready to help. Hosted by author Mary Hunt, this site is a companion to her monthly print newsletter.

Learn tricks and tips to make every dollar last longer at the Cheapskate Monthly.

Although much of the site is accessible by members only (for a modest annual fee), you will find a lot of free tools and tips to explore on the site. Check out the preview issue, for instance, or the interactive tools and calculators in the "Activity Center."

How Can You Start a Saving and Investing Plan When You Have All That Debt Hanging Over Your Head?

One of the biggest myths about investing is that you have to have a lot of money to get started. It's just not true! In fact, you can start with just $10 or $25 a month. Even if you are mired in debt, why not start your saving plan somewhere, even if you just put away a few dollars a month on a regular basis. At the same time, continue to pay off your debts. You will reap the rewards as you begin to see your savings grow and realize just how terrible it is to let yourself fall back into the debt quagmire.

If you get the idea into your head that it's far better to save than to spend, maybe you will think twice the next time that you pull out your credit card! By cutting your monthly expenses, you will have more to contribute to paying down your existing debt and to fund your long-term savings plan.

Online Debt Reduction Calculators and Planners

After you've made up your to eliminate your bad spending habits, you need to make a plan of attack to pare down the debt you've already rung up. Your first stop on the Web should be Quicken.com's Debt Reduction Planner (http://www.quicken.com/saving/debt). This calculator will help you to tally up your existing debts, and then create a strategy to help you pay off your debts.

Before you begin using the planner, gather up all your credit card statements and other paperwork related to all your debts. Then enter all your current debts in the program. This includes credit cards, mortgages, auto loans, home equity loans, personal loans, and any other debts you might have. You will need to enter the interest rate, current balance, and payment details in the program, clicking the **Save** button after each item. Then click the **Next** button to go on to the next screen.

QFN Debt Reduction Planner – Netscape

Quicken .com
Debt Reduction Planner

SOFTWARE
business intelligence by **transi•m**

Introduction

Debts

Debts
Enter information about your debts here. When you're done, click Next.

		Your debts
Lender	MasterCard	Visa
Type of loan	Credit Card	Optima
inual percentage rate	16.5%	MasterCard
Current balance	4895.00	First Bank
Typical monthly pmt	800.00	Bank & Trust
Minimum monthly pmt	110.00	

Summary

Payment

Savings

Expenses

Results

Action plan

Next steps

Restore   Save

Delete   New

Exit

Next ▶

Add up all your debts using Quicken.com's Debt Reduction Planner, and build a step-by-step plan to eliminate them.

The Debt Reduction Planner then calculates how long it will take you before you are 100% debt free. Don't get too depressed, however, because the Planner has a few tips for you. Click **Next** to go on to the next page.

The planner walks you through strategies that can save you money and reduce your debt faster. It shows you how much you will save by paying off high-interest credit cards first, by using some of your savings to pay down debts, and by reducing your monthly expenses. As you enter the amount of cash you can direct toward reducing your debt, the Planner recalculates your savings and the time required.

Americans Love to Charge!

As of August 1998, Americans had racked up $545.9 billion on their credit cards, a 4.8% increase over the figure a year earlier.

Source: Federal Reserve Board

Finally, the Planner shows you a "before" and "after" chart, illustrating how the plan you've just created can save you money. You also get an "Action Plan" that details how much to pay each month to each of your obligations for the next year.

31

Quicken.com's Debt Reduction Planner demonstrates how quickly your action plan can get you completely out of debt.

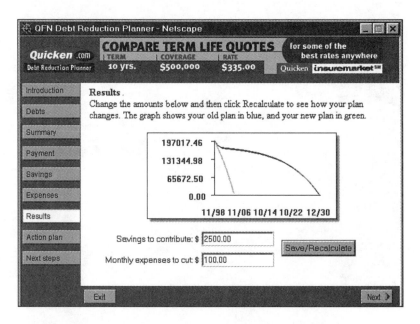

Finding Great Credit Card Rates on the Web

Another strategy that can help you better manage your debts is to switch to a credit card with a lower interest rate. Let's go back to that $5,000 you're carrying on the credit card. At 18%, your $128 monthly payment will cost you $2,635 in interest over five years. If you switch to a card that pays 14%, you will only pay $1,980 in interest (a savings of $655), and you will finish paying off your debt seven months earlier!

If you've got high-interest-rate credit cards, maybe it's time to switch to a card with a lower rate. Bank Rate Monitor (http://www.bankrate.com) offers a free credit card search engine that lets you zero in on the best credit card deals.

Excessive Credit Card Switching Can Be Hazardous to Your Credit History

Although switching to a lower-cost credit card can save you money in the long term, you shouldn't switch too frequently. Credit card companies don't necessarily like to see customers who continually open and close accounts, so you could be denied for a new card on this basis, even though the rest of your credit report is sound.

To search for a low-rate card, click on the "Credit Cards" section of its site, and then select your state (not all cards are offered in all states) under the heading "Find the best rate for you."

Now you can customize the search to display only those cards that meet your objectives. You can search for cards with no annual fees, low annual percentage rate (APR), or the best overall deals. You can also decide whether you want a personal or business card, and whether you need a gold or platinum card, or whether a standard card will do.

Click **Go** and the cards that fit your specifications display, ranked from best to worst. In addition, click the **Details** button to get the full scoop on any card's rates, fees, and information about the issuer.

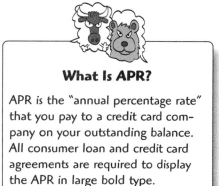

What Is APR?

APR is the "annual percentage rate" that you pay to a credit card company on your outstanding balance. All consumer loan and credit card agreements are required to display the APR in large bold type. Comparing the APR of different credit cards makes it easier to find the best card for you.

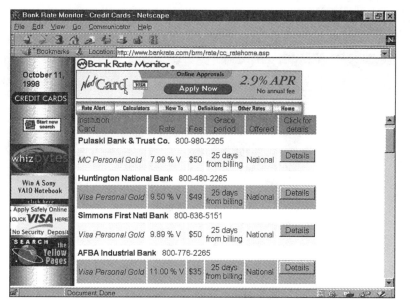

At the Bank Rate Monitor Web site, you can find the credit cards with the lowest fees, the lowest interest rates, and the overall best deals.

After you have your new, lower-interest card, consider transferring debt from your other cards to the new one. Many credit cards allow you to transfer these balances.

If You Need More Help Climbing Out of Debt

If you've added up all your debts, plugged them into an online debt reduction planner, and are still feeling completely overwhelmed, perhaps it's time to get in touch with a pro. Debt Counselors of America (http://www.dca.org) is a not-for-profit

Avoid Cards with Annual Fees if You Pay Your Bills in Full Each Month

If you don't carry a balance each month, look for a credit card with no annual fee. Because you won't be paying any interest on your card balances, the APR isn't as important. Go for a card with no annual fee and a reasonable interest rate instead.

group that has a special program for individuals who are overburdened by debts. Its service could help you avoid more drastic actions such as bankruptcy.

When you visit the DCA Web site, click on the link to its "One-Pay" service to learn more about the plan. When you enroll, DCA works with your creditors to help to stop collection calls and organize your debts into one manageable monthly payment. Often, they can get the interest rates you pay significantly reduced or eliminated, as well.

The Debt Counselors of America Web site should be your first stop if you're feeling overwhelmed by your debt load.

If you enroll in the DCA's program, you will have access to your account information on its Web site to see complete information about payments received and individual payments sent to creditors.

The Debt Counselors of America Web site features plenty of materials and publications to help you learn more about ways you can deal with unpleasant experiences like bankruptcy, repossession, and collection agencies.

One Downfall of Working with a Credit Counselor

If you decide to work with a credit-counseling agency such as Debt Counselors of America, some creditors may add a comment to your credit report that indicates you are working with a payment service. This negative factor is certainly not worse than filing for bankruptcy, however.

The Least You Need to Know

➤ Unless you get your debts under control, your saving and investing plan will be impossibly bogged down.

➤ Develop a plan to reduce your debt, and then stick to it. But don't put off starting a plan of regular saving—start setting aside a small amount for your long-term savings even while you whittle away at your debt load.

➤ As a last resort before bankruptcy, consult a credit-counseling agency to help get your financial affairs in order. You can reach out to these groups on the Web, and they can help you develop a strategy to eliminate your debts.

Chapter 4

How the Stock Market Works

In This Chapter

➤ Why companies sell stock

➤ How the stock market works

➤ Stock exchanges and market simulations on the Web

For many years, average Americans just didn't concern themselves with notions of investing in the stock market. Why should they have? For many, a job in a good company was a permanent position. There were no layoffs or downsizing or restructuring to worry about; and after retirement, pensions and Social Security could provide for the family. Others, who might have considered investing on their own, were scared off by their childhood memories of the "Great One," the Great Depression of the 1930s. If they didn't recall the hard times directly, their parents were sure to remind them of the years of suffering and hardship. And because the Great Depression is forever linked to the 1929 stock market crash, all too many individuals turned their backs on "speculating" in the stock markets. Fear drove investors and potential investors from buying stocks.

Investing for Your Future

Today, the specter of job insecurity and of a crippled Social Security system haunts many investors. Pension plans (known as defined benefit plans) are going the way of Cadillacs with fins, in favor of retirement plans that employees themselves must fund (such as 401(k) accounts). And with each passing generation, memories of the Great Depression are fainter, lingering mostly in the history books.

How Bad Was the Stock Market Crash of 1929?

The Dow Jones Industrial Average hit a peak at 386 on September 3, 1929 just weeks before the October 28th crash. And although the crash was bad, the market continued to decline for nearly another three years, reaching a low of 40.56 in July 1932, and a drop of 89% from the September 1929 high. It took another 24 years until the Dow finally returned to the 386 level.

All those changes add up to a nation of investors who are afraid of never being able to retire, yet aren't afraid of the markets. Individuals are taking control of their financial destinies—by turning to the stock market.

Boy, how times have certainly changed. With the changing attitudes of Americans, a whole new industry devoted to those individual investors has arrived. Today you can turn on the television and tune in to any of the number of channels devoted to the financial markets. Thousands and thousands of Web sites are devoted to financial topics. New financial newspapers, magazines, and newsletters seem to appear every week, and subscriptions are soaring. And let's not forget books that aim to help beginners get their feet wet in the stock market (like, for instance, this one).

Unfortunately, too many people are still laboring under the misconception that investing is a complicated subject. Although there are plenty of tricky concepts in the world of corporate finance, the basics of investing can be easily understood by just about anyone with a seventh grade education.

Maybe you don't even need a seventh grade education, either. In his book, *Beating the Street*, Peter Lynch immortalized the seventh grade class at St. Agnes School in a Boston suburb and their teacher, Joan Morrissey. As part of their Social Studies class, the students managed a hypothetical $250,000 portfolio. Although the portfolios were hypothetical, the returns were terrific. From 1990 to 1991, the student portfolios returned 69.6%, trouncing the S&P 500's 26.1% return.

Buy a Bunch of Stocks, and You've Got a Portfolio!

A *portfolio* is any group of investments that you own, or the total of all your investments. You can divide up your holdings into portfolios in whatever way makes sense to you—by thinking of your retirement plans as one portfolio, your college savings investments as another, and your regular brokerage account as your third. Or, you could lump them all together and just call it "My Portfolio."

You can take a moment now to recall what you were doing when you were in seventh grade. Pretty depressing in contrast to the story of Ms. Morrissey's class, huh? But don't worry, even if you weren't lucky enough to learn about investing when you were in junior high school, there's still hope. Just keep reading.

Sometimes people confuse investing with other, more difficult subjects. Take economics (please!). Economics is hard. There's a story about a college graduate who took the opportunity of his 25th class reunion to visit his economics professor. While the two were pleasantly recounting old times, the former student noticed a test on the professor's desk, and, leafing through it, remarked, "I see you're still using the same test you gave us 25 years ago."

"Ahhhh," the economist replied, "the test is the same, but the answers are completely different."

Yes, economics can be a difficult subject to learn. But investing can be mastered by anyone who is willing to spend some time learning how the stock market works. Consider the members of the National Association of Investors Corporation (NAIC), a group devoted to investor education, mainly through investment clubs. NAIC's membership is made up of ordinary people—just like you—who invest in the stock market as members of a club, or in

> ### Investment Clubs Work!
>
> In 1997, 45% of investment clubs surveyed by NAIC outperformed the Standard & Poor's 500 Index. In comparison, only 10% of all mutual funds beat the S&P 500 in the same year.
>
> *Source: National Association of Investors Corporation*

their own portfolios. Few NAIC members are economists, and most know nothing about the market before joining an investment club. (You can learn more about investment clubs and the NAIC in Chapter 6.)

So how do these novices (and former novices) fare in the markets? According to NAIC's annual surveys, more investment clubs than mutual fund managers beat the Standard & Poor's 500 Index. As these investment clubbers have found, it is entirely possible that you can beat the pros of Wall Street at their own game, too.

It comes down to this: Investing isn't rocket science. You can invest successfully. After you believe this, you will be on your way to building a profitable portfolio.

Understanding the Stock Market

When people talk about investing, they usually mean the stock market. You probably can name several stocks without much difficulty: Microsoft, IBM, Coca-Cola, General Electric, and General Motors. These are all publicly traded companies, corporations that have issued stock that investors can buy and sell in the open market.

A *stock* is nothing more than a share of ownership in one of these public companies. So how does the stock market work, and how do investors buy and sell these shares? These are a couple of the questions that you will need answered before you start investing yourself.

Why Do Companies Go Public?

When a company sells shares of stock to investors through a stock market (a process known as *going public*), they're no longer privately owned, and become what's known as a *publicly traded company*. So why does a company like General Electric go public? To answer that question, consider the following: Let's say that you are the manager of a department store, and one day you decide to go into business for yourself and open your own store. It takes money to start such a business, to acquire or lease or rent a building, to stock inventory for your shelves, to hire personnel, to advertise your new business, and to pay the myriad other costs involved with the operation of your business.

Where do you get the money to pay all those expenses? You have a couple of options:

➤ You could use your own savings.

➤ You could borrow from the bank, friends, or family and pay back the loan with interest.

➤ You could sell a stake in the business to a partner who would run the business with you, sharing in any profits (as well as any losses).

These are all sources of capital, and are essentially the same ways that corporations such as McDonald's, Exxon, American Express, and Sears-Roebuck get their hands on money for their operations, but on a much bigger level.

You can get your new business up and running with your own savings and a little from the bank. Business is good, and your new store is popular. In a few years, you can build and operate a few more stores until finally you are sitting on a little retail empire. It's clear you're on to a big new concept in retailing. Now, you're ready to take your chain to a national level. As you look at the costs of building hundreds of stores across the country, however, you are amazed at how much more capital you need.

Although you could go back to the bank and ask for a big, fat loan, you see a couple of problems with that plan. First, banks want a solid business plan; then they want some kind of repayment guarantee and collateral. That is a lot of leverage for a bank, giving them the ability to foreclose on your loan if you fall behind on payments.

A few bad months, and the bank could be knocking on your door with a foreclosure notice. Banks also charge interest—that's how they make their money, after all—but those interest payments could have a serious drain on your cash flow in the crucial expansion stage of your business.

So what do you do? The next step is to turn to people outside your company and ask them to invest in your business. In return for their investment, you will give them a piece of your company. If the company were profitable, they would be eligible to share in those profits with you. They would also have some say in the operation of your business.

Companies Like to Get Their Hands on Other People's Money

Going to the trough is the term sometimes used to describe what companies do when they look for outside financing, whether from venture capital sources or in a public offering.

When it comes time to look for outside investors, you could turn to the private firms and individuals that specialize in helping businesses to grow. These investors provide what's known as *venture capital*, and will put up millions of dollars in return for a stake in the company.

You could also go public. You will offer shares of your company for sale to the general public, in the form of stock that trades on a stock exchange. This sale of stock is your initial public offering, and the proceeds from the sale go into your company's bank account (after you pay the investment bankers who helped manage the offering).

Your new shareholders each own a piece of your business, and can elect a Board of Directors to oversee the management of your business. (Of course, you will probably maintain a majority stake in your business and have some pull in the nomination and election of the Board's directors and officers.)

A Stock Is Born

An *initial public offering* (also known as an IPO) is the first issue of stock to the general public.

By going public, not only have you raised money for your company, you've also raised money for your own wallet! Because you were the owner of the business, the shares that were sold to investors belonged to you.

By the way, the preceding story is essentially the tale of how a pickup truck–driving small businessman in Arkansas named Sam Walton turned a small chain of stores into one of the biggest companies in America—Wal-Mart Stores—with sales of $119 billion in 1997. Wal-Mart was added to the Dow Jones Industrial Average in 1997, representative of its ascendance to the pinnacle of American business.

Inside a Stock Exchange

If you'd like to buy a share of stock in Wal-Mart Stores—or any other publicly traded company—you will most likely need the services of a brokerage firm. Although it's possible to buy and sell shares of stock on your own, this approach risks some practical and legal problems. The securities industry is highly regulated, so you can't just hang a shingle and start selling stocks to the general public unless you're properly registered and licensed.

What's a Security?

A *security* is anything that represents ownership in a company (such as a stock), a debt that is owed (such as a bond), or a right of ownership (such as an option or warrant).

When you want to buy groceries, you go to the grocery store. When you want to buy a sofa, you go the furniture store. And when you want to buy stocks, you need to do business with a brokerage firm.

A *brokerage firm* is a dealer of stocks and other securities that acts as your agent when you want to buy or sell stocks. (You will learn more about brokers in Chapter 14.)

Most trading of stocks happens on a stock exchange. These are special markets where buyers and sellers are brought together to buy and sell stocks. The best known stock exchanges are the New York Stock Exchange and the American Stock Exchange.

The Total Value of the Companies Listed on the New York Stock Exchange Is Larger Than the Gross Domestic Product of Many Countries!

At the end of 1997, there were 3,656 securities listed on the New York Stock Exchange, with a total market value of $11.8 trillion dollars.

Source: New York Stock Exchange

Besides these two national exchanges, there are many smaller regional stock exchanges, such as the Pacific in Los Angeles, the Philadelphia, the Boston, the Cincinnati, and the Chicago. Some small companies are listed only on a regional exchange; some NYSE and AMEX companies are listed on these smaller exchanges, as well, to help trades happen faster and cheaper for investors.

When most people think of a stock exchange, they picture a scene of frantic activity, with traders in funny-looking jackets simultaneously jostling for position, shouting commands, making strange hand signals, and writing up orders.

Behind this frenzied spectacle, however, is a methodical and organized system of trading in which the price of any stock is set purely by rule of supply and demand in an auction setting. Specialists help match buyers and sellers, but shares are always sold to the highest bidder.

How Did "Wall Street" Come to Be Used to Describe the American Financial Markets?

Wall Street is located in the southern tip of Manhattan Island in New York City, and is so named because of the wall that early settlers built in the late 1600s to protect themselves from northern-approaching marauders. The street next to the wall was descriptively named "Wall Street." Years later, traders gathered near the street, and eventually built the New York and American Stock Exchanges right there. Today, when you hear the term "Wall Street," it most likely is referring to the entire financial industry, and not just a short street in Manhattan.

How a Trade Is Made

From the perspective of an investor, buying and selling stocks seems pretty simple. If you use a full-service broker, just call her up on the phone and place an order for 100 shares of Coca-Cola. Within a few minutes, you will receive a confirmation that your order has been completed, and you will be the proud new owner of Coke's stock.

Behind the scenes, however, a lot of action takes place between your order and the confirmation. Here's what has to happen before you actually become the owner of Coca-Cola stock:

1. You place the order with your broker to buy 100 shares of the Coca-Cola Company.
2. The broker sends the order to the firm's order department.
3. The order department sends the order to the firm's clerk who works on the floor of the exchange where shares of Coca-Cola are traded (the New York Stock Exchange).
4. The clerk gives the order to the firm's floor trader, who also works on the exchange floor.
5. The floor trader goes to the specialist's post for Coca-Cola and finds another floor trader who is willing to sell shares of Coca-Cola.
6. The traders agree on a price.
7. The order is executed.
8. The floor trader reports the trade to the clerk and the order department.
9. The order department confirms the order with the broker.
10. The broker confirms the trade with you.

43

That's how a traditional stock exchange works, but much of the action that takes place when you buy or sell a stock is being handled with the assistance of computers. Even if you bought a stock that trades on a stock exchange, it's possible that your order could be executed with little or no intervention by humans. You can log on to a brokerage firm's Web site, enter an order, have the trade be executed, and receive a confirmation all within 60 seconds or less!

A Tour of Stock Exchanges on the Web

There are stock exchanges all over the world and across the U.S., from Boston to New York to Chicago to California. Most offer tours to groups of visitors, and these can be educational and entertaining events.

But it's also possible to visit stock exchanges without leaving your desk. Many exchanges produce full-featured sites on the Web, providing a glimpse into the workings of the financial markets.

The New York Stock Exchange (http://www.nyse.com) is known as the "Big Board" because it's the preeminent stock exchange in the world. Its Web site provides plenty of information about the exchange and the stocks listed on it.

To understand how an auction market works, visit the New York Stock Exchange Web site.

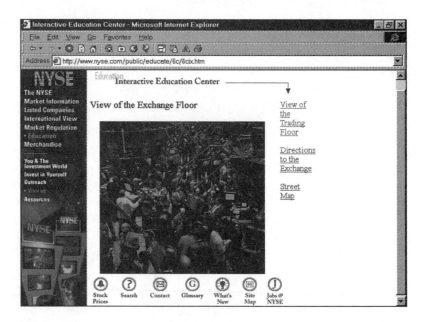

Start your exploration of the NYSE site by selecting the Education link and reviewing the online publication, "You and the Investment World." In seven chapters, the tutorial describes how companies raise capital in the stock market, how the market works, and why stocks go up and down.

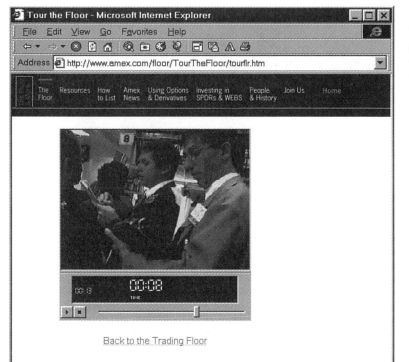

You can watch live video of the activities that happen on the floor of the American Stock Exchange, right from its Web site.

The American Stock Exchange is another major stock market in the United States. You can refer to the Exchange as the AMEX if you want to sound like a pro! If you really want to get a taste of how a stock market works, check out the Web site (http://www.amex.com). Each day, while the market is open, you can tune in to live video of the action from the floor delivered over the Internet. You can also view market reports that are created each morning and afternoon.

Elsewhere on the AMEX Web site, visit the "Resources" section for interactive tutorials, glossaries, and facts about the American Stock Exchange and how it works.

The ABCs of Ticker Symbols

Ticker symbols of stocks on the NYSE have three letters or less. Single-ticker symbols are the most-prized, but the New York Stock Exchange is holding two such symbols, *I* and *T*, in the hopes that it can someday from Nasdaq lure two big companies to list on its exchange. The companies? Tech giants Intel and Microsoft!

In 1998, AMEX and the National Association of Securities Dealers (NASD, the operator of the Nasdaq trading system) approved a merger of their two companies. Although AMEX will continue to operate as an auction market, it will also offer new electronic order services from the floor of the exchange, courtesy of Nasdaq.

Before You Tune In on the Web, You Need to Install a Video Player

Many sites offer video broadcasts of news or market reports on the Web. Many use a technique called *streaming video*, which enables you to view the video at the same time it is delivered to your computer (instead of requiring you to download the entire file first and then watch it). To take a peek at these video feeds, you need to have a video player installed in your browser. The most common programs are RealVideo, VivoActive, Videogram, VDOLive, Vxtreme, or Microsoft Media Player. When you encounter a site that requires a viewer that isn't installed on your machine, you will be provided with a link to the appropriate software. Just install it and tune in!

Nasdaq is the abbreviation for the tongue-twisting and grammatically incorrect phrase "National Association of Securities Dealers Automated Quotations." Nasdaq is not a stock exchange, however; it's a completely electronic market. Known from its advertising campaign as "the stock market for the next generation," trading on Nasdaq is done by computers over a vast network that connects brokers and investment banks.

The Nasdaq system connects "market makers" of Nasdaq stocks. Market makers are brokerage firms that agree to maintain an inventory of shares of stock in a particular company. They are always willing to buy, as well as sell, shares in the company for which they "make a market."

What's an OTC Stock?

Some stocks don't trade on Nasdaq or a stock exchange. These are known as *over-the-counter* (OTC) stocks, and prices for these are printed on pink paper and distributed to brokerage firms each day. Often, these stocks are known as *pink sheet* stocks.

Companies are willing to be market makers because they earn a "markup" on every share they sell from its inventory. They sell shares at a higher price than other investors are willing to pay for that company, and buy shares at a lower price than other investors are willing to sell its shares. A market maker could buy 100 shares of stock from an investor for $10, and immediately sell those 100 shares to you for $10 1/8. The broker keeps the difference, one-eighth of a dollar in this case, for his services. Although it might not sound like a lot of money, market makers handle thousands and thousands of trades a day, and all those little fees add up to lots! The Nasdaq Web site (http://www.nasdaq.com) can tell you more about how its market works. Click **About Nasdaq** to learn more about the organization, and how trades are made in the Nasdaq market. Be sure to visit the "Nasdaq Facts" section here for its "Ask the Economist" feature, which answers common questions about the Nasdaq market. Nasdaq's "Investor Resources" includes tips and lessons about investing, and the "Reference" area offers links to other stock markets and investing sites. When you're learning about a new subject for the first time, there's nothing like actually doing it to really teach you what you need to know. Investing in the stock market is no different. To do that, however, you need a bundle of money, right? Wrong! A number of Web sites feature market simulators that can help you to understand how stock markets work.

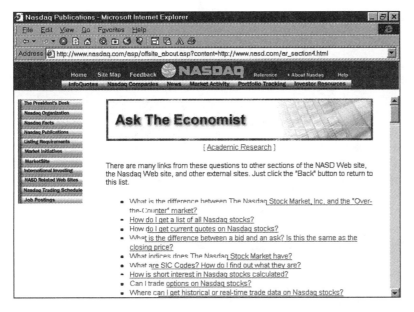

The Nasdaq Web site can answer many of your questions about how its stock market works.

These sites are not only educational, they can be fun to play, too! And you won't necessarily practice trading with stocks, either. Some sites allow users to buy and sell shares of celebrities, politicians, and sports stars!

One of the most popular and educational stock market simulations on the Web has nothing to do with the stock market at all! Do you think Leonardo DiCaprio's star is rising? On the Hollywood Stock Exchange (http://www.hsx.com), you can "buy" shares of hot stars like DiCaprio, while you "sell" the bonds of that just-cancelled television sitcom or movie bomb.

This simulated marketplace is based on the entertainment industry, and it's surprising how similar Hollywood and Wall Street can be—this year's hot actor might be tomorrow's has-been (the same thing that happens to stocks sometimes). After you register on the site, you will have $2,000,000 in play money to begin buying and selling your favorite movies and actors.

On the Hollywood Stock Exchange, you can try your hand at "investing" in your favorite movies and stars.

In no time at all, you will begin to get the hang of how the laws of supply and demand work (just like in the stock market). If you would prefer a more serious approach to learning about the stock market, try MarketPlayer (http://www.marketplayer.com). Each month, MarketPlayer hosts the HedgeHog Competition, a free contest that lets you build a portfolio of stocks and begin to understand how the market works.

MarketPlayer allows you to build a stock portfolio, and then will provide a graph of the performance of your picks over time.

When you arrive at the MarketPlayer Web site for the first time, click the **Register Free** button to open your account. You then receive $1,000,000 in "cash" to begin buying and selling stocks. But that's not all: Besides providing the capability to build a portfolio and test your skill, MarketPlayer has a host of tools for searching and studying stocks. Each week, the editor of the site offers commentary about the status of the U.S. stock market, too, with ideas about which sectors and industries look like potentially good investments.

The Least You Need to Know

➤ Companies sell shares of stock to investors to raise capital to expand their businesses.

➤ The stocks of public companies trade on organized markets or exchanges. The major U.S. stock exchanges are the New York Stock Exchange, the American Stock Exchange, and Nasdaq, and each one has a Web site where you can learn more about how they operate.

➤ You can learn more about stock markets and how they work by trying your hand at a market-simulation Web site. These sites allow you to buy and sell shares in a fake portfolio, track your performance, and teach you how the laws of supply and demand can affect the price of a stock.

Chapter 5

Principles of Investing for the Mathematically Challenged

Does the mere mention of "algebra" bring painful memories to mind? Or did you have a bad run-in with calculus in high school or college? If so, you will be happy to know that even if you were never a math whiz in school, you can still be a successful independent investor. You need to master (or at least understand) just a few simple principles before you set foot on the investing trail. Being "mathematically challenged" is no obstacle!

The Riddle of Risk and Return

Sure, you would like to make a fortune in the markets—who wouldn't? The first thing you need to understand, before you commit even a dollar to a portfolio or begin surfing investment Web sites—is that it is impossible to realize a return on any investment without facing some amount of risk.

No matter what you decide to do with your savings and investments, your money will always face some risk. You could stash your dollars under your mattress or in a cookie jar, but then you would face the risk of losing it all if your house burned down. You could keep your money in the bank, but the buying power of your dollars would barely keep up with inflation over the years, leaving you with little more dollars in real terms than when you started. So, you must face the fact that increased return from your investment portfolio comes from taking an increased amount of risk. And, although risk in your portfolio may be unavoidable, it is manageable. The riddle of controlling risk and return is that you need to maximize the returns and minimize the risk. When you do, you ensure that you will make enough on your investments, while facing an acceptable amount of risk.

You'd Better Understand Beta

One measure of investing risk is known by professionals as the *beta coefficient*, often referred to as simply *beta*. The beta of a stock or mutual fund is determined by comparing its returns to the overall market (usually that means the Standard & Poor's 500 Index). Sound complicated? All that it means is that a security with a beta of 1.0 rises and falls in perfect sync with the market. A security with a beta of greater than 1.0 will be more volatile than the market in general; a security with a beta below 1.0 *is* less volatile than the market. Is a higher beta better? Not necessarily, because it all depends on how much risk you can take—and beta gives you a way to measure that risk.

So what constitutes acceptable risk? It's different for every person! A good rule of thumb followed by many investors is that you shouldn't wake up in the middle of the night worrying about your portfolio. If your investments are causing you too much anxiety, it's time to reconsider how you're investing, and bail out of those securities that are giving you insomnia in favor of some investments that are a little more calming. When you find your own comfort zone, you will know your personal *risk tolerance*—the amount of risk you are willing to take on to achieve your financial goals.

What's an Asset Class?

An *asset class* is a broad category of securities, such as stocks, bonds, or cash. These are often broken down into more specific categories, such as large-cap stocks and small-cap stocks, or corporate bonds and government bonds.

Every type of security carries a different amount of risk. In this table, you can see how some different asset classes stack up against each other as far as risk is concerned.

Risk Levels of Different Asset Classes

Less Risky	More Risky	
U.S. Treasury Bonds	Blue-chip stocks	Small-cap stocks
U.S. Treasury Bills	Highly rated	IPO stocks
U.S. Treasury Notes	Corporate bonds	Junk bonds
U.S. Savings Bonds	Domestic stocks	Commodities
Municipal bonds	Stock and Index	
Certificates of Deposit	options	
Money market funds	International	
Mortgage-backed	stocks	
securities	International	
	bonds	

When it comes to your long-term financial future, however, the biggest risk of all may be just to do nothing. If you *don't* invest for retirement, or for the college education of your children, or to help meet your personal financial goals, you are most likely guaranteed a future of just scraping by.

Not Putting All Your Eggs in One Basket (a.k.a. "Diversification")

Before you commit to burying Mason jars of cash in the backyard, read on to learn some strategies you can use to manage risk in your portfolio. The first rule is a trite saying, but it's true. The advice to "don't put all your eggs in one basket" is sound. The image of a basketful of eggs cracking in unison all over your kitchen floor is pretty vivid. The message for investors in this advice is that risk can be managed by diversifying your portfolio.

Diversification means building a portfolio that includes securities from different asset classes. Because bonds tend to do well when stocks don't, you could construct a portfolio that includes a certain percentage of stocks and bonds. When bonds are doing well, that part of your portfolio would do well. When stocks do well, the other part of your holdings would do well.

Over-Diversification Can Cause Problems, Too

Make sure that your portfolio isn't *over-diversified*. Research shows that the benefits of diversification can be lost if your portfolio has too many holdings. The returns of your portfolio are likely to slide toward the average of the overall market, while your risk level remains the same.

Another way to diversify is to buy securities in the same asset class that are not affected by the same variables. Entertainment companies, utilities, grocery stores, and airlines, for example, are completely different businesses. Depending on the country's economy, one or more of these industries might perform better than the other industries. If you built a portfolio that included securities from a number of sectors, chances are that one or more would always be doing better than average.

What Is Noncorrelation?

Noncorrelation is a fancy way of saying that different types of securities, or stock markets in different countries, tend to move in different directions at the same time.

When you diversify, you try to ensure that at any given time, the value of some of your holdings might be down, and some might be up, but overall your portfolio is doing fine. The trick is to find securities that don't have tendencies to increase or decrease in price at the same time.

The trade-off for the balancing of risk and return in a diversified portfolio is that your overall return might be somewhat lower than you could get in an undiversified portfolio. Along the way, however, a diversified portfolio will have less volatility and steadier returns.

Allocating Your Assets

Asset allocation is the primary tool in the battle to build a diversified portfolio. This is the task of figuring out how much of your portfolio will be invested in different asset classes such as stocks, bonds, or cash.

What's the Difference Between "Tactical" and "Strategic" Asset Allocation?

Tactical asset allocation is an attempt to shift the assets in your portfolio based on a prediction of where the market is headed in the short term, such as moving into bonds when you think a bear market is coming. This usually doesn't work. On the other hand, *strategic asset allocation* is a long-term approach to investing where you create a plan for the asset allocation of your portfolio, and rarely make changes to the percentages you initially established.

Asset allocation has been recognized as a very important part of the process of building a portfolio. In fact, one study has found that your decision as to how you will divide up your portfolio into several classes is more important than the process of choosing the actual stocks, bonds, and funds that you will own!

In developing your asset allocation strategy, you should remember that, generally, the younger you are, the more risk you can afford to take. As you get older and closer to retirement, you will probably be less interested in growth and more interested in the *capital preservation* of your portfolio—protecting it from any declines. One rule of thumb that many experts use is to subtract your age from 100 to determine the percentage of investments to invest in stocks. If you're 45, you might put together a portfolio that's 55% stocks and 45% bonds and cash.

You Can't Completely Eliminate Risk

Even if you use the principles of Modern Portfolio Theory to build a portfolio, you can't entirely eliminate risk from your portfolio. You can, however, manage to reduce the risk to an acceptable level—all any of us can hope to do!

Most full-service brokerage firms maintain a suggested asset allocation for their customers. The firm's chief investment strategist determines the optimal percentage of a typical portfolio that should be invested in particular asset classes at any time, and then updates the asset allocation strategy on a regular basis. When it comes time to design your portfolio, resources on the Web can help you figure out the best asset allocation plan for you. You will learn more about these in Chapter 17.

Making the Most of a Buck—With Dollar Cost Averaging

The funny thing about investing is that, too often, investors react to the stock market quite differently than they react to other money decisions. If you went to the grocery store and found that some essential item was on sale for a terrific price, you wouldn't hesitate to stock up. But when you log on to your portfolio and see a good stock fall in price, you're likely to hesitate, or even sell your holdings—the complete opposite of how you would react to a sale in a grocery store!

Dollar cost averaging is the antidote to emotional investing. This method of investing involves two steps. First, select a good, quality stock or mutual fund. Second, make a commitment to invest the same amount of money each month to purchase shares in that fund, say $50 or $100 a month. Now, whenever the price is low, your set investment will buy a lot of shares. When the price is high, that same amount will buy fewer shares. It may sound too easy, but the end result of regular investing in this fashion is that you're likely to end up with a greater number of shares at a lower average cost per share than if you had invested the same amount of your money all at once.

In fact, you may come way ahead if you use dollar cost averaging. In 1998, *Money Magazine* commissioned Value Line to do a study of how investors would have fared if they had invested $100 a month in domestic stock mutual funds over the past 5 and 10 years. The results? Investors would have received an average annual return of 25.7% over 5 years and 23.7% over 10 years if they invested each month—compared to average annual returns of 17.4% and 13.3% for a lump sum invested in the same funds at the beginning of the periods. That's a big difference!

The Institute for Systematic Investing Research (ISIR) is a private, independent, not-for-profit research organization devoted entirely to research about dollar cost averaging. Its Web site (`http://www.isir.com`) is filled with educational articles, applications, and research about the topic. If you want to really dig in, or see some examples of how dollar cost averaging works in specific mutual funds, drop by this site.

The final word on dollar cost averaging is that it commits you to investing regularly, and not trying to guess the market's future direction. Sure, it's boring! But it works, and that's what's most important to remember.

It's Hip, It's Now, It's Mod—Modern Portfolio Theory

You can divide the history of investing in the United States into two periods: before and after 1952. That was the year that an economics student at the University of Chicago named Harry Markowitz published his doctoral thesis. His work was the beginning of what is now known as Modern Portfolio Theory.

How important was Markowitz's paper? Well, he received a Nobel prize in economics in 1990 as a result of his research and its long-lasting effect on how investors approach investing today. In fact, the principles of asset allocation and diversification outlined in this chapter really derive from Markowitz's work.

So here's the crux of Modern Portfolio Theory, and why it's important to you. Markowitz starts out with the assumption that all investors would like to avoid risk whenever possible. He defines risk as a standard deviation of expected returns (see the sidebar for more about standard deviation).

Rather than look at risk on an individual security level, Markowitz proposes that you measure the risk of an entire portfolio. When considering a security for your portfolio, don't base your decision on the amount of risk that carries with it. Instead, consider how that security contributes to the overall risk of your portfolio.

Markowitz then considers how all the investments in a portfolio can be expected to move together in price under the same circumstances. This is called "correlation," and it measures how much you can expect different securities or asset classes to change in price relative to each other.

High fuel prices might be good for oil companies, for example, but bad for airlines who need to buy the fuel. As a result, you might expect that the stocks of companies in these two industries would often move in opposite directions. These two industries have a negative (or low) correlation. You will get better diversification in your portfolio if you own one airline and one oil company rather than just owning two oil companies.

When you put all this together, it's entirely possible to build a portfolio that has a much higher average return than the level of risk it contains. When you build a diversified portfolio and spread out your investments by asset class, you're really just managing risk and return.

What Is Standard Deviation?

In the context of investing, *standard deviation* is a term that's used to describe the level of risk that comes with investing in a particular security, usually a bond or mutual fund. To figure an investment's standard deviation, first you need to calculate the average returns of a security over a long period. Then you compare the actual returns during a short period to the long-term average, and measure the difference. In the past two years, for example, bond "A" has returned 15% in the first year and then 5% in the second year. Its average annual return is 10%. But bond "B" has returned 9% and then 11% in the same two years, and its average annual return is also 10%. Obviously, investors who invested in either bond in either the first year or the second year would see very different results in their portfolio! Bond "A" appears to be much more volatile in these two years than bond "B"; and bond "A" has a higher standard deviation than bond "B." The higher the standard deviation of a particular security's returns, the greater the risk that comes with investing in that security.

The Least You Need to Know

➤ You can't avoid risk in your portfolio if you want to earn a respectable return. You can balance risk and return, however, with some simple strategies.

➤ Diversifying the assets in your portfolio can help steady your overall return, and smooth out the bumps as you reach your goal. Diversification can cushion the inevitable bottoms.

➤ Dollar cost averaging can help increase your returns. By investing a regular amount of money according to a set schedule, you can smooth out the bumps in your portfolio holdings.

Chapter 6

Learning More About Investing

In This Chapter

➤ Organizations and educational Web sites you should know about

➤ You can learn more about investing by participating in a mailing list or message board

➤ An investment club can be a great learning experience

It's easy to be overwhelmed by many of the financial sites you will encounter on the Web. At some sites, however, you will receive a kinder, gentler welcome to the world of investing. Several organizations focus on helping individuals learn about investing, and some sites have been built with the sole aim of educating investors. With their focus on newbies, these sites are worth visiting—and revisiting—as you expand your own understanding of investing.

Educational Web Sites

If you need help learning to manage your new portfolio, don't worry—you won't need to go back to school to get a degree in finance! But you will need to spend some time on your investment education. Fortunately, a number of organizations are devoted to investor education. These groups also have Web sites that you can explore to help you learn much more about investing.

A Membership in NAIC's Computer Group Can Expand Your Investment Education

When you join NAIC, you have the option of joining its Computer Group as well. A Computer Group membership offers a subscription to its monthly newsletter, filled with tips for using software and the Internet, stock studies, and a regularly updated list of growth stocks to study. It's a good deal for any Internet investor!

One of the best investments you can make if you're a new investor is a membership in the National Association of Investors Corporation (NAIC) . NAIC is a not-for-profit investor education group that has been around for nearly 50 years. They support investment clubs as well as individual investors with an educational program that focuses on investing in the stock market. Millions of investors have learned to invest using NAIC's principles following an approach of growth stock investing that anyone can understand with a little study and a little practice.

NAIC has created a library of manuals, videotapes, worksheets, and software that can aid you in building a portfolio of stocks. An annual membership is inexpensive, and it is worth the price just for the subscription to *Better Investing* magazine (an undiscovered gem of a financial publication) that you will receive.

Members also can participate in its Low Cost Investment Plan and the NAIC Stock Service Plan, two programs that can enable you to invest in stocks without a broker. (You will learn more about these plans in Chapter 16.)

NAIC welcomes new investors with a site filled with articles and resources also including information about NAIC membership and its privileges.

The NAIC Web site (`http://www.better-investing.org`) is chock full of information that's all for your benefit as long as you're willing to explore it! Click on Learn to Invest to get a directory of the educational articles available on the site, including reprints from *Better Investing* magazine. The search engine can help you locate articles of interest as well.

NAIC also hosts a popular discussion mailing list, the "I-Club-List," which is an ongoing and dynamic source of investor education. I-Club-List is short for Investment Club List. The list welcomes any investors who follow NAIC's approach to the market, regardless of whether they are club members.

As long as you have an email account, you can subscribe to the list (for free) and join more than 2,500 other investors in discussions about growth stock investing. Each month, a moderator leads an online workshop, either a study of a particular stock, an analysis of an industry, or a lesson on a related investing subject. Questions from beginners are welcome, which makes the I-Club-List a friendly online home for many investors.

You Can Communicate with Other Investors by Subscribing to a Mailing List

One of the popular methods of connecting people on the Internet is by means of a *mailing list*. A discussion mailing list is made up of a group of people who use email to talk about a particular topic. The group could be two people or 2,000 people—it doesn't make a difference! To participate on a particular list, you just need to "subscribe."

```
Eudora Pro - [Mark Robertson, 10:20 AM 9/30/98 , Challenge Analysts All-Time St]
File  Edit  Mailbox  Message  Transfer  Special  Tools  Window  Help

                        Subject Challenge Analysts All-Time Standings

X-Sender: manifest@better-investing.org (Unverified)
X-Mailer: QUALCOMM Windows Eudora Light Version 3.0.5 (32)
Date: Wed, 30 Sep 1998 10:20:38 -0400
To: i-club-list@better-investing.org
From: Mark Robertson <manifest@better-investing.org>
Subject: Challenge Analysts All-Time Standings
Reply-To: i-club-list@better-investing.org
Sender: owner-i-club-list@better-investing.org


SPECIAL EDITION - HOW ARE WE DOING?

The Challenge has been running since October 1997.
It's time, once again, to check in on our favorite pundits.
The difference between those forecasts that you read in
your newspapers and magazines, is that we actually keep
track.  Who has identified the best-performing stocks since
we started this?  Analysts are entered into the "all-time
standings" when their challenge selections are at least
three months old.  (Those of you that scooped up the
opportunities on September 1-8 have to wait until
```

The I-Club-List is a community of investors who are willing to share what they've learned.

Don't Get Flamed!

A *flame* is an angry, insulting, and offensive message sent by email or posted on an Internet message board. You can get "flamed" if you post an inappropriate message to a mailing list, or if you post an insulting message. A *flame war* can erupt if tempers flare and angry messages begin volleying back and forth between users. To avoid getting flamed, follow these basic rules of the Net. Make sure you know the guidelines of any message board or mailing list before you send a message. Don't insult other users no matter how much you think they deserve it. And, make sure you've got your facts straight before you click the Send Mail button.

To subscribe to the I-Club-List, use the form on the NAIC Web site (http://www.better-investing.org/iclub/iclub.html), or send an email message to listproc@better-investing.org. In the body of the message, type the following:

```
SUBSCRIBE I-CLUB-LIST "YOUR FULL NAME"
```

Remember to replace "YOUR FULL NAME" with your first and last name; do not use quotation marks. Do not include a subject in the header or a signature in the body of the message. If your mail program requires a subject line, enter a blank space or type the word *blank*. If you fail to follow these instructions exactly, the list processor software will refuse your request.

You will receive a confirmation message from the list processor software that includes other information about the list and how to eventually unsubscribe from it. Be sure to save this message for future reference!

After you successfully sign up, you will start receiving mail, as many as 50 messages a day (or more!). The list has an option to receive messages in "digest" mode, which means you will get a single message a day that includes all the other posts to the list. This can help cut down on the volume of mail in your inbox.

The NAIC's primary tool for investment analysis is the Stock Selection Guide (SSG). This two-page paper form helps investors to identify a stock that is growing faster than the market in general, and then it helps them to determine the best price at which to buy that stock. Used for more than 40 years, the SSG is a tried-and-true tool for the analysis of stocks, even for beginning investors.

Although the NAIC publishes a handbook and other information to help investors understand the SSG, you can also learn more about the SSG by checking out the Stock Selection Guide Tutorial at Investment Club Central (http://www.iclubcentral.com/ssg). This illustrated tutorial walks through the entire process of completing the SSG, and then helps you to understand the information and draw conclusions about the suitability of a particular stock for your portfolio.

Don't worry, you will learn more about selecting stocks and building a portfolio later in this book. But it's still worth a glance at this tutorial to see the potential that lies on the Web to help you with your investment education!

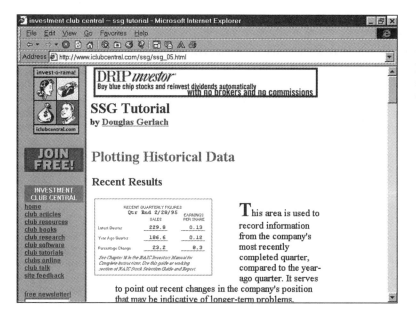

The Stock Selection Guide Tutorial at Investment Club Central can help you learn the NAIC's approach to stock analysis.

Other sites on the Web are focused on investor education. By making a few pit stops at these sites, you will be able to learn more about the basics of investing, as well as terms you should know and how the stock market operates.

If mutual funds are more your style, a Web site called Mutual Funds Interactive features an area called "Funds 101" devoted to new fund investors (`http://www.fundsinteractive.com/newbie.html`). You will find articles, crossword puzzles, trivia quizzes, and other resources focused on funds.

The Armchair Millionaire (`http://www.armchairmillionaire.com`) is a good example of a site that aims to help beginning investors without overwhelming them with big words and fancy terms. The Armchair Millionaire looks to provide common sense saving and investing strategies for people who are just getting started in the stock market, or for experienced investors who are still looking for a sensible approach to the stock market.

The "Getting Started" area on the site is home to articles and resources for beginning investors, as well as message boards with names such as "There Are No Dumb Questions." The "Fund-amentals" area of the site is devoted to mutual fund basics and features a resident expert who responds to user questions each week.

One unusual feature of the Armchair Millionaire is the real money model portfolio featured on the site. The site's founder has invested his own portfolio according to a strategy that's laid out on the site for all to see—and if you like it, you can emulate the approach in your own portfolio!

Another interesting and educational Web destination is InvestSmart (`http://hyperion.advanced.org/10326`), an educational site that addresses stocks, bonds, and mutual fund investing. The "Investment Basics" and "Investment Lessons" sections offer sound advice and plenty of tips to extend your knowledge of the markets.

InvestSmart was built by high school students and provides a comprehensive resource for beginning investors.

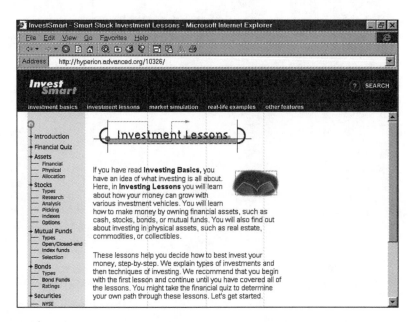

You may be surprised to learn that not only was InvestSmart built *for* young people, it was also built *by* young people! InvestSmart was an entrant in a national competition, ThinkQuest, held to encourage high school students to explore the collaborative and interactive nature of the Internet. The team that built InvestSmart consisted of students at three high schools in California.

Students from a high school in Maryland joined forces to create another site that was a finalist in the ThinkQuest competition. EduStock (`http://tqd.advanced.org/3088`) is a site designed to teach young people about the stock market. It includes a tutorial about the stock market, a market simulation program where you can build your own practice portfolio, and sample company profiles. Click on The Stock Market to let these students teach you about investing in stocks!

For more education about stocks, visit The Motley Fool (`http://www.fool.com`). The Fool's motto is "To Educate, Amuse, and Enrich," and its Web site is filled with ample selections of each. At the core of the Fool's philosophy is the premise that it's quite possible for individual investors to do better in the markets than the experts of Wall Street. Because the so-called wise men of the financial world are so often wrong with their predictions and analysis, it's far better not to follow in their footsteps, and to be a "fool" instead! In the Motley Fool's world, there's no higher compliment than to be called "foolish."

The Fool's School on the Motley Fool site can teach you the basic principles of "foolish" investing.

One of the Motley Fool's strengths is its extensive community. On the Fool site, you will find hundreds of message boards on topics ranging from individual stocks to inheritance strategies. Just click on the Community link to join in the discussions and network with other investors.

As you continue your investment education, be sure to visit the "Fool's School." This area is where the Fools teach their principles of investing, beginning with their "13 Steps to Investing." By following these simple steps, you can be well on your way to starting a portfolio of your own.

Investment Clubs—Online and Off

"There's strength in numbers," as the old saying goes, and that just might be the motto of thousands and thousands of investment clubs now in existence. An investment club is a small group of individuals which pools its money and invests in a single portfolio. Most clubs are formed by groups of friends, neighbors, coworkers, church members, or relatives, who meet once

Are You a Lurker?

If you read messages on message boards or mailing lists, but never send or post any messages of your own, you are a "lurker!" There's nothing wrong with being a lurker, but if all the people on a list or board were lurkers, it would be awfully quiet! An online community is only as strong as the interaction and participation of its members. Your thoughtful contributions (when appropriate) would only enhance the experience, both for you and all other members of the community.

a month and decide how the club will invest its money. Clubs have their own bank and/or brokerage accounts, and elect officers to run the meetings and handle the club's operations.

Female Investment Clubs Do Best

All-female investment clubs outperform both all-male and mixed-gender clubs. In 1996, they boasted an average annual return rate of 21.3%, compared with 18.1% for clubs with females and males. All-male investment clubs came in last, with an average annual return of 15%.

Source: NAIC

You don't need a lot of money to be a member of an investment club. Many clubs require their members to contribute just $20 to $50 a month. When you add up the contributions of a dozen or so members, however, you can see how clubs can quickly build up a sizeable portfolio.

But the biggest advantage of investment clubs is that they provide a terrific educational opportunity for their members. Most successful clubs don't focus on "making a lot of money," but rather on contributing to the investment education of their members. Fortunately, these clubs usually find that profits will follow!

The National Association of Investors Corporation (NAIC) can provide much of the information you need to know about starting your own investment club. Its Web site (`http://www.better-investing.org`) includes an area all about investment clubs; just click the Investment Club Support icon from the main page of the site.

Another source of information about clubs can be found online at Investment Club Central (`http://www.iclubcentral.com`). This site provides a directory of resources about investment clubs from all over the Web. Click on Articles to learn more about clubs and how they work, or click on **Software** to find computer programs that can help your club in its operations or stock analysis.

Another feature of Investment Club Central is its directory of Web sites of investment clubs. Although you might think that this listing might be great to find an existing club to join, you should remember that most clubs are close-knit groups and don't always welcome outsiders as members. With that in mind, you can still visit the sites of over one hundred clubs linked here at Investment Club Central to see firsthand how other clubs work. And maybe, just maybe, you will find a club in your area that might be looking for new members.

As you scan this list of investment clubs, you will notice that a handful of clubs meet in cyberspace. That's right, there are clubs that exist and meet exclusively online!

Many members of online clubs have never met in person; the clubs discuss stocks, make investing decisions, vote, and carry out all their business using a message board or mailing list. There's not much difference between online clubs and "living room" clubs beyond this electronic aspect to their communications, however. Online clubs have brokerage accounts, bank accounts, officers, and disagreements, just like other clubs!

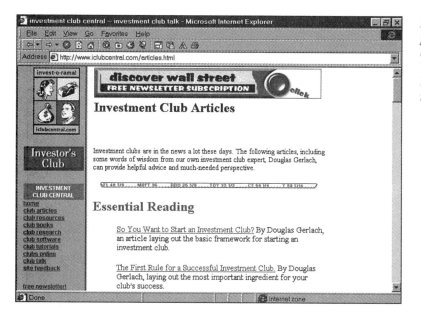

Investment Club Central provides helpful articles and links to hundreds of Web sites to help you learn more about investment clubs.

The biggest advantage of an online investment club is that members can participate whenever it's most convenient for them: at 2:00 a.m. dressed in their bathrobes, or during their lunch break at the office. Because there's no set monthly meeting time, each member can set aside time when it best fits his or her personal schedule.

Whether you join or start a regular or online investment club, you're sure to find that being a member of a club is a great learning experience!

The Least You Need to Know

➤ The National Association of Investors Corporation (NAIC) is an organization that can help you learn more about investing. Its Web site includes plenty of information.

➤ You can learn more about investing at a number of sites devoted to investment education. You will find tutorials, articles, and message boards where you can add to your knowledge about stocks, bonds, mutual funds, and just about any financial topic.

➤ Joining or forming an investment club is a great way to further your investment education. You can learn how to start and run a club by visiting the Web sites of NAIC and Investment Club Central.

Part 2
Investing in Mutual Funds

Okay, so you probably know that mutual funds are one type of investment, but do you know anything more about them? Wouldn't you want to? Mutual funds appear everywhere in the investment world and they make a lot of money for a lot of people, so it is time to learn all about these gems.

The ABCs of Mutual Funds

What Mutual Funds Are (and What They're Not)

When most individuals finally decide to start building an investment portfolio, they usually turn to mutual funds. After you have decided to invest in the stock market, you should consider mutual funds. Mutual funds are an easy way to own stocks without worrying about picking and choosing individual stocks. As an added bonus, you can find plenty of information on the Internet to help you learn about, study, select, and purchase funds.

What is a mutual fund? It sounds like an easy question to answer, and it's not so hard, really. A dictionary definition of a mutual fund might go something like this: a single portfolio of stocks, bonds, and/or cash managed by an investment company on behalf of many investors.

What Is an Investment Company?

Although the term *investment company* sounds official, it really refers to any bank or brokerage house that offers mutual funds for sale to the public. Some investment companies are firms whose sole business is to manage mutual funds. You might be surprised to learn that any individual or company could theoretically start a mutual fund and offer shares to the public—there is no particular expertise required. Fortunately, in the real world there are some pretty serious financial, legal, and logistical obstacles that make it a bit more complicated.

The investment company is responsible for the management of the fund, and it sells shares in the fund to individual investors. When you invest in a mutual fund, you become a part owner of a large investment portfolio, along with all the other shareholders of the fund.

Every day, the fund manager counts up the value of all the fund's holdings, figures out how many shares have been purchased by shareholders, and then calculates the *Net Asset Value (NAV)* of the mutual fund, the price of a single share of the fund on that day. If you want to buy shares, you just send the manager your money, and he will issue new shares for you at the most recent price. This routine is repeated every day on a never-ending basis, which is why mutual funds are sometimes known as *open-end funds*.

If the fund manager is doing a good job, the NAV of the fund will usually get bigger. Your shares are worth more!

But exactly how does a mutual fund's NAV increase? Well, a mutual fund can make money in its portfolio in a couple of ways—the same ways that your own portfolio of stocks, bonds, and cash can make money!

A mutual fund can receive dividends from the stocks that it owns. *Dividends*, of course, are shares of corporate profits paid to the stockholders. The fund could

Don't Be Alarmed If a Fund's NAV Goes Down—If The Decline Is Due to a Distribution

When a mutual fund makes a distribution to shareholders, the NAV of the fund is immediately reduced by the per-share amount of the distribution. It doesn't mean that your investment is worth less, because you would have received the difference in the price of the fund in cash!

also make money from bank interest, or on the interest payments that it receives from the bonds that it owns. Mutual funds are required to hand out (or *distribute*) this income to shareholders. Usually they do this twice a year, in a move that's called an *income distribution.*

At the end of the year, a fund makes another kind of distribution, this time from the profits they might make by selling stocks or bonds that have gone up in price. These profits are known as *capital gains*, and the act of passing them out is called a *capital gains distribution.*

Watch Out When You Buy Shares near the End of the Year

Mutual funds typically distribute capital gains to all shareholders at the end of the year. What happens, however, if you buy shares after the *record date* of the distribution (the day the fund determines all the owners of record of the fund) but before the *payable date* of the distribution (usually several days later)? You would not receive the distribution of gains and income, but the NAV of the fund would still be reduced, leaving you with a loss on your investment. If you buy shares at the end of June or December, you should make sure you don't hit the few days in between the record and payable dates of the fund's distribution.

These are all ways that a fund can share any profits from the sale of securities with all the fund's investors. Unfortunately, funds don't always make money—sometimes they lose money, too. These are *capital losses.* Everyone hates to have losses, and funds are no different. The good news is that these losses are subtracted from the fund's capital gains before the money is distributed to shareholders. If losses exceed gains, a fund manager can even pile up these losses and use them to offset future gains in the portfolio. That means that the fund won't pass out capital gains to shareholders until the fund has at least earned more in profits than it has lost. (Although you might want to reconsider your decision to remain invested in a fund that's losing money if the rest of the market is growing!)

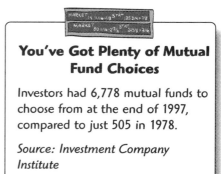

You've Got Plenty of Mutual Fund Choices

Investors had 6,778 mutual funds to choose from at the end of 1997, compared to just 505 in 1978.

Source: Investment Company Institute

Now that you understand the basics of mutual funds, it's time to dig in a bit deeper—particularly if you want to learn how to separate the winners from the losers!

All mutual funds share three basic characteristics:

➤ An investment objective

➤ An investment plan

➤ Professional management

A fund's investment objective is not merely to make money for shareholders (although that's certainly important). Each mutual fund has a specifically defined mission that tells you its overall approach to investing. A fund might have an objective to produce current income; another might strive to generate long-term growth. But, some mix the two approaches.

Choosing the right one is important. If you were retired and were looking to supplement your pension and Social Security, it would be very important for you to buy an *income fund*. The manager of an income fund tries to generate gains, usually from dividends or interest, that are paid out to shareholders on a regular basis.

You Can't Compare Apples to Oranges

When you compare two mutual funds, you should make sure you're comparing funds that have similar characteristics. It's not fair to compare a growth fund to an income fund, for instance—they have different objectives and reasons that you might choose to own one over the other.

On the other hand, the manager of a *growth fund* doesn't care about producing income for shareholders. A growth fund manager will probably want to invest in fast-growing stocks. Shareholders hope to profit when they eventually sell their shares in the fund at a much higher price than they purchased them. If you have 10 or 20 years until retirement, you will probably want to go for the growth! There's no need to be taking income from the fund right now.

Growth and income fund managers try to balance the two objectives, maybe by buying some bonds to provide current income and some stocks that are rapidly growing. The notion of *balance* is key to these funds, as the fund manager hopes to protect you from big bumps in the stock market.

Well, that's the investment objective. Now, what about the investment plan? This plan describes how the fund's manager will invest to meet the fund's objectives. Will the manager buy blue-chip stocks, small-cap stocks, municipal bonds, government bonds, or some combination of several different security types?

When you begin researching a mutual fund on the Web, you may not know these answers, but the investment plan will tell you. It describes all types of securities the fund will purchase in its portfolio and states the minimum and maximum percentages that the fund can invest in any particular type of security.

Finally, the main advantage of investing in a mutual fund is that your money has the attention of professional management. A fund can be managed by an individual or by a team of managers. In fact, when you buy shares in a mutual fund, you're really hiring a manager to invest your money in a portfolio of his or her design. Of course, your investment is immediately thrown into the pot with the investments of thousands of other shareholders, so you can't expect personalized attention from the manager. But it can be very helpful to think of investing in a fund as paying a professional to manage a part of your investment portfolio.

After professional management, the second most important benefit of a mutual fund is that it provides instant *diversification* to its shareholders. As you may recall from Chapter 5, diversification is how you can spread out your eggs in different baskets. When you buy a fund, your new portfolio is likely to be made up of hundreds of eggs—or rather, stocks. Because the fund's portfolio contains so many stocks, the entire portfolio won't be dragged down if one or two stocks do poorly. You would certainly have your hands full trying to manage that many stocks in your own portfolio!

Another benefit of investing in a mutual fund is that you can concentrate your investments in a particular area if you wish. This seems to contradict the advantages of diversification, and it does! But if you have a hunch that now is the time to invest in Japan, or healthcare stocks, or emerging markets, you could buy a fund that invests solely in those areas. (Not that you would ever invest on the basis of hunches, mind you.)

There's plenty more to learn about mutual funds, and with a computer and a Web browser, you should head straight to the Web site of the Investment Company Institute. The I.C.I. is the trade group of the mutual fund industry, so it's not entirely nonobjective! Its Web site (`http://www.ici.org`) offers lots of meaty educational information about mutual funds and how they work.

Besides a compendium of facts, figures, and statistics about funds, the I.C.I also publishes dozens of brochures and booklets that you can download from its site. Click on **About Mutual Funds** and you can grab your choice of publications that describe how funds work and everything you need to know before you buy a fund.

Many of the brochures and booklets are available only in Adobe Acrobat format, however. Acrobat is a special computer file format that enables you to download a document and view it exactly as it is in a printed version. You will have to make sure you have the free Acrobat reader software installed before you can access these files.

The Investment Company Institute can answer many of your questions about mutual funds.

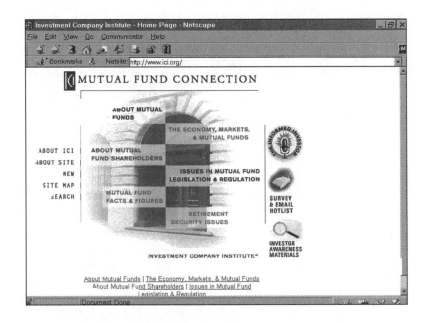

There's No Such Thing as a Free Fund

Mutual funds are businesses. Period. Fund companies are in business to make a profit, just like any other business. So how do fund companies make money? They don't necessarily make their income from wise investing, but more likely from the fees that they charge you and other investors.

It's important that you understand the many different types of fees that funds charge. These fees will be outlined in a fund's prospectus, on its Web site, or in reports from Morningstar or Value Line. You will learn more about the online sources where you can find information on a fund's fees in Chapters 8 and 9.

To help you understand how fees work, you can separate a fund's expenses and fees into three categories: ongoing expenses of operating the fund, which are already accounted for by the return figures you see in newspapers and fund reports; *loads*, charged when you buy or sell shares, and which aren't included in return calculations; and miscellaneous fees and charges.

It costs money to operate a mutual fund! Ongoing expenses include the salaries and advisory fees paid to the investment managers, as well administrative expenses (such as preparing and mailing statements and confirmations, staff to answer the phones, office expenses, and so on). These costs are known as the fund's *expense ratio*. You will usually find that they range from 0.2% to more than 2% of a fund's net assets.

Another ongoing expense that some funds charge is a 12(b)-1 fee. This ambiguously named fee (so dubbed after the legislation that allows it to be charged to shareholders) is used to pay costs of advertising and distribution. By law, a 12(b)-1 fee can't exceed 1% a year.

Some Fund Managers Increase Returns by Waiving Their Fees

One practice that is becoming more popular, particularly for new funds, is for a fund company to temporarily waive its management fee or absorb all operating expenses, and thereby inflate the fund's return. If a fund is waiving its fee, you might be in for a surprise when the fund starts paying its manager and its returns decline by a percentage point or two.

The second category of fund expenses, the load, is the fee for buying, selling, or just owning shares in the fund. *Load* is certainly the right term, too, because there are light loads, heavy loads, and downright backbreaking loads that you might have to carry as a shareholder of these funds.

Loads are either front-end or back-end. The difference between the two comes down to whether the fee is charged when you buy a fund (front-end) or when you sell it (back-end). Usually, these loads are paid to the advisor who sells you the shares.

Many investors don't like loads, for a number of reasons. First of all, mutual fund companies aren't required to include the impact of loads when calculating the total return of their funds. That makes it harder for investors to evaluate the true return of a load fund. You need to make sure that you consider any loads when you are comparing the returns of different funds.

This distaste for loads has spawned a new type of fund, the *no-load fund*. These are funds that don't charge sales charges at all, and they appeal to investors who are turned off by excessive sales charges.

Beware "No-Load" Funds That Charge Fees to Shareholders

Funds that charge 12(b)-1 fees of up to 0.25% are legally permitted to call themselves no-load funds. The only way to determine whether a fund is truly a no-load fund is to read its prospectus carefully.

Here's an imaginary example that demonstrates just how much of a problem a load can be. Let's say the Consolidated Conglomerate Sector Fund is a no-load fund, and its main competitor, the Occidental Oligopoly Specialty Fund, charges a 4.5% back-end load. The fund managers of both have done pretty well lately, turning in a five-year average 16% annual return on their portfolios.

If you had invested $10,000 five years ago in Consolidated's fund, you could sell your shares today for just over $21,000. If you had invested in the Occidental fund, however, the 4.5% back-end load would have cost you less than $1,000, lowering your actual annual return to about 14.95% after the load.

To keep up with its no-load competitor and give its investors the same return, the Occidental fund needed to generate an annual 17.1% rate of return over the period. It doesn't sound like much, but think of it this way: For every $100 that Consolidated made in profit, Occidental needed to earn $114.40, just to end up giving shareholders the same return in the end! Too many load funds just can't compete with their no-load brethren.

Learn more about no-load mutual funds from the No-Load Mutual Fund Council.

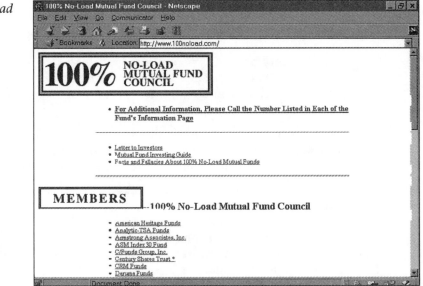

The 100% No-Load Mutual Fund Council (http://www.100noload.com) is an industry group made up of mutual fund companies that offer no-load funds. Obviously, their mission is to point out the superiority of no-load funds for individual investors. The Web site includes a directory of their members, as well as a handy guide to mutual fund investing that explains the advantages of investing in no-load mutual funds.

The third category of fees includes maintenance fees, transaction fees, and redemption fees. A typical account maintenance fee is $10 or $25 a year, and is usually applied to smaller accounts. Vanguard, for example, charges a $10 maintenance fee for accounts less than $10,000. If you don't have a large amount invested, these maintenance fees can add up and that can lower your returns.

Not All Load Funds Are Bad

Load funds are not necessarily always the worst choice for your portfolio. Because you usually purchase these funds from a financial professional, you may be able to receive other financial services as a client of that broker or advisor. But the bottom line is that the performance of any load fund should outperform comparable no-load funds, after the loads have been paid—and that can be a tall order to fill.

Transaction or redemption fees are different than loads, in that they generally go back into the pot (the fund's portfolio) rather than to the fund company's pockets. These fees are designed to discourage market timers and more active traders from moving in and out of the fund to the detriment of long-term shareholders.

What Funds Are Not

Now that you know what mutual funds are, let's go over what mutual funds are *not*.

Mutual funds are not securities, as are stocks and bonds. Funds invest in securities, however, and the share price of a fund is determined by the value of the securities it owns.

Mutual funds are not an asset class. Back in Chapter 5, you learned how to divide up your portfolio among such assets as stocks, bonds, and cash (to name some of the more common classes). As part of your asset allocation decision, you can't decide to allocate 75% of your portfolio to mutual funds and 25% to stocks—you have to consider what the funds own. If all the funds you bought invested in stocks, your portfolio would be 100% invested in stocks. And that's not asset allocation!

When you choose to buy shares in mutual funds, you need to be aware of the asset classes of the securities they own. If you so desire, you can build a diversified portfolio by investing 100% of your money in mutual funds that each own different asset classes.

Mutual funds are usually not short-term investments. Fund companies put up all sorts of barriers to prevent shareholders from buying and selling funds too frequently—and it's for good reason. Frequent buying and selling wreaks havoc with a manager's portfolio plan, making it hard to figure out how much cash the company might need on hand to take care of withdrawals, as well as generating lots of extra activity that raises costs for all shareholders.

Growth, Balanced, Specialty, Bond, International, Yada-Yada-Yada

So far, you have learned that there are funds that own stocks, bonds, or some combination of those two assets. Most mutual funds specialize in much more specific approaches to investing than just buying stocks or bonds, however. Before you begin your research about mutual funds on the Web, you will need to know what you're looking for, and how to identify the various kinds of funds.

Mutual funds are generally categorized by *what* they invest in, *where* they invest, and *how* they invest.

First, let's look at the kinds of investments that mutual funds make. Most mutual funds invest in stocks, and these are called *equity funds*.

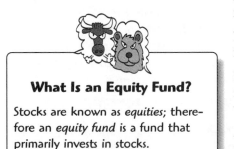

What Is an Equity Fund?

Stocks are known as *equities*; therefore an *equity fund* is a fund that primarily invests in stocks.

Although mutual funds most often invest in the stock market, fund managers don't just buy any old stock they find attractive. Some funds specialize in investing in large-cap stocks, others in small-cap stocks, and still others invest in what's left, mid-cap stocks.

"Cap" has nothing to do with hat size or what your spouse left off the tube of toothpaste (again). On Wall Street, cap is shorthand for capitalization, and is one way of measuring the size of a company—how well it's capitalized. Large-cap stocks have market caps of billions of dollars, and are the best-known companies in America. Small-cap stocks are worth several hundred million dollars, and are newer, up-and-coming firms. Mid-caps are somewhere in between.

It's Easy to Figure Out a Stock's Market Cap

There's no big secret about how the market cap of a stock is determined. You can do it yourself! Just multiply the current price of a single share times the number of shares the company has issued.

Other funds have a narrower focus and only invest in stocks in a particular *sector*, such as technology or healthcare companies. That Consolidated Conglomerate Sector Fund, mentioned earlier, would belong in this category.

Still, there are other funds out there, and not all of them are interested in stocks. *Money-market funds*, for instance, typically invest in short-term government bonds and aim to provide a modest return to investors, comparable to a savings account in a bank. These are quite safe investments, but won't give you a big bang for your buck.

How Big Is Large?

Mutual funds are often categorized by the market capitalization of the stocks that they hold in their portfolios. But how big is a large-cap stock? Formulas differ, but here are some guidelines:

Small-cap stocks   < $500 million

Mid-cap stocks $500 million to $5 billion

Large-cap stocks   > $5 billion

Bond funds, on the other hand, purchase and hold bonds issued by corporations, municipal governments, or federal government agencies. You can invest in tax-free bond funds, just as you can buy tax-free bonds, and the interest you earn is exempt from federal and perhaps state and local income taxes.

The second way that funds are categorized is by geographic location—where in the world does a fund invest? Funds that invest specifically in the United States are known as *domestic funds*, and these include domestic equity funds and domestic bonds funds.

Some funds specialize in securities outside the United States, as well. These are known as *international funds* or *global funds*. There is a subtle but important distinction between these two types of funds. The international fund invests only in companies outside the United States, but the global fund invests both internationally and domestically.

International and global funds can specialize in bonds, stocks, or some mix of the two. An international fund can also specialize in a particular country or region of the world, such as the Pacific Rim, Latin America, or Germany.

Your Global Fund Might Not Be as Global as You Think

Because global funds can invest in stocks from the United States, you need to be aware of the how much the fund has invested in and out of the United States. If you bought a global fund to provide a little international diversification to your portfolio, you might be surprised to learn that the fund's major holdings are American stocks!

More Americans Are Investing in the Stock Market

In 1997, a total of 32.4% of Americans' total financial assets was invested in the stock market. In 1968, at the peak of the so-called go-go years of the American stock market, this figure peaked at 34.25%, and then declined to a low of 14.0% in 1984.

Source: Investment Company Institute

How Many Types of Funds Are There?

Morningstar classifies mutual funds into 44 different categories, from Diversified Emerging Markets to Small Blend to Ultrashort Bond.

Those are the *what* and *where* of mutual funds; next comes the *how*. Equity fund managers usually employ one of three particular styles of stock picking when they make investment decisions for their portfolios.

Some fund managers use a *value* approach to stocks, searching for stocks that are undervalued when compared to other, similar companies. Often, the share prices of these stocks have been beaten down by the market as investors have become pessimistic about the future potential of these companies.

Another approach to picking is to look primarily at *growth*, trying to find stocks that are growing faster than the market as a whole or than their competitors. These funds buy shares in companies that are growing rapidly, often well-known, established corporations.

Some managers buy both kinds of stocks, building a portfolio of both growth stocks and value stocks. This is known as the *blend* approach.

After you gather your information from the Web, you will have a good idea of how that fund works. Put it all together, and you can identify whether a fund is a domestic small-cap growth fund, or an international large-cap value fund, or a mid-cap value fund, or a specific-country sector fund. And the combinations go on and on!

Strategies for Getting Started in Mutual Funds

If you are ready to buy shares in that Consolidated Conglomerate Sector Fund, or even an index fund that tracks the S&P 500, you have two choices:

➤ Buy shares through your discount or full-service broker.
➤ Buy shares from the fund directly.

If you buy shares through a broker, you will probably have to pay a commission. However, many discount brokers, including Schwab, Waterhouse, and Jack White, now offer *mutual fund supermarkets* where you can buy shares with no transaction fees. These brokers have made agreements with hundreds (or even thousands) of mutual funds to offer shares to customers without charging commissions or fees.

Another advantage of buying fund shares through a broker is that you can consolidate all your investments in one portfolio, and on one statement. Sometimes, the minimum initial investments are lower in these fund marketplaces than if you bought shares from the fund directly!

If you buy shares from the fund company directly, you won't have to pay a commission (although there may be an annual maintenance fee for your account). You will be able to easily make transfers between different funds in the same family. If you want to sell your shares of Consolidated Conglomerate and buy shares of Consolidated Growth instead, you just have to call the company or log on to your account. There probably won't be a charge for the transfer, either.

Mutual Funds Are More Popular Than Ever

Investors had 171.3 million active accounts at mutual fund companies at the end of 1997, compared to just 8.7 million accounts in 1978.

Source: Investment Company Institute

One disadvantage of purchasing shares directly from a fund company is that you're usually limited to buying that company's funds. This isn't always the case, however. Fidelity Investments, the largest mutual fund company in the country, offers a FundsNetwork of 3,300 funds, including their own funds and funds from other firms. More than 800 of the funds are available with no transaction fees.

Some funds are only available through brokers or financial advisors. These are almost always load funds—the advisor's compensation comes from the sales charge. The downside of buying funds from an advisor like this is that the advisor has an incentive (to earn the sales fee) to sell you a fund that might not be the best choice for you.

Investing in Funds on the Cheap

One of the advantages of mutual funds is that you don't need thousands of dollars to begin investing. Do you have $250 or less to start your investing plan? More than 900 funds will accept an initial investment as low as that. Another 1,000 funds will let you start with $500 or less.

The Quicken.com Mutual Fund Finder (`http://www.quicken.com/investments/mutualfunds/finder`) enables you to search for funds with low minimum investments. Select the amount that you have to invest, and then you will see a list of all the funds that will sell you shares. You learned how to create a mutual fund search in Chapter 5.

You Can Beat High Minimums with an IRA Account

Mutual fund companies often accept smaller initial investments in Individual Retirement Accounts (IRAs) and Roth IRAs than in regular, nonretirement accounts.

After you've established your account, most mutual funds have minimum amounts for additional purchases. Often these are as low as $50, or perhaps $100. This can be an important consideration when you select a fund—if minimum subsequent investments are too high, it may be difficult for you to invest on a regular basis.

It Can Be Tough to Get into a Hot Fund

The more popular and successful a mutual fund is, the more likely that it will require high minimum initial and subsequent investments. The demand for the fund means that the management can demand (and receive) a more substantial commitment from investors. Conversely, a fund that has been less successful or is just starting out may have low minimums to make it as easy as possible for investors to invest.

Fundomatic Investing with Automatic Investing Plans

If $250 is a stretch for you to come up with all at once, there is another way to get started in mutual funds. Many fund companies will allow you to invest in their funds with as little as $50, as long as you make a commitment to invest that amount each month for a year or so. This is called an *automatic investment plan* (AIP).

Get Acquainted with This Method of Regular Investing

Investing using an automatic investment plan is sometimes known as *systematic investing*.

How do fund companies make sure that you honor your commitment to invest each month? They require that your monthly investments be automatically deducted from your paycheck or checking account. Each month, a preset amount is automatically transferred to the fund company and invested in the fund that you've selected, purchasing shares at whatever the price might be on the date of the investment.

Besides allowing you to start investing with small amounts, the beauty of AIPs is that they make it extremely easy to invest regularly. You don't have to worry about writing a check each month. When you "pay yourself first" automatically, you will make sure that your investment plan is being funded, before you've had a chance to buy that new outfit you have had your eye on or a new set of golf clubs.

As you work toward your goals, step by step, you will also put the power of dollar cost averaging to work for you. Remember that when you invest the same amount in a mutual fund on a regular basis, you buy more shares when the price is lower, and fewer shares when the price is higher. Over time, this can reduce your average cost per share. It can also make market fluctuations work for you, not against you.

To get started with an AIP, just ask your mutual fund company for an application, or download one from its Web site. If you're having money transferred from your bank account, you will probably need to send along a voided check with the application. Before you sign up, be sure that you understand how long you need to continue in the AIP before you can stop, and what the procedures are for stopping the plan altogether.

Dollar Cost Averaging Works Great with Stock Funds!

Dollar cost averaging works best with investments that fluctuate in price. Because stock market funds tend to be more volatile than other types of funds, an automatic investment plan can be a great way to invest in these funds.

In a Down Market, Dollar Cost Averaging Won't Protect You from Losses

In a declining market, not even dollar cost averaging or an automatic investment plan can protect you from losses on your investments. That's why it's best to implement your AIP with an eye to the long term, and invest an amount that you can continue to invest no matter what happens in the market.

The Least You Need to Know

➤ You can invest in your choice of thousands of mutual funds. There are funds that strive to meet many different investment objectives.

➤ You can buy mutual funds through a broker or directly from a fund company. Many brokers offer mutual fund supermarkets that allow you to invest in funds from many families with little or no transaction fees.

➤ You can get started in many funds with $100 or less, as long as you invest in the fund automatically each month for a year or so.

Chapter 8

Finding and Researching Mutual Funds on the Web

In This Chapter

➤ What to look for on a mutual fund's Web site

➤ Where else on the Web you can find information about mutual funds

➤ Key points to consider in evaluating a fund's prospectus

Now that you understand how mutual funds work, it is time to find out more about the funds that are out there. On the Web, you can learn plenty about mutual funds, from the fund companies' own Web sites to independent services that rate and review mutual funds. You can even poke around in an online government database to get the "official" scoop about most any fund.

It's a Family Affair

When you are ready to hit the Web to learn more about mutual funds, you will find that most fund families have Web sites that are a great source of information about their funds.

MARKET 14 11/16 +1/8 STAT 135 3/4 + 7/8

MARKET 50 11/16 -2 3/16 STAT 245/8 + 3/16

The Largest Fund Families Manage Billions and Billions of Dollars

The following are the top mutual fund groups ranked by the total assets each has under management:

Fund Family	Assets ($Mil)
Fidelity Distributors	427,381
Vanguard Group	336,476
American Fund Distributors	251,467
Franklin Distributors Inc.	176,601
Putnam Investments	173,214
T. Rowe Price Investment Svcs.	89,211
Merrill Lynch Asset Management	87,463

Source: Financial Research Corporation, June 1998

You probably recognize the names of some of the largest and best-known fund families, such as Vanguard, Fidelity, and T. Rowe Price. All three firms have terrific sites on the Web that provide plenty of information to potential investors.

Some Fund Families Offer More Than Just Funds

Vanguard (http://www.vanguard .com) and Fidelity (http://www. fidelity.com) are among a small group of fund families who offer discount brokerage services to their clients, as well as financial planning and other investment services.

Online Mutual Funds and Families

The first place to start your online search for a mutual fund on the Web is the listing of mutual fund Web sites on Invest-O-Rama!, at http:// www.investorama.com/funds.html.

Before you set off on an exploration of a fund's Web site, ask yourself what kind of information you hope to find about this fund. If you expect a revealing look at the fund itself, think again. Fund companies will gladly tell you all the good things about their fund, but what if the fund has performed poorly?

Do you really think that a mutual fund company's Web site will just "tell" you that their funds are weak performers? The Securities and Exchange Commission and the National Association of Securities Dealers watch over how funds present their track records to investors, even on the Web, so you will rarely find a fund that will come right out and shamelessly lie to you about its history.

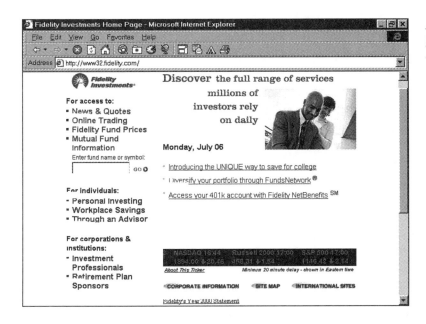

Fidelity is the largest fund family in the United States.

And could it be possible that a bit of glitz and glamour on a Web site might distract you from uncovering the essential truths? Could your attention be easily diverted by flashy graphics to another section of a site—away from that page that describes a fund's lousy performance?

If you are the kind of person who is never fooled by a magician who tries to distract you with chatter while he slides the ace of spades up his sleeve, you are all set. For the rest of you, remember that a glossy brochure—or a snazzy Web site—doesn't mean that a mutual fund is a good investment.

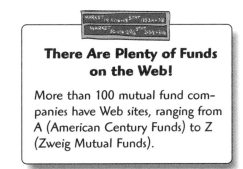

There Are Plenty of Funds on the Web!

More than 100 mutual fund companies have Web sites, ranging from A (American Century Funds) to Z (Zweig Mutual Funds).

Value Line's (`http://`
`www.valueline.com`*)*
Web site offers educational
articles, as well as infor-
mation about their funds.

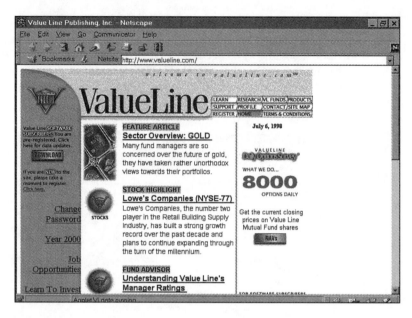

Keep that thought in mind as you navigate mutual fund Web sites. On most sites, you can find a lot of good information that can be important in helping you make a decision to buy (or not to buy) a particular mutual fund. The key is that you have to know what to look for.

Here are the key items that you should search for on any mutual fund's Web site.

General information about the fund company, the fund managers, and contact information. Here's where you can learn about the company and the people who are offering to manage your money. Some firms publish mission statements. These can be informative and illuminating articles that help you understand a fund company's character. On the other hand, you might find just a sentence or two of over-simplistic babbling, such as "Our mission is to serve our shareholders." Every fund company should have that mission!

Often, a fund Web site will publish a photograph of a fund's managers, just to let you know that fund managers are people too. Just don't be deceived by their smiling faces—remember that fund managers usually are paid a salary regardless of whether the fund performs well.

Specific information about the company's funds. Although this information may not seem like much more than spin, you can learn much about a specific fund by reading through the general information on its Web site.

Many sites, such as American Century's Web site (`http://www.americancentury.com`) group their funds by categories: stock funds, bond funds, specialty funds, growth funds, international funds, and so on. You can browse through all the funds a family offers, or zero in on funds in which you are especially interested. This can be a quick way to compare the different funds offered by the same company.

Online fund profiles can be easier to read than the prospectus, but they are not nearly as complete, either. On American Century's site, you can learn about a fund's performance, investment strategy, top holdings, expenses, and minimum investments, for instance. After you have reviewed a profile, you can then download the prospectus for further study.

Many families skip the fund profiles altogether and just reprint their prospectus on the site.

The fund prospectus. The most important thing to look for is the fund's *prospectus*. Investment companies are legally required to outline the fund's objectives and operating procedures in a formal document called a prospectus. (You will learn more about the kind of information that's in a prospectus a bit later.) Most fund companies now offer Web surfers the chance to download a copy of their prospectus right from their sites.

Past Performance Figures May Not Be All They Seem

The SEC has allowed some mutual funds to tout the past performance of their fund managers—even if those managers racked up their records at the helm of an entirely different fund! In a well-known case, Elizabeth Bramwell used her admirable record at the Gabelli Growth Fund to promote an entirely new fund she had left Gabelli to run. The Commission requires that funds be run in a "substantially" similar manner. Investors should be wary of a fund that advertises the successes of its management rather than the performance of the fund itself (and vice versa!).

Most recent Net Asset Value (NAV) of the funds. On the Web site of T. Rowe Price (http://www.troweprice.com) and other fund families, you can sometimes find the closing NAV of a fund posted even before it reaches other quote servers on the Internet. Often, you can access an archive of historical NAV data, or the fund company will calculate performance figures for the funds on a daily, weekly, monthly, yearly, or multiyear basis.

Application to open an account. Most fund companies include an account application that you can download from their site. At the least, every fund Web site provides easy instructions for requesting an application. Other forms, such as those required to open an IRA or establish an automatic investing program, may also be provided. If the company doesn't sell its funds directly to investors, the site will direct you to those brokers and advisors where you can purchase their fund.

Commentary from the fund managers. Many funds publish the current market outlook of their management or interviews with managers. Here, fund managers share their perceptions about the markets and how their funds will perform in the future. Some companies produce audio versions of market commentary so that you can listen to the fund manager describe his or her views. In these reports, you can often get a better understanding of a manager's approach to the stock market.

Getting Rid of the Legalese in Financial Documents

The Securities and Exchange Commission has released new rules that will require the nation's 3,400 mutual funds to use simplified, user-friendly prospectuses for all funds they offer. The new "Plain English" prospectuses will be in use by the end of 1999.

Annual, semiannual, and quarterly reports. Mutual funds are required to keep their shareholders informed about their activities in reports produced at least twice a year. This is helpful information for analyzing a fund's history and learning about where the fund's managers plan to take it.

Press releases and news stories. Mutual funds typically issue press releases that detail the fund's year-end or semiannual distributions of capital gains and dividends or describe changes in management and other news about the fund and its operations. You can often find archives of these stories on a fund company's site.

Calculators, quizzes, IRA analyzers, educational articles. Many fund sites provide educational information and decision-making tools for investors. It is not uncommon to find calculators to help with developing a financial plan, such as determining how much you need to save to put your children through college or when you will likely be able to retire comfortably. If you have questions about whether to convert your traditional IRA to a Roth IRA, many sites have analyzers that can outline the best scenario for your personal situation. Interactive quizzes test your knowledge of the markets (and hopefully you will learn a thing or two, too!). These "added bonuses" can really contribute to your investment education.

Online account access (for shareholders). If you are a shareholder of a mutual fund, many sites offer access to your accounts. You can log on and check your account balances, review a history of your transactions, and even make transfers between funds. Although you probably shouldn't buy a fund just because it offers online access, this feature can be very convenient in keeping track of all your purchases and account balances.

Contact information. Nearly every fund company Web site provides (at the very least) a phone number that you can call to request a prospectus, application, or other information. If you have any questions, go ahead and send an email message or telephone the fund company. And don't worry that your question may be too "basic" or "simple"—most funds have trained customer service representatives who can answer any questions you might have and patiently walk you through the process of completing an account application or selecting a fund from within their family.

Getting Acquainted with a Fund's Prospectus

A mutual fund prospectus is your best decision-making tool. The Securities and Exchange Commission requires certain information be contained in a fund's prospectus, and that each prospectus be updated on a regular basis. Often, a fund company prospectus will include information about a company's entire family of funds, or a particular "portfolio" of funds in that family.

The SEC considers the information in a prospectus to be so important that it won't allow a fund company or broker to offer to sell you a mutual fund without giving you the prospectus first. If you place an order to buy a mutual fund with your broker, you will get a copy of the prospectus in the mail along with or soon after you receive your order confirmation.

Companies like Vanguard and Fidelity provide downloadable versions of their prospectuses in Adobe Acrobat format. You must have Adobe Acrobat installed on your computer to read the prospectus. But don't worry—the Acrobat reader is available for free from Adobe, and publishers who use Acrobat files provide a link to Adobe's Web site so you can download the reader program.

The advantage of publishing documents in Acrobat is that the prospectus you download to your computer looks exactly the same as the printed version a fund company might send you in the mail, including any charts, graphics, and fonts used in the publication.

Some companies, such as T. Rowe Price (http://www.troweprice.com), require investors to provide their name and address even before they can view prospectuses on the T. Rowe Price Web site. This is because the SEC won't let a fund company sell you a fund without sending you the prospectus. When you register, you are providing proof to the fund that you have had the chance (at least) to read the prospectus.

Be Patient! Acrobat Files Can Be Big

Adobe Acrobat files are large, so it can take a few minutes to download a prospectus or application from a fund Web site, especially if you have a slower connection to the Internet.

Adobe Acrobat Is a Graceful Way of Delivering Information over the Internet

If you have ever tried to open a file that was created on someone else's computer, you might be familiar with the problems that this seemingly simple task can create. If you want to open a spreadsheet file, for instance, you need to have the same application installed on your computer as the one that originally created the spreadsheet. Even then, new wrinkles can pop up if different versions of software or different operating systems (Macintosh versus Windows) are involved, often making a file unusable on some computers. And if specific fonts are used in the file, those have to be installed on both computers; otherwise, it won't look the same. Printing adds another level of complication, because not all printers work within the same margins. All in all, if can be tough to share information with others—at least so that it looks exactly the same no matter what kind of computer a user has.

Adobe Acrobat tackles this problem by letting information publishers convert any document into an Acrobat file. Acrobat files are created in something called a "portable document format." This means that these files can be viewed on any type of computer by any user, regardless of the fonts or printers that might be installed on a machine—and the document will look almost exactly the same on screen and in print. Brochures, application forms, and legal documents are often converted to Acrobat files so that they can be distributed online and ensure that all users get exactly the same information. The best news is that the Adobe Acrobat reader program is free to users (the program that creates Acrobat files must be purchased if you plan on creating Acrobat files). Just go to the Adobe Web site at http://www.adobe.com and download the correct version for your computer.

Other Web sites, including American Century (http://www.americancentury.com) and Robertson Stephens (http://www.rsim.com), publish their prospectuses in HTML format. That means that you can just read the prospectus in your browser.

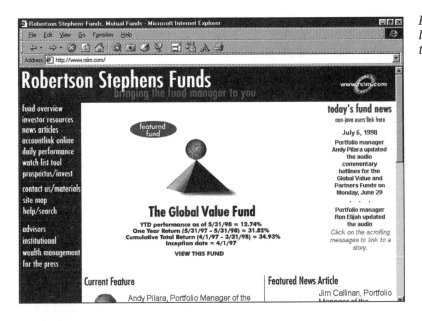

Robertson Stephens publishes their fund prospectus on their Web site.

EDGAR Is Ready to Serve You

If you can't find a prospectus on a fund company's Web site, another source could be the Security and Exchange Commission's EDGAR. EDGAR is an acronym for Electronic Data Gathering, Analysis, and Retrieval, and it is the SEC's system of collecting information from public companies and investment companies via computer links. In days not so long ago, companies used to prepare voluminous reports on paper (and multiple copies, of course) and submit them to the SEC.

Today, companies can just send their filings to the Commission via modem. Although this certainly cuts down on the mountains of paper that used to be generated, another side benefit is that the SEC can provide copies of all these reports to individual investors on its Web site.

The SEC has made it easy for investors to search for mutual fund prospectuses on its site, with a form designed for just that search (http://www.sec.gov/edaux/prospect.htm). Enter a few letters of the fund family name, select how far back you would like to search (all filings or just last month, for instance), and the search program will find the prospectus you are looking for. Another form (http://www.sec.gov/edaux/mutual.htm) enables you to search for all available information for a particular fund.

The SEC makes it easy to search for mutual fund prospectuses on their EDGAR Web site.

```
EDGAR Prospectus Report - Microsoft Internet Explorer                    _ 🗗 ✕
File  Edit  View  Go  Favorites  Help                                        🄴
← · → · ⊗ 🖪 🏠 | 🔍 📷 📀 💲 | 🖅 🗞 🄰 🖨
Address 🄴 http://www.sec.gov/edaux/prospect.htm                                 ▼
```

EDGAR Prospectus Report

This page gives you all "485" filings pertaining to a mutual fund of your choice.

enter a mutual fund...

> (do NOT enter more than 20 characters of the company, or you run the risk of getting no hits even if you typed in the name properly):

> Examples of input: "de" gives you Dean Witter, "dr" gives you Dreyfus, "van" gives you Vanguard...

Vanguard

```
              │Now
              │Last Week
              │Last Two Weeks
              │Last Month
What date range?│Entire Database (since 1/1/94)
```

Learn the Form Numbers and Abbreviations Used by EDGAR

EDGAR filings are often labeled by form number. Some of the more common abbreviations in use for mutual fund filings include the following:

N-1A: Registration statement (prospectus) for mutual funds.

497: Supplements to a previously filed prospectus.

N-30D: An annual and semi-annual report mailed to shareholders.

PRE 14A: Preliminary proxy statement.

DEF 14A: Definitive proxy statement.

One thing you will notice right away if you access a prospectus from EDGAR is that it is not the easiest document to read. All EDGAR filings have headers and footers with special codes, but you can safely ignore these. The documents themselves are just text files—but text files with line breaks at the end of lines (so the lines don't wrap as they might in your browser or word processor) and page breaks that may not coincide with your printer.

You can learn to navigate and read EDGAR documents in your browser—it just takes practice! Some people like to print out these files (although just clicking the Print button in your browser can result in pages that are still difficult to read).

Just the Facts, Jack—Understanding a Fund Prospectus

No matter where or how you access a fund prospectus—from a company's Web site, from the SEC EDGAR Web site, or in the mail—the same information will be included in the document. Getting your hands on a fund prospectus is the easy part—interpreting all the facts and figures in a prospectus is another story, however.

All mutual fund prospectuses follow the same general format. If you can get through the following information in a prospectus (and understand it), you will be well on your way to making better decisions about your fund purchases.

Expense Summary. It costs money for a company to run a mutual fund—but those costs are passed right along to shareholders in the form of "expenses." Some funds directly charge shareholders certain fees for services and transactions, or just for managing the fund.

All prospectuses include a summary of these fees and expenses near the beginning of the document. Fees can be divided into several categories:

➤ All funds have an annual management fee. This fee typically varies from under 1% to more than 2% of the fund's assets. These are the costs of administrating the fund, and are they passed along to shareholders.

➤ Distribution fees (called 12b-1 fees) are used to cover the expenses of marketing and advertising the fund to new investors.

➤ A sales load is a charge you pay when you buy a fund.

➤ A deferred sales load is a charge you pay when you sell a fund. Often, this charge disappears if you hold a fund longer than a specific period, such as five years.

➤ Redemption fees (also known as back-end loads) are assessed when shares are sold. These fees are sometimes used to discourage frequent trading of a fund.

Get a Load of This!

A *load* is a charge that you pay to the fund when you purchase or sell shares in it. Loads come in two varieties: front-end loads, charged when you buy a fund; and back-end loads, charged when you sell a fund. These charges are usually a percentage of the total amount you are investing in the fund.

The total of these fees can range anywhere from a low of 0.2% (for no-load bond funds and index funds) up to 8.5% (for an international stock fund with a load) of the fund's assets.

The key point to remember is that fees reduce your profits (or increase your losses). If the managers of two mutual funds can both generate returns of 10% on the investments in their portfolios, but one fund has a 1.5% expense ratio and the other charges 4%, you will be better off with the fund that has lower expenses. The actual return of the fund with lower expenses is 8.5%, compared to a 6% return of the more expensive fund. The best thing to do is compare the fees and expenses of several similar funds and see how they stack up. You can also compare a fund's expenses to the averages for that type of fund (see the sidebar for average expense ratios of many types of funds).

Fees aren't included in total return calculations, so you will have to figure out for yourself what investing in a specific fund really costs you. Comparing the prospectuses of all the funds you are considering is a way to figure out which fund may be better for you.

Financial Highlights. Each prospectus includes a 10-year table of the fund's results over the last 10 years (or for the life of the fund, if it is been around for fewer than 10 years). The table shows the fund's total return in each fiscal year, as well as each year's expense ratio, distributions, dividends, and portfolio turnover rate (this is how frequently the fund manager buys and shares securities in the portfolio).

Investment Objectives and Policies. The next section that you will encounter in a prospectus is an outline of the fund's basic investment objective. You will also hear how the managers expect to meet those objectives.

A fund's objectives are usually very broad. A fund might seek "long-term growth," or "capital appreciation," or "the highest rate of current return on its investments." You need to make sure that your personal objective and the fund manager's are in sync.

The prospectus also details the policy that governs the kinds of securities that the fund expects to own, often with minimum or maximum percentages for different classes or categories. An intermediate-term bond fund might invest in "securities issued or guaranteed by the U.S. Treasury and maintaining a weighted average portfolio maturity, which ranges from 3 to 10 years." A growth stock fund might invest in "small- and mid-cap companies, to create a portfolio of investments broadly diversified over industry sectors and companies."

Other Investment Practices and Risk Considerations. If the fund manager is permitted to own speculative investments, such as derivatives or use "hedging strategies" to manage the portfolio's risk, those points will be covered here.

Management of the Funds/Portfolio Managers. Who is the company and who are the people who would be managing your money in this fund? This section provides information on the fund manager, his or her experience and length of service, and details of the firm behind the fund. Remember when you buy a mutual fund, it is like you are paying the fund manager to handle your investment decisions. Read through this section as if you were interviewing a job candidate!

Expenses Vary Widely Depending on the Type of Fund

The average expense ratios for various categories of mutual funds are as follows:

Category	Average Expense Ratio
Sector - Tech/Communications	2.28%
Emerging Market Equity	2.23%
Sector - Other	2.02%
Global Equity	1.88%
Non-U.S. Equity	1.85%
Sector - Energy/Natural Resources	1.83%
Sector - Precious Metals	1.79%
Aggressive Growth	1.77%
Sector - Health/Biotechnology	1.71%
Sector - Real Estate	1.67%
Sector - Financial Services	1.62%
Small Cap	1.54%
Mid Cap	1.52%
Sector - Utilities	1.51%
Growth - Domestic	1.45%
Equity Income	1.43%
Growth & Income	1.33%
S&P 500 Index	0.66%

Source: Findafund.com, June 1998

An Easy-to-Read Prospectus Is on the Way!

In 1998, the Securities and Exchange Commission approved a plan to permit a mutual fund to offer investors a new "mini-prospectus" document called a "profile." A profile summarizes key information about the fund in a concise, standardized format. Funds can offer a profile to investors rather than the full prospectus, and investors can purchase shares in the fund after reviewing only the profile. Of course, to make the best-informed decision about your fund purchases, you should still read the full prospectus first.

Investment Methods. Now it is time to get down to the nitty-gritty of investing in a fund. This section of the prospectus explains how to buy and sell shares in the fund, the minimums for initial and subsequent investments in the fund, and whether the fund offers services such as check writing. Other details may be stated here, as well, such as whether exchanges within the fund family are free, whether an automatic investing plan is available, and how to redeem shares. If you are investing on a shoestring budget, it is important to know whether you can manage the minimum investment amounts. This is where you can get the scoop.

Dividends, Distributions, and Taxes. The prospectus will explain the tax consequences of the investment for the shareholder, and the fund's policies regarding distributions of gains, income, and dividends.

The Least You Need to Know

➤ Check out a mutual fund company's Web site for important information about a fund—before you invest.

➤ Several Web sites provide important details about a fund and its performance.

➤ You can find the prospectus for nearly every mutual fund on the Web. The prospectus is the single most important document you should review before investing in a fund.

Chapter 9

Getting Cyber–Advice About Funds

In This Chapter

➤ Research particular funds on the Web

➤ Get advice and information to help you build a portfolio of mutual funds

➤ Talk with other investors about mutual funds

➤ How to find mutual funds that meet your objectives

Although the information on a fund company's Web site may help you to learn about one of their mutual funds, let's face it: Before you invest any of your hard-earned dollars, you will probably want to check out some information provided by an unbiased third party. Fortunately, a number of Web sites are happy to oblige your quest for more information. And plenty of the fund research on the Web is free!

Mutual Fund Reports

Start your fund research at Morningstar.Net (`http://www.morningstar.net`). Morningstar is an independent analysis firm that reviews and rates mutual funds. They produce software as well as printed guides to funds, and their "star" rating system is widely regarded as one of the best overall measures of a fund's potential future performance.

The Morningstar.Net Web site is one of the richest online sources of information about mutual funds. Commentary and tutorials from Morningstar's analysts and staff writers can help you to learn more about fund investing, or you can ask your questions in the site's message boards and get responses from Morningstar's staff or other users. You can track your own customized portfolio of stocks and funds on the site, too.

The highlight of the site is the QuickTake report, available on any mutual fund. Enter the ticker symbol of your fund on the front page of the site, and you will see a comprehensive report. Each QuickTake includes details of a fund's performance, its risk and return ratings, the top holdings in the fund's portfolio, recent news stories, an overview of the fees and expenses charged by the fund, and information about contacting the fund manager and investing in the fund.

In these reports, Morningstar also provides the "star" rating assigned to that fund. Morningstar rates mutual funds on a one-star to five-star basis, based on a mathematical calculation of each fund's risk and return in the past. If your fund is rated four or five stars, you have found one of the best!

Morningstar.Net provides ratings and reviews of mutual funds.

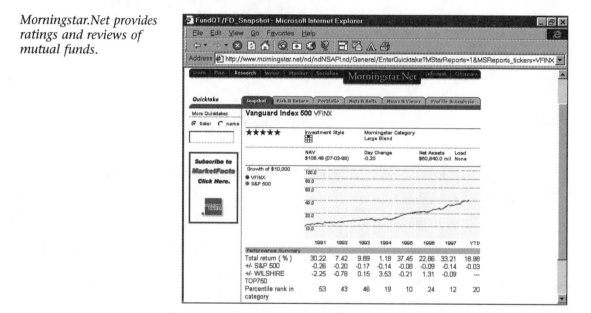

Most of the resources on the site are free, although Morningstar also offers some additional services in a Premium subscription package.

Downloadable versions of Morningstar fund reports are not available from the site, however. Morningstar's mutual fund reports are highly esteemed for their analytical insights, but a subscription to the printed edition is a whopping $425 a year! One alternative that can save you money is to purchase only the Morningstar Mutual Fund Reports you need for just $5 each from INVESTools (http://www.investools.com).

INVESTools is like a shopping mall for investing newsletters and reports. Instead of subscribing to several pricey market letters or advisory services, investors can purchase individual issues from the INVESTools Web site. You will need to establish an account with INVESTools, using a credit card, but you won't be charged until you purchase a specific item. Immediately after you have purchased a report, you can download it in Adobe Acrobat format to your own computer desktop.

Granted, it might not be economical to purchase 30 Morningstar fund reports while you are trying to decide on the fund that's best for you. So explore the Morningstar Web site, and the others described in this chapter, and invest $5 in a complete Morningstar Mutual Fund Report from INVESTools before you make the final decision to invest thousands of dollars.

Value Line (`http://www.valueline.com`) is probably best known for its "Value Line Investment Survey," a stock analysis and rating service used by many investors. However, the company also produces a "Mutual Fund Survey" that rates and reviews 1,500 funds, both in a printed edition and as a data/software service. Although the company doesn't publish any free fund research online, they do offer some good educational material that makes the site worth a visit. Select **Learn** from the menu bar on the site to explore this section. (Value Line does license some of its information to other sites, as you will see later in this chapter.)

Millions of people are familiar with the Quicken line of financial software, programs that help balance a personal or business checkbook or keep investing records. The Quicken.com (`http://www.quicken.com/investments/mutualfunds`) online financial network is a robust Web site featuring articles, message boards, and data, available for free.

The "Mutual Funds" section of the site provides research reports on funds using data provided by both Value Line and Morningstar. One handy feature of Quicken.com's fund charts is that they can be customized by date to plot the NAVs of up to nine separate funds on a single chart.

Quicken.com's Fund Finder is the best way to zero in on the right funds for your portfolio (see the following section for more on this feature). The combination of reports from the two major fund analyzers, as well as quotes and charts, makes Quicken.com a convenient, informative, and essential resource for fund investors.

Mutual Funds Online (`http://www.mfmag.com`) is an online companion to *Mutual Funds Magazine*, a popular monthly devoted to fund investing. Registration is required to use the site, but there is no cost for access to much of the information on the site, including reprints from the magazine, bulletin boards, and daily fund picks. A Charter Membership option provides additional tools for screening and researching stocks for a monthly fee (mostly useful if you are a hard-core fund addict).

Mutual Funds Interactive (`http://www.fundsinteractive.com`) is an online community for mutual fund investors, offering discussion boards, chats, and columns from an array of contributors. The site also offers truncated Value Line mutual fund reports that include a few performance numbers and some descriptive information. You can find a lot of helpful information here, as long as you are willing to explore!

Find-a-Fund (`http://www.findafund.com`) publishes a lot of fund information on its site, including all kinds of performance charts and presorted lists of funds, but the standout feature is its "Similarity Portfolio Analysis" tool. Enter the tickers of two mutual funds and the program examines the similarity between two funds by comparing their sector weightings and individual holdings. You may be surprised! Your portfolio's diversification can be thrown askew if you own two funds that are very similar in objective and that own the same stocks—and it happens more than you think.

Find-a-Fund's "Similarity Portfolio Analysis" tool pinpoints funds in your portfolio that own too many of the same securities.

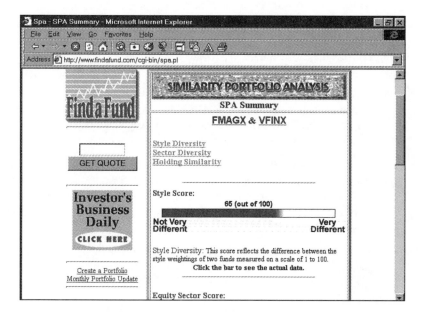

You could say that a mutual fund price chart is worth a thousand words. Taking a peek at a chart of a mutual fund's net asset value over time at BigCharts (http://www.bigcharts.com) can give you a good idea of how the fund has performed for investors. BigCharts is a fast, easy-to-use, and customizable charting service for stocks and funds. Enter the ticker symbol or part of the fund's name, and BigCharts will deliver a graph in seconds.

Online Guides Through the Fund Forest

If you are the type of person who likes to get advice from a pro before making a final decision about where to invest, the Web is home to plenty of pundits. As always, figuring which experts you *should* listen to is a problem, especially if you are paying for it! Most sites provide samples of their newsletters or advisory services, or a free trial subscription. These examples are usually enough to give you an idea of whether the advice you are getting is worth the cost.

The following few sites are just a sampling of the wide range of experts waiting to guide you through the fund maze—hopefully making your portfolio more profitable in the process.

The Association of Mutual Fund Investors (http://www.amfi.com) has created several mechanical trading systems that indicate when to buy or sell growth funds, sector funds, or bond funds. The Association seeks to achieve higher-risk adjusted returns than just buying and holding an S&P 500 Index Fund. After you join the group by paying an annual membership fee, you will receive a manual that describes its approach and regular updates on their site. You can also subscribe to additional "hotlines," manuals, and research reports that can all add up to an expensive purchase.

The Cedar Group (http://www.cdrgrp.com) is an advisory firm that aims to help individuals invest successfully in their 401 or 403 retirement accounts, or for an individual portfolio. But rather than just send the same monthly newsletter to each subscriber, Cedar Group prepares rankings of the funds in *your* company retirement plan, and recommends the particular funds you should purchase. It also offers a more standard fund advisory service.

Don't Be Fooled by the "Credentials" That Some Advisors Hold

Anyone can advertise his or her services as "Registered Investment Advisor"—anyone can become an RIA if he submits an application (with the appropriate fee) to the Securities and Exchange Commission signifying that he intends to provide investment advice to the general public. But there are no other requirements to becoming an RIA— no tests to pass, no experience, and no particular financial knowledge is necessary.

For the ultimate investing couch potato, Sensible Investment Strategies (http://www.seninvest.com) is a service that will tell you how to put together a portfolio using highly rated, no-load mutual funds. Just fill out a brief questionnaire, pay a one-time fee of $50, and your customized portfolio strategy will be on its way to you via mail within a few days. All you have to do is buy those funds and you will be the proud owner of a new portfolio!

Yakking About Funds

If you have questions, chances are that someone has answers. At least that's the philosophy behind the numerous message boards and chat rooms on the Internet. Online discussion groups are often referred to as *bulletin boards* because users *post* messages on a site and wait for other users to post responses (think of a cork board with notes on index cards hanging by thumbtacks).

Who Is FundGenius1234, Anyway?

Although you can never be sure who exactly is behind a particular nickname, the best message boards are truly virtual communities, with members who know each other, know whom to avoid, and know whom to listen to. If you hang around long enough, you can usually figure out who is the loud-mouth (and who is the quiet genius).

If you are a fund investor, you can choose from several sites where you can talk to others who are fond of funds. You can ask for recommendations from other investors, or "eavesdrop" on the conversations and try to soak up the knowledge. Online discussion groups provide a good place to ask your questions about mutual fund investing, and meet other people who have been in your shoes as a beginning investor—and who are willing to share what they have learned with others.

The Armchair Millionaire (http://www.armchairmillionaire.com), for example, hosts message boards that are particularly useful for beginning mutual fund investors. In fact, one of the first message boards you will see when you arrive on the site is titled "There Are No Dumb Questions." The Mutual Fund boards feature a lot of beginner questions and lively responses from more experienced fund investors. The site also features an asset allocation strategy using stock market funds (often called index funds) to build a long-term portfolio.

After you have learned a bit more about funds, drop by Mutual Funds Interactive (http://www.fundsinteractive.com). This site is home to six newsgroups, each devoted to mutual funds. Investors can talk about specific funds, retirement planning, the market and the economy, and related topics on these Web discussion boards. Mutual Funds Interactive claims that its boards are the "most popular hangout for mutual funds investors" on the Web, so you are likely to find someone to chat with you on just about any fund-related topic.

Most Message Boards Require Registration

Nearly all these message boards on the Web require that you register before you can post a message on their boards. That's to make users more accountable for the messages they post on the board, and to make it difficult for anyone to post messages anonymously.

If you want to meet shareholders of a particular mutual fund family, check out Quicken.com's online forums at (http://www.quicken.com/forums). In conjunction with Web search engine company Excite, Quicken.com offers investors a chance to discuss mutual funds in a structured message board. Here, folders have been set up for major funds and fund families; just find the fund that you want to talk about and ask your questions. Other users are likely to chime in with their opinions of that particular fund.

Searching for Funds in All the Right Places

If you have decided to do it all yourself and design your own portfolio of mutual funds, you need to start picking some funds. Although it is relatively easy to find information about mutual funds on the Web, you must first understand your own goals. Among some of the questions that you must ask of yourself are the following:

➤ How much risk can I stand?

➤ What are the objectives of my entire portfolio?

➤ When do I need the money that I'm investing?

➤ What's my asset allocation strategy?

➤ How will my portfolio be diversified?

Answering those questions can guide you toward the right funds for you.

The Charles Schwab Guide to Investing (`http://www.schwab.com/invest/invest-index.html`) features an "Investor Profile" questionnaire, with seven simple questions about your approach to the markets and your risk tolerance. The program analyzes your responses and then determines the type of investor you are, such as "Aggressive," "Moderate," or "Conservative," and how much you should consider investing in stocks, bonds, and/or cash.

Online Mutual Fund Screening

After you have determined your strategy, you need to find the funds that complete the puzzle. Fortunately, computers and the Internet make one particular investing task much, much easier—the job of sifting through the 8,000 available mutual funds to find the handful of funds right for you. This process is known as *screening*.

Don't Forget the Importance of Proper Asset Allocation When Choosing Funds

Don't get too caught up in picking the perfect mutual fund. Academic studies have shown that the most important part of building a successful portfolio is your asset allocation strategy—not your stock- or fund-picking prowess. Particular stock or fund selections determine only about 5% of your long-term return. The remaining 95% is determined by the way you allocate your assets among stocks, bonds, and cash.

Screening is the process of determining the particular qualities that you want in your funds, thus enabling you to spend your time studying a handful of funds most likely to meet your criteria, instead of the thousands of funds that are wrong for you.

On the Web, you can screen mutual funds at a number of different Web sites. The big advantage of online screening is that you don't have to worry about maintaining or updating an enormous database on your own computer. The site that offers the screening tool will keep its database up to date, which means you will be accessing current information.

The Quicken.com Mutual Fund Finder (http://www.quicken.com/investments/ mutualfunds/finder) is one of the easiest screening tools to use on the Web. Using a database provided by Morningstar, users can screen on any of the following criteria:

➤ Morningstar category

➤ Morningstar rating

➤ Front load

➤ Net assets

➤ 12b-1 fees

➤ Minimum investment

➤ Expense ratio

➤ Year-to-date return

➤ 1-year return

➤ 3-year return

➤ 5-year return

➤ 10-year return

You Still Have More Work to Do

After you have run a screen, the funds in your search results are not immediate candidates for purchase. You still need to do your research on the funds, because some other factors may make some funds unsuitable for your portfolio.

Just click and select the factors important to you, and how you would like the results sorted (by return or expense ratio, for instance), and the program walks through the database, ignoring those funds outside the scope you established. In a few seconds, you will be looking at a list of mutual funds that passed your screen.

Let's say you were looking to add a no-load, large-cap growth fund to your portfolio. You might build this screen in the Fund Finder:

➤ Morningstar category: Large Growth

➤ Morningstar rating: Three stars or better

➤ Front load: No front load

➤ Net assets: Any

➤ 12b-1 fees: No 12b-1 fees

➤ Minimum investment: Any

➤ Expense ratio: 2.0% or less

Sometimes, You Just Can't Seem to Go Back!

You may occasionally try to use the Back button on your Web browser to return to a page you have already visited, only to be greeted with an ominous-sounding message such as `Warning: Page Has Expired` or `Data Missing`. Although they sound grim, these messages mean only that the page you are trying to view was created on-the-fly just for you. You probably entered some information on a form on the site, or made some selections in a search tool, for instance. The page that you viewed after that was built by a program on the Web site using your input. As a security precaution, and to keep Web servers from needlessly re-creating the same page time after time, your browser may not save these pages in its cache. If you want to view the page again, you need to click the Reload button on your Web browser, and the customizing information will be sent from your browser back to the Web server to create the page again.

If you stopped right there and clicked the Search button, you would see that 50 funds meet these criteria. You would certainly spend a lot of time looking at those funds if you thoroughly researched them all!

Quicken.com's Fund Finder enables you to search using a dozen different criteria.

So, let's make the criteria a bit more restrictive. At the bottom of the Web page, you can adjust your criteria (your current criteria are maintained so that you don't have to start all over from the beginning).

Let's upgrade our Morningstar rating to only show funds that have a four-star rating or higher. Click the Submit button, and you will see that half of the funds disappear. If you change the screen to only display funds with a five-star rating, you will end up with about 10 funds. We have gone from several thousand funds down to less than a dozen. That's more like it!

Quicken.com's Fund Finder makes searching for funds a snap.

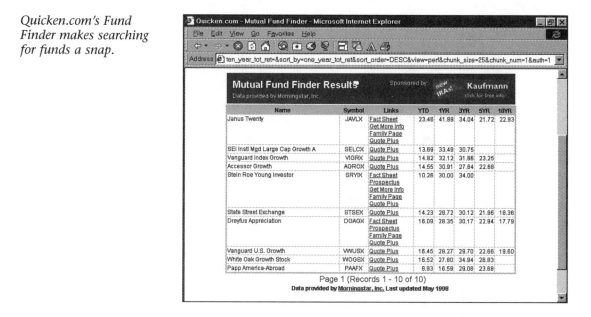

Quicken.com provides several ways to view the results: sorted by return, fund name, or expense ratio. It also provides several ways to display data: performance numbers, fees, ratings, or your search criteria. Depending on what's most important to you, you can look at the final list of candidates in a number of ways. After you have narrowed the list, you can click to get more information from Quicken.com's fund reports.

Remember these two rules of thumb about screening. First, it is always good idea to start your search with broad criteria—three-star funds rather than five-star funds, for instance—and then whittle your search down to become more restrictive.

Second, don't use search criteria that cancel each other out or aren't even possible. You could build a search that looks for a municipal bond fund with a 1-year 40% return, for example, but it would be exceptionally uncommon for a municipal bond fund to have that kind of return.

Morningstar.Net Fund Selector (http://www.morningstar.net) is an online fund screening tool takes a slightly different approach to searches. Its basic screen enables you to select a broad category of funds and a single screening field, and the results are only the top funds in that search. The advanced screens are only available to registered members of the site, and use Java to enable you to build a screen one factor at a time. Each time you select a field, it adds that criteria to the screen and displays a new results set.

Although this sounds plausible in concept, it is a bit hard to work with in real life. There is no button labeled Search—as soon as you select the final field, your search is executed.

Mutual Funds Interactive (`http://www.fundsinteractive.com`) uses a subset of Value Line's database to enable you to screen for mutual funds. One drawback is that you have to enter your email address every time you enter the screening area. Another drawback is the very cursory information provided.

As part of their subscription package, Microsoft Investor (`http://www.investor.com`) offers an Investment Finder that enables you to select from several "canned" searches or build your own. You must also download some software to your computer before you can access the search capabilities, and you have to wait while Investor checks that you have the software installed each time you access the site (although the software does do some nifty tricks).

The Least You Need to Know

➤ You can learn more about particular mutual funds by visiting sites that offer research reports, many for free. You can visit sites where you can discuss ideas and ask questions with other fund investors.

➤ Online advisors and newsletters can lay out a blueprint with specific directions for building your portfolio of mutual funds.

➤ You can use the Web to search for mutual funds using several screening tools. These screening sites are quick and convenient ways to find the funds that warrant further research.

Part 3
Investing in Stocks

Ever wished that you were lucky enough to have bought stock years ago in the little company with the big idea that made everyone rich? Then, this section is just for you. Remember, clever investing isn't always about buying stock in that one, magical company with the exploding profits. Sure, picking good stock is important, but the reward is in investing in a variety of stocks to create a portfolio with stamina. On the Internet you can find sources to help you make those money decisions that really matter.

Chapter 10

Strategies for Investing in Stocks

In This Chapter

➤ Understanding fundamental and technical analysis of stocks

➤ The dangers of penny stocks

➤ Investing in the "Dogs of the Dow"

Ah, the allure of the stock market! For the hardcore, do-it-yourself investor, there's nothing more satisfying than picking a stock that turns out to be a winner.

But a successful portfolio takes more than merely trying to buy stocks that you hope will go up in price. If you want to consistently beat the market, you need to choose a methodology of investing, and then stick with it. The most successful stock investors are the ones who never waiver from their selected approach.

You can use a number of different approaches to select stocks. You can look for stocks that are growing faster than the market in general, or stocks that are undervalued compared to other similar stocks. You can look for stocks with prices that are moving up really fast, or stocks that are being publicly sold to investors for the first time. Investors use dozens of methods and techniques when deciding which stocks to buy.

The approach to the stock market that you ultimately select will be determined by a couple of factors. For instance, do you want to spend hours a day on your portfolio? Or would you rather spend a few hours a month researching and following the stocks you own or would like to own? Do you want to build a solid blue chip portfolio? Are you a computer buff who really wants to maximize the capability of that expensive piece of hardware on your desktop to analyze stocks?

To help you figure out the best approach to use, here's an overview of the most common methods that investors use in building a portfolio of stocks.

Fundamentally Speaking

One of the most popular ways of studying stocks is called *fundamental analysis*. Investors who use this approach like to learn as much as possible about a company and its management. They read annual reports and study financial statements and the industry in an effort to figure out what they think is the true or "fair" value of that company's stock. By comparing the current stock price to that "fair value" you can determine whether it might be a good time to buy that stock—or if it's a stock to avoid like the Black Plague!

The Internet can deliver just about all the information that you need to make a decision to buy or sell a stock based on fundamental analysis. In the rest of Part 3, you will learn more about these sites. Some of the best-known investors in history have been fundamental analysts, including Peter Lynch, the legendary manager of the Fidelity Magellan mutual fund. Under his management, Magellan was the best performing mutual fund in history. Another famous fundamentalist is Warren Buffet, the brilliant investor behind Berkshire Hathaway. Berkshire Hathaway was once a textile company, but Buffet turned it into a vehicle in which he could invest in other stocks, with phenomenal success. A single share of Berkshire Hathaway now trades for more than $65,000!

Most individual investors use fundamental analysis in some way to pick stocks for their portfolios. If you are looking for a way to build a "buy-and-hold" portfolio of stocks, made up of companies that you can purchase and then own for years and years without losing too much sleep at night, you will probably use the methods of fundamental analysis.

Investors who use fundamental analysis usually focus on two separate approaches to picking stocks: *growth* or *value* (or sometimes a combination of both). On the Internet, you can learn more about both varieties of fundamental analysis, and determine which is best for you.

Going for Growth or Seeking Out Value?

When you gaze into your crystal ball, what future do you see for the stock market? Investors who focus on growth try to predict which companies will grow faster in the future—faster than the rest of the stocks in the market, or faster than other stocks in the same industry. If you're successful in buying a company that does grow faster than other companies, it's likely that the price of that company's stock will increase as well, and you can make a profit!

Peter Lynch primarily used a growth stock approach in managing the Magellan mutual fund. Individuals who invest in growth stocks often prefer this approach because

116

their portfolio will be made up of stocks in established, well-managed companies that can be held for many, many years. Companies such as Coca-Cola, IBM, and Microsoft have demonstrated great growth over the years, and are the cornerstones of many portfolios. The National Association of Investors Corporation (NAIC) teaches its members a method of stock selection that focuses on building a portfolio of growth stocks. (You can learn more about NAIC at `http://www.better-investing.org`.) Also, Investment Club Central features a tutorial about NAIC's Stock Selection Guide (SSG) that details how you can use this approach to evaluate and select growth stocks for your portfolio. Just surf on over to `http://www.iclubcentral.com/ssg` to check out this free lesson in fundamental stock analysis.

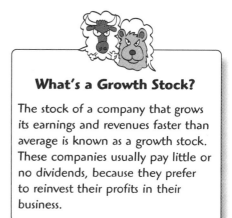

What's a Growth Stock?

The stock of a company that grows its earnings and revenues faster than average is known as a growth stock. These companies usually pay little or no dividends, because they prefer to reinvest their profits in their business.

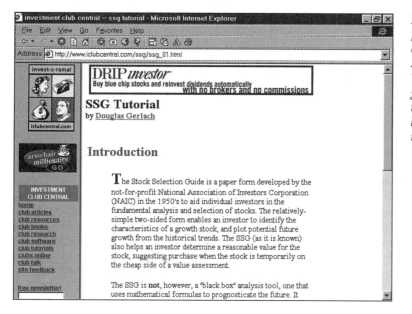

Investment Club Central features a tutorial that explains NAIC's Stock Selection Guide in detail. This approach to picking growth stocks has been used for nearly 50 years by NAIC members and investment clubs.

Value investors, on the other hand, look for stocks that have been overlooked by other investors and that may have a "hidden value." These companies may have been beaten down in price because of some bad event, or may be in an industry that's looked down on by most investors. However, even a company that has seen its stock price decline still has assets to its name—buildings, real estate, inventories, subsidiaries, and so on. Many of these assets still have value, yet that value may not be reflected in the stock's price.

Value investors look to buy stocks that are undervalued, and then hold those stocks until the rest of the market (hopefully!) realizes the real value of the company's assets.

Warren Buffet is usually recognized as one of the greatest investors of all time, and his approach to buying stocks is grounded in the value approach. As Chairman of Berkshire Hathaway, Inc., headquartered in Omaha, Nebraska, Buffet has managed to increase the book value (the total net worth of the company on its books) at a compounded annual growth of 24.1%.

The Berkshire Hathaway Web site isn't flashy, but the "Chairman's Letters To The Shareholders" are required reading.

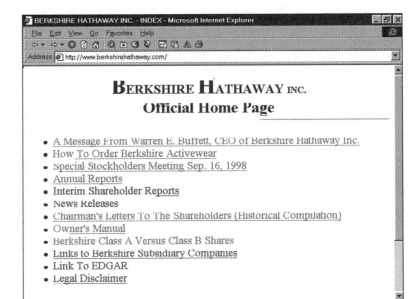

Even if you're not a shareholder of Berkshire Hathaway stock, you can still benefit from his expertise. Each year, Buffet pens a "Letter To The Shareholders" for the company's annual report, and these missives have become legendary for their wit, insight, and education. The Berkshire Hathaway Web site (http://www.berkshirehathaway.com) is low on pizzazz—at least the visual kind—but high on substance, featuring all the letters to shareholders for the past 20 years. The site also features the "Owners Manual," outlining Buffet's philosophy and rules for running the business. Every investor should spend some time here to learn from the master.

Although some investors stick closely to either the value or growth approach, many investors look at characteristics from each side, and look to buy growth companies that they think are temporarily undervalued by the market.

Getting Technical

If you're a "numbers person," or a heavy-duty computer geek, you might be more interested in a method of picking stocks known as *technical analysis*. Technical analysis looks at the relationships that exist between a stock's price, its volume (the number of shares that trade hands during a single day), and other factors. When they plot all these numbers on a chart, or do some other calculations, technical analysts hope to be able to predict future changes in the price of a particular stock.

By looking for particular patterns on a price chart of a stock, for instance, technical analysts try to figure out the direction that the stock's price is likely to move in the future. These patterns often have unusual names such as "cup and handle," "head and shoulders," or "double top." If you can identify any of several dozen different established patterns in a stock's price, you might have a good chance of knowing whether a stock is about to "breakout" (that's technical analysis talk for "rise in price") or "retreat" ("fall in price").

This Kind of Technician Can't Fix Your Stereo

A *technician* or *market technician* is someone who practices technical analysis.

To learn more about this method of investing, check out the online book *Technical Analysis from A to Z* by Steve Achelis, available free on the Web site of Equis International (`http://www.equis.com/free/taaz`). Equis is a maker of a popular software program for technical analysis called MetaStock. Company president Achelis's tutorial will explain the details of technical analysis, along with illustrations of all the various chart patterns and other indicators.

Equis International's online book, Technical Analysis from A to Z, can help you learn all about this method of analyzing stocks.

After you have the basics of technical analysis under your belt, you will need a couple of things before you start investing. You need access to charting software, access to price data, and plenty of time!

A stock's price chart is the primary tool of technical analysis. You can use many technical analysis software programs if you want to study stocks using these methods. Besides MetaStock, you can also choose from Windows on Wall Street, Omega TradeStation, and many others. You can subscribe to your pick of many services on the Web that provide daily price updates that can be imported into these programs. (You will learn more about downloading price data from the Internet in Chapter 18.)

These programs can be quite expensive, however, so another option for savvy Internet investors is to take advantage the Web's free charting programs. One of the best is ProphetCharts (`http://www.prophetcharts.com`), a complete online charting application built using the Java programming language. Using this free service, you can create a chart of any stock, for one to five years, in any of several formats (such as bar charts, line charts, or a fancy format called "candlestick" charts). You can add the customized indicators of your choice to the display, and even draw trend lines right on your screen. After you've reached a conclusion about a stock, you can print the chart for future reference.

You can try your hand at technical analysis using ProphetCharts.

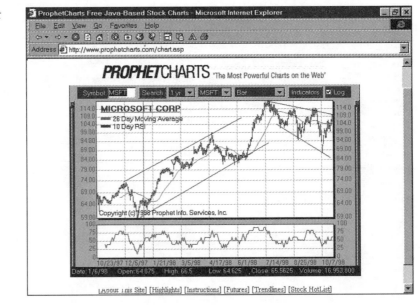

To use technical analysis successfully, you need to be able to spend time on your portfolio on a regular basis. You need to be able to consistently sit down and analyze charts, or perform the calculations necessary to update the indicators you use. And after you've bought a stock, you need to be vigilant in watching that stock's chart to know when to sell. There's no time to relax if you're a technician.

What a Difference a Day Makes

A recent phenomenon that has surfaced in the stock market is a method called "day trading." Day traders buy and sell dozens (or even hundreds) of different stocks in a single day, usually never owning any of those stocks for more than a few seconds or minutes. Traders make their profits by locking in very small profits—pennies per share—on, say, $50,000 worth of stock at a time. Some day traders make tens of thousands of dollars in a single week, a few dollars at a time. Before you jump onboard this train, however, better take a closer look. Trades can go down as well, leaving you thousands of dollars in the hole when the week ends.

If you're still interested and have a bundle to start out with (you will need about $25,000), pay a visit to the Day Traders of Orange County (http://www.worldwidetraders.com). Although the group is headquartered in California, they provide plenty of resources about day trading, as well as links to similar groups elsewhere in the country. In day trading, you can look forward to sitting behind a special computer trading terminal in a high-pressured, noisy, windowless office that's been set up to service a roomful of day traders, and you will pay for the privilege of being there. You will rarely have a chance to sneak a bite to eat or run to the bathroom while the market is open. You've got to be able to think fast, and react even faster with nerves of steel (and a cast iron stomach, too!).

The Day Traders of Orange County provides support for people who are trying to make sense of the hectic world of day trading.

Common Cents or Nonsense

Does this sound like a bargain to you? You discover that shares of Fabulous New Products, Inc. are selling for just 32 cents per share. You try to do a little research to find out more about this company, but there's not much available on the Internet. So you go ahead and buy 2,000 shares, at a cost of $640 plus commission. How much could you lose, you figure?

Well, you could lose $640, that's how much! And in the world of "penny stocks," chances are good that you *will* lose out on your investment! Penny stocks are those companies whose share prices are below a dollar. Although many investors are attracted to them because of their low prices, they are actually some of the riskiest investments you can purchase.

Warning: Penny Stocks Can Be Manipulated!

Because they have lower share prices and fewer number of actively traded shares, it's not too difficult for someone to use a variety of techniques to stir up interest (and the price) of a penny stock. The Internet is fertile territory for manipulators who try to get investors excited about a particular company and drive up the share price. When the stock's price peaks, the manipulators dump their shares and make a tidy profit. But they also stop promoting the stock, and the lack of interest now causes the share price to fall, leaving the investors who bought at the high with nothing but a hefty loss. (You will learn more about protecting yourself from these schemes in Chapter 20.)

In nearly ever case, penny stocks are penny stocks because they've had a miserable life as a public company. These stocks had to fall long and hard to get from their initial offering price of $10 or more a share. Penny stocks are the remnants of the stock market, and although some of these companies may claw their way back to the top, many will languish and ultimately die.

Some investors specialize in penny stocks. Typically, these are aggressive individuals who are willing to speculate, and can tolerate huge losses. Most sensible investors will stay away from penny stocks altogether.

Investing on Auto-Pilot

If all of this stock-picking business sounds like it might be way over your head, don't worry! There is a way that you can build a portfolio of stocks without worrying about doing research on individual stocks. As a bonus, you will only need to spend less than an hour a year on your portfolio, and you will never own more than 10 stocks. And the end result of this "auto-pilot" investment approach is a portfolio that will provide excellent returns, beating the market averages year in and year out.

Does this sound like your idea of investing nirvana? This approach goes by the lowly sounding name of "the Dogs of the Dow." And you can learn more about it at a Web site devoted just to this investment strategy.

Running with the Dogs of the Dow

Visit the Dogs of the Dow Web site (`http://www.dogsofthedow.com`) and you will get some quick training about this popular and low-maintenance method of investing.

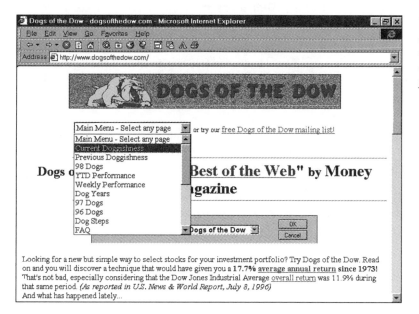

The Dogs of the Dow Web site lays out this popular and easy approach to building an investment portfolio.

The "Dow" part of this strategy refers to the Dow Jones Industrial Average, an index of 30 companies that is used to measure the performance of the overall market. These companies represent some of the biggest companies in America, including Sears, Hewlett-Packard, General Motors, Exxon, and AT&T.

The "dogs" part of this approach refers to the 10 companies (out of the 30 in the Dow) that you must invest in once a year. You see, the idea here is to invest in the 10 recently worst performing stocks out of the 30 in the Dow—the "dogs" of the Dow.

Invest in worst, you ask? Why would any investor do that, you wonder? Well, the answer is fairly simple. Because these 30 companies are among the best-known companies in the country, even the 10 worst of the bunch have proven to be exceptional recovery acts, year after year. Although a handful of the Dow might be beaten down at any point in time, they usually rebound quite handily.

On the Dogs of the Dow site, click on Dog Steps and you will be presented with an explanation of how you can invest in the dogs. Once a year, you need to review the dividend yields of all 30 stocks in the Dow. The dividend yield of a stock is figured by taking the total annual dividend that's paid per each share of stock, and then dividing it by the current share price. You can find this figure in any newspaper's stock listings, or many Internet quote servers (or on the Dogs of the Dow Web site—just click Current Doggishness for an update).

Next, identify the 10 Dow stocks with the highest dividend yields. These are the stocks that have had their prices knocked down (that's why the dividend yield is so high).

Finally, buy an equal dollar amount of all 10 of these stocks. Hold them for one year, and then repeat the process. That's all there is to the Dogs of the Dow approach!

So, does it work? From 1973 to 1996, the dogs approach would have earned an annual return of 17.7%, compared to a return of 11.9% for the entire Dow Jones Industrial Average during the same period. That's quite a difference! And with no worries about deciding when to sell, the Dogs of the Dow method is truly a couch-potato investor's dream come true!

The Least You Need to Know

➤ Fundamental analysis is a common method used by individual investors to evaluate stocks, and to identify companies with strong growth and/or that are undervalued in the marketplace.

➤ Technical analysis is more of a "by the numbers" approach to investing. By using charts and statistics, technicians hope to pinpoint the right times to buy and sell stocks.

➤ Stay away from penny stocks!

➤ The Dogs of the Dow can be an easy way to invest in the stock market, and can help you achieve better-than-average returns.

Chapter 11

Building a Portfolio of Stocks

In This Chapter

➤ What is a portfolio of stocks?

➤ The importance of a diversified stock

➤ How to evaluate your portfolio's balance

A stock is a stock—but a portfolio is where the real money is! Even the name "portfolio" suggests the idea of power and wealth. Your father or grandfather may have had a portfolio of genuine, thick, well-worn leather, stuffed with ledgers and account statements and other important documents. Within this portfolio would have been meticulous records of all the investments he had made, row after row of numbers and calculations.

Today, a portfolio refers to any group of investments that you can make. You can consider all your stocks as one big portfolio, or you can group your investments by the different goals you're trying to achieve. If you've decided to invest in the stock market, it's a good idea to pay attention to all the stocks you own and what happens to your risk and return when they all come together.

Diversify, Diversify, Diversify

When you build a portfolio of stocks, it's very important to consider the diversification of your holdings. Remember the discussion about diversification back in Chapter 5? Diversification is the process of spreading out your investments so that you decrease risk as much as you can while still maintaining an acceptable rate of return.

Don't Forget the Importance of Asset Allocation

While many investors are comfortable with a portfolio that's made up solely of stocks, other investors will be more comfortable with a portfolio that includes bonds as well.

One of the fundamental truths about stocks is that their share prices will fluctuate. Even if you're right about a particular stock you've picked, you might not be right at the right time!

Stock prices rise and decline for lots of reasons, often through no fault of the company at all! The overall status of the economy, the condition of a company's industry group, and a thousand other factors can influence share prices, turning a stock you've just bought into a loser, at least on paper.

There's nothing worse than seeing your entire portfolio decline all at once. If you diversify your portfolio, you will be more likely to have at least one or two winners in your portfolio whenever the rest of your holdings fall in price.

You can look several ways at the diversification of a portfolio of stocks. The first way is to buy stocks from several different sectors or industries. That way, if the entire tech sector is in a slump, transportation stocks might be doing very well. If you own one technology stock and one airline, your portfolio could experience less "bouncing around" as stocks in one sector fall and rise in another.

To find out which sector or industry a particular company belongs to, or to learn what companies make up a particular sector, visit Market Guide (`http://www.marketguide.com`). The site's "Research" area includes lists of all sectors and industries, as well as the companies that each include. And it works the other way, too. If you search for a company report, you will find out what sector and industry that stock belongs to.

The second way you can look at the diversification of your holdings is by buying companies of differing sizes. Remember the concept of "noncorrelating markets" that was explained back in Chapter 5? Well, studies have shown that the stocks of small companies tend to increase in price at completely different times than large companies. When large company stocks are rising in price, small company stocks tend to stagnate, and vice versa.

Also, small company stocks are generally more volatile than large company stocks. You can expect a portfolio that's made up of nothing but small stocks to experience big swings in price. But a portfolio that includes large, small, and medium-sized companies can have less overall risk and still provide a good return.

What's the Difference Between a Sector and an Industry?

A *sector* is a broad classification used to group companies that share common characteristics. For instance, Market Guide classifies companies into the following sectors:

Basic Materials	Financial
Capital Goods	Healthcare
Conglomerates	Services
Consumer/Cyclical	Technology
Consumer/Non-Cyclical	Transportation
Energy	Utilities

Each of these sectors is made up of several different industry groups that further define the operations of companies. The Healthcare sector is made up of the following industries, according to Market Guide:

Biotechnology and Drugs	Major Drugs
Healthcare Facilities	Medical Equipment and Supplies

Be aware, however, that different data providers use different classification systems when it comes to industries and sectors.

You can determine a company's size two different ways. The first is to determine its *market capitalization*. Market cap (as it's known) is calculated by multiplying a company's current price per share by the number of shares of that company's stock that are outstanding. Although there are no hard-and-fast rules for how to categorize companies after you know their market cap, here are some general guidelines:

Small-cap	Less than $500 million
Mid-cap	Between $500 million and $5 billion
Large-cap	Greater than $5 billion

What's a Micro-Cap Stock?

Some analysts consider a fourth category of stocks, the micro-caps. These are very small companies with market caps smaller than $100 to $250 million.

Although investors commonly use this method, sometimes it provides a distorted picture of a company's size. A company that has just gone public may see its share price climb to the sky as investors are optimistic about the company's future prospects, for example. And although that same company may not yet have any profits, it could still be considered a large-cap stock if you do the math.

For this reason, some investors like to use a company's revenues (sales) rather than market cap to determine its size. A mid-sized company has revenues between $500 million and $5 billion—anything smaller is small, and anything larger is large!

Market Guide provides lists of all the stocks in a particular sector and industry group, as well as which industry and sector any stock belongs to.

Finding the Right Balance

Now that you know how to diversify your portfolio of stocks, what's the right percentage you should allocate to each category? The key is to find the right balance.

The National Association of Investors Corporation teaches its members that it is possible to build a well-diversified portfolio with just 7 to 12 stocks, spread out among a half dozen or so sectors. It also recommends that a portfolio of growth stocks should ideally be made up of 25% small companies, 25% large companies, and 50% mid-sized companies.

In NAIC's experience, a portfolio with this general makeup will provide an optimal rate of return.

So how do you figure out how your portfolio measures up? One way is to use the portfolio tracking tool available at Quicken.com (http://www.quicken.com). After you have entered the stocks that you own into its online portfolio program, you can view charts and tables of your holdings, arranged by company size and by sector. Click the Portfolio Analysis link and you will be presented with a pie chart of your portfolio.

Even though Quicken.com doesn't include mid-cap stocks in its analysis, you can still get a good idea of how your portfolio is balanced.

Then, click the **Sector Diversification** link to view a chart of your portfolio's holdings by sector. Below the chart is a table of the percentages of your stocks that fall into different sectors. You can tell in an instant whether your portfolio is out of balance!

Everybody's Got a Different Definition of Big and Small

Investors use a lot of different breakpoints when categorizing companies by market cap. Some analysts consider small companies to have market caps of less than $250 million; others might push that figure to $1 billion. Some investors consider a stock a large-cap if it's bigger than $1 billion, and others think $10 billion is closer to the mark. You should know the definitions that a particular data service or analyst uses.

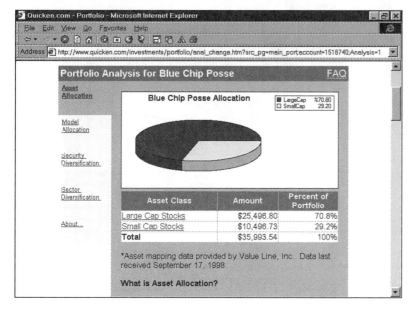

Quicken.com's Portfolio Analysis tool provides a quick way to calculate your portfolio's balance.

Don't Sweat Your Portfolio's Diversification If You're Just Getting Started

When you first start investing in stocks, your portfolio is likely to be way out of balance. Gradually, however, as you purchase more stocks, you will want to buy stocks that fit into your plan, and eventually you will have a well-balanced portfolio. Don't feel like you have to buy a bunch of stocks all at once just to have a diversified portfolio. It's probably better to take your time, do your homework, and make wise stock choices. In time, you will achieve the optimum balance.

As you build your portfolio, it's important to keep the balance of your holdings firmly in mind. If you own a few stocks that have performed well and increased in price significantly, you might see that you have become overweighted in a particular part of the market. Likewise, a stock that has fallen in price may cause your portfolio to be underweighted in one sector.

The "Sector Diversification" chart details how well your portfolio is invested according to different sectors of the market.

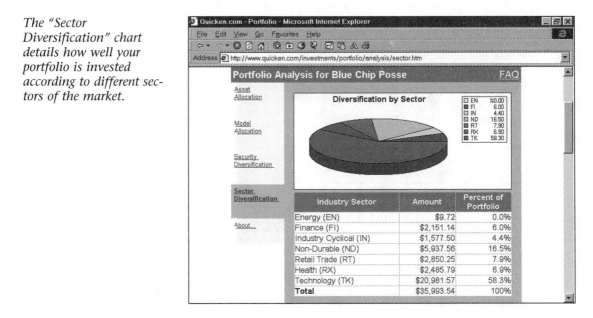

How Do Mutual Funds Fit into a Diversified Portfolio?

The same principles of balance and diversification also apply to portfolios that include mutual funds. Funds already have the diversification element taken care of, because they own hundreds of different stocks. You should still consider the holdings of each fund you own as part of your overall diversification plan, however. A single small-cap mutual fund might take care of all the small company stocks that you need to own in your portfolio. But if you own a mutual fund that primarily owns large companies, and your stocks are also all large companies, your portfolio could be dangerously out of balance.

To correct the imbalance, you could sell some of your holdings in the overweighted sector. What's probably more appropriate, however, is to designate future investments to purchases of stocks in underrepresented sectors.

The Least You Need to Know

➤ A diversified portfolio can help smooth out the bumps in the overall market.

➤ You should aim to build a balanced portfolio of stocks, one that includes companies of different sizes and from different sectors.

➤ You can evaluate your portfolio's balance and diversification by using the tools available on the Web.

Chapter 12

Finding the Right Stocks on the Web

In This Chapter

➤ Getting advice from pros and newsletters

➤ Using stock-screening tools on the Web

➤ Analyzing stocks with online tools

➤ Sharing tips with other investors on the Internet

If you're ready to start building a portfolio of stocks, your next step is to find some stocks to buy! The Internet can help you in your search, by providing tools, tips, and advice about stocks that you can consider.

Getting Tips from the Pros

Many money managers, financial planners, and investment advisors use the Web as a platform to reach clients and potential clients. Sometimes, these pros maintain a model portfolio of stock picks, or publish email newsletters that allow individual investors to follow along—and hopefully profit from the wisdom of the pros!

One financial professional who has established an informative and educational Web site is Bob Bose. Bose is a Vermont-based money manager who follows the value-investing principles of Warren Buffet for clients of his Green Mountain Asset Management.

You can get advice from a pro at Green Mountain Asset Management.

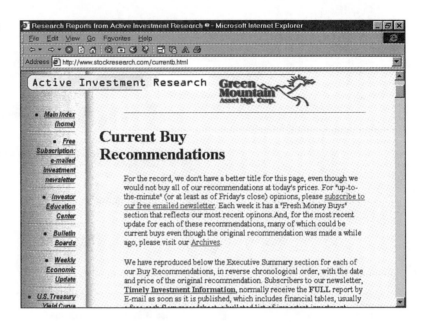

The Green Mountain Asset Management Web site (http://www.stockresearch.com) includes a weekly economic update, current buy recommendations for a portfolio of stocks that Bose tracks, and an Investor Education Center. What's more, you can sign up for Bose's free weekly email newsletter, too!

Hot Tips and Chilly Dogs

If you're searching for hot stock tips, you might consider subscribing to a stock market newsletter. In fact, you might even get offers in your mailbox that tout the success of a market pundit and urge you to subscribe to a printed newsletter.

Plenty of advisory services and newsletter publishers have turned to the Internet, however, to distribute their advice to investors. Now you can get instant recommendations via email or on the Web from market experts of all sorts—for a price, of course.

The good news is that many stock market letters publish free editions to help promote their paid services. Often these newsletters contain only excerpts from the full edition, or they may be published on a delayed basis. But these free newsletters give you a chance to sample the wares of a particular service before you shell out big bucks for a subscription.

Tip Sheets and Advisory Services

For a sampling of the market commentary you can find online, surf over to Invest-O-Rama!'s market commentary section (http://www.investorama.com/commentary.html).

Here you will find an assortment of opinions, news, and perspectives on stocks (as well as mutual funds and options). Besides offering advice about individual stocks, many of these experts also provide an overview of the entire market.

The newsletter publishers listed on this page provide samples of their products for free on Invest-O-Rama! so that you can get a taste of their advice. After you have reviewed a particular offering, you can also check out each publisher's own Web site, as well. Here are some highlights.

Bedford & Associates Research Group provides several investment advisory services, all delivered by email or on its Web site (`http://www.baresearch.com`). This group focuses on stocks, options, and day trading for serious investors. Its newsletters are direct, no-nonsense affairs that give direct recommendations on particular stocks.

You Might Not Get the Same Rate of Return That a Newsletter Advertises

Most stock market newsletters will provide statistics about their past performance. Although the old adage holds true—"past performance is not indicative of future results"—other reasons might cause you to not get the same return in your own portfolio even if you follow the newsletter's recommendations. First of all, a newsletter's track record includes *all* its investments. Because no expert can boast a 100% accuracy rate in picking stocks, if you pick and choose particular stocks from among all the recommendations you may end up missing out on some of the biggest winners. Second, even if you follow a particular service's picks to the letter, you may not be able to make purchases at the same price as the recommended price in the newsletter.

Dohmen Capital Research Institute (`http://www.dohmencapital.com`) publishes 10 different newsletters under the direction of Bert Dohmen. Dohmen uses both fundamental and technical analyses of the overall economy and particular markets to pinpoint stocks, bonds, options, and mutual funds that are poised to rise—or fall! Dohmen excels at providing insight into the direction of the world stock markets and how they will impact the U.S. markets. Subscribers to his newsletters can receive editions by email, in print, or on the Dohmen Web site.

The Inger Letter is a stock market newsletter published daily, and available to subscribers on the Internet.

Gene Inger is one of the original "market mavens" of financial television network CNBC, and his two newsletters are available to subscribers on his firm's Web site (http://www.ingerletter.com). Inger uses technical analysis to identify short-term trading opportunities for investors.

Separating the Wheat from the Chaff—Online Stock Screening

Another way of finding stocks that might be worthy of consideration for your portfolio is to use a stock-screening tool. Screening is the process of looking at the whole universe of stocks and then "screening out" those stocks that are most likely to meet your criteria.

More than 10,000 different stocks trade on the NYSE, AMEX, and Nasdaq, so where do you begin when you're trying to find stocks for your portfolio?

Basics of Stock Screening

The first thing you need to know about stock screening is what kind of stocks you're looking for. Are you looking for stocks that pay a high dividend, or ones that have had good earnings growth in the past? Are you looking for large or small companies? Would you like to invest in stocks in a particular sector or industry?

After you've identified the characteristics of the stocks that you would like to own in your portfolio, you can proceed to the process of building a stock screen.

You can find many stock-screening programs on the Web. The big advantage of these online tools is that you will always know that the database you're using is current. Before the Internet, if you wanted to use a stock-screening program, you had to maintain your own database of thousands of stocks, an often expensive and time-consuming task. Today you can just connect to a stock-screening Web site!

Building a Successful Stock Screen

One stock-screening site that is easy to use is Hoover's Stock Screener (http://www.stockscreener.com). StockScreener provides 20 variables for you to choose from, including financial ratios, growth rates, rates of return, and margins. All you need to do is fill in the maximum and/or minimum parameters for the criteria you select, and you will get a list of stocks that fit the bill.

Some Stocks That Pass a Screen May Not Be Suitable for Your Portfolio

Stock screening is the process of eliminating companies that are unlikely to be sound candidates for purchase. But some of the stocks that pass the screen may have other qualities that might make them undesirable for your portfolio. You need to do your homework before you make any investment decision, and that includes analyzing the stocks that pass your screening.

Here's how you can build a stock screen using StockScreener. Let's say you are looking for established companies that have had good growth of sales and earnings in the past, have low debt, and are selling for Price/Earnings (P/E) ratios that are low relative to the expected growth of the company's earnings. It might be a good idea to get rid of very small companies, because micro-cap stocks tend to be dangerous territory. This basic screen could present you with some stocks that currently are undervalued but have good growth potential in the future.

In StockScreener, you would enter the following criteria:

Price/Growth Rate, Maximum 1.0

Debt/Equity Ratio, Maximum 0.5

1-Yr. Revenue Growth Rate, Minimum 15

1-Yr. Earnings Growth Rate, Minimum 15

5-Yr. Revenue Growth Rate, Minimum 15

5-Yr. Earnings Growth Rate, Minimum 15

Latest 12 Mos. Revenue, Minimum $100 (million)

Enter your screening criteria in StockScreener by just filling in the blanks.

After you have entered those values, click the **Search** button and see how many companies pass muster. In this example, 108 companies passed the screen—you've eliminated more than 9,000 companies from consideration! Even though it's a lot easier to look through a list of 100 companies, that's still a lot of stocks. You can adjust your screening parameters still further, however, just by clicking the **Refine Search** button at the top of the page. This will give you a chance to refine your screen, perhaps by increasing the growth rates or requiring a lower debt/equity ratio.

The results of a stock screen are displayed on StockScreener.

A particularly useful feature of StockScreener is the capability to sort your results by criteria. Click on the arrow beneath the column headers to sort by that criterion, either in descending or ascending order.

Another online screening tool is Market Guide's NetScreen (`http://netscreen.marketguide.com`). This Java-driven application provides 20 variables, and each parameter can be customized to enable you to create complex searches. Advanced screeners will find this tool to be more robust than StockScreener.

After you have successfully whittled your list down to perhaps 30 or 40 stocks, your next step is to review the list of companies, and select a few for more study. Some Web sites can help you analyze your potential investments.

Hard, Cold Analysis Tools

Sometimes it's hard not to get emotional about your stocks. That's why there's a saying on Wall Street: "Don't fall in love with your stocks." One way to keep your head about you when you're studying stocks is to take advantage of analysis tools that enable you to make rational decisions about potential purchases.

VectorVest is a complete system of evaluating stocks, based on identifying stocks that offer low risk but high reward. Its service is available by subscription, but the company provides a taste of its analytical methods for free to visitors of its Web site (`http://www.vectorvest.com`).

Click on the **Free Stock Analysis** button at the top of the main page, and then enter the ticker symbol of the stock that you're studying.

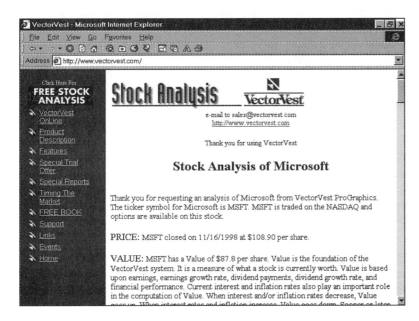

VectorVest can give you a buy, sell, or hold rating on nearly any stock.

Getting a Second Opinion Can Be a Good Idea, But...

It can be very helpful to get another opinion before you invest in another stock, and an analysis tool such as VectorVest's can be very helpful. Beware of the tendency of investors to try to confirm a decision you've already made, rather than trying to find valid reasons that might mean that you're better off not making a particular purchase.

VectorVest instantly presents you with a report that provides an analysis based on more than a dozen different criteria. VectorVest identifies the value of the stock, and whether the current price makes it over- or undervalued. It also identifies the safety level of the stock and its record of past returns.

VectorVest limits the free use of these reports to just three times a day. If you like what you see, however, you can subscribe to its service and use the service on an unlimited basis. Even a limited use of its service could provide information that you may have overlooked in your own analysis.

Another example of an online stock evaluation tool is the Value Point Analysis Financial Forum (http://www.eduvest.com). This site enables investors to enter a dozen criteria about a particular stock, and determine the stock's "intrinsic" or "fair" value (a theoretical price for stocks given a level of interest rates and corporate earnings). It's not a "black-box" program, however, so you have to understand the various criteria you choose to use for any stock.

The Value Point forum offers the results of other investors' stock studies for your review, as well as a description of the Value Point financial model and how it works. This tool can provide an important double-check before you make a stock purchase. If you learn that a stock's fair value is too low according to the model, you may want to reconsider making an investment at the current time.

An Investing Software Program May Be Just the Ticket

Many software programs can help you with your analysis of stocks. One that's particularly recommended is the NAIC Investor's Toolkit, the official software of the National Association of Investors Corporation. This program follows NAIC's approach of investing in growth stocks for the long-term, and features terrific tutorials incorporated into the program. Although the software is only available from NAIC, you can download a demo version and learn more at the Web site of the company that created the program, InvestWare (http://www.investware.com). Buying a piece of software such as Investor's Toolkit could be the best investment a beginning investor makes!

Getting Social About Stocks

One common way that many investors get ideas about possible investments is though the advice of friends, family, and coworkers. On the Internet, it is also possible to talk about stocks and even find people whose opinions you trust when it comes to investing!

You can find thousands of investing communities on the Internet—investors who use mailing lists, newsgroups, and message boards to talk to other like-minded investors. The key to the success of these groups is the concept of community. Groups of anonymous people who "mouth off" on a message board with a lot of bluster but few facts are not a community.

What's the Difference Between a Moderated and an Unmoderated Community?

Some online communities are *moderated*. This means that someone is responsible for approving and reviewing each message that's posted in an online forum, either before or after it appears publicly. Other forums are *unmoderated*, which means that anyone can say anything, and no one is responsible for overseeing the contents of messages posted in that forum. It is important that you recognize whether a particular form is moderated or unmoderated, because that might affect how you find the messages in that community. Unmoderated communities can be much "noisier." With no one to keep participants on track, discussions can stray off into other areas, or users can behave in a nasty manner, or messages can contain blatant lies.

Groups of individuals who respect the opinions of others and engage in thoughtful, meaningful dialogues together can find that sharing ideas and information can be profitable to many. But these communities are most successful when they are focused on a particular subject or their members share a common approach to the market.

You can find online communities around just about every corner on the Internet! One top spot to talk stocks is at Yahoo! Finance (`http://messages.yahoo.com/yahoo/Business_and_Finance`). Here you can find more than 8,000 message boards, each one devoted to a particular stock. You will have to know the sector and industry group of your stock to navigate to the board where discussions take place, or you can use the search engine to find the right board.

Talk about any stock on the Yahoo! Finance message boards.

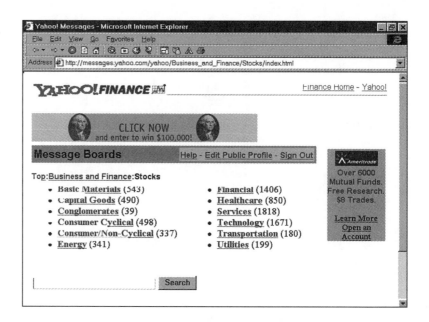

Another useful site to know about when you want to talk stocks is The Silicon Investor (http://www.techstocks.com). Tapping into the very heart of the tech sector, The Silicon Investor is the largest financial discussion site on the Web, and it is *the* place to talk about tech stocks. (Anyone can read messages that have been posted on the site, but a subscription is required if you would like to create your own messages on its boards.)

The Silicon Investor also features research tools and articles, but the real strength is the collective wisdom of its membership. Tune in to the talk here, and you can learn to evaluate stocks in the volatile technology sector.

How Can You Tell Whether a Message Is True?

Often, you can't! There will always be people with ulterior motives who post deceiving messages on public discussion boards. The best way to make sure that you've got the facts is to independently verify all online information that you find before you choose to invest in that stock. Assume that nothing is true, and then prove it to yourself. Remember, just because someone said it online, doesn't make it true. Be sure to review Chapter 19 for ways to protect yourself from online hype.

The Least You Need to Know

➤ You can find many financial advisors on the Internet. Even if you aren't a client, you may be able to take advantage of their expertise by reviewing the stock tips they provide online. Stock market newsletter publishers are taking advantage of the Internet to offer immediate delivery of their publications. No more waiting for the mailman to bring you stock recommendations—now you can get them in real-time as soon as your favorite newsletter publisher issues them!

➤ Take the time to learn how to use the stock-screening tools available on the Web. These are a powerful way to find stocks that meet your criteria.

➤ Some Web sites have begun to offer online stock analysis tools. These can be helpful in determining whether a stock is a reasonable candidate for your portfolio.

➤ Message boards can provide communities of investors the chance to swap ideas and trade barbs (before trading stocks).

Chapter 13

Researching Stocks on the Web

In This Chapter

➤ EDGAR provides the official word on a company's performance

➤ Annual reports can be real page-turners

➤ News sources provide clues you can use

➤ Price charts give you a picture of past performance

➤ Analyst earnings estimates offer a glimpse of the future

There's an old saying among investors who prefer stocks: "You should always do your homework before you buy." That doesn't mean you have to go back to elementary school, but it does mean that research is the core of good stock selection. It doesn't matter what method of stock analysis that you use, you'll still need the right information—and the know-how—to interpret that information and to make sure you're buying the right stocks.

One of the biggest strengths of the Internet is its capability to deliver information about publicly traded companies. No matter what you want to know about a stock, you can probably learn it on the Web.

The Data, Just the Data, and Nothing But the Data

If you base your stock purchase decisions on technical analysis, then you'll only need to get your hands on data about the stock's daily trading volume and share prices for the past several months. There are many subscription services that you can use to maintain this data, which you'll then plug into your charting software. But that's all you'll need—many chartists couldn't tell you any more about the stocks in their portfolio other than the name and ticker symbol!

When you use fundamental analysis to examine a stock, whether from a growth or value perspective, you'll want to become intimately familiar with a company. For that, you'll need access to all kinds of financial information about a company. One of the quickest ways to access stock research on the Web is to use the "Research a Stock" tool on Invest-O-Rama! (http://www.investorama.com/research.html). Just enter a stock's ticker symbol and you'll get links to more than 75 Web sites with news, quotes, charts, and more about that company. The information you'll find here can keep you busy for hours—but more importantly, it will help you learn as much as possible about any stock.

Getting Acquainted with EDGAR

Fortunately for investors, public companies prepare financial statements on a regular basis so that their owners (the shareholders) can be kept informed about the companies' activities and their financial condition. In fact, the U.S. Securities and Exchange Commission (SEC) requires that publicly traded companies file these reports on a regular basis and that shareholders receive a copy of the company's annual report. These documents can provide a wealth of background material about a company and its operations.

The SEC maintains a Web site where you can find reports about nearly any publicly traded company (http://www.sec.gov/edgarhp.htm). EDGAR (Electronic Data Gathering, Analysis, and Retrieval) is the system devised by the SEC that enables companies to send required reports to the Commission by modem. Within 24 hours after the SEC receives these reports, they are made available on the Web site for investors to download.

You can learn a lot about a stock by studying the information in these reports. And because you can get these reports online, and at no cost, they are a rich source of research for investors. Some of the reports that you'll find on the EDGAR system are the following:

➤ 10-Q: This is a company's quarterly report, filed three times a year (the fourth quarter report is included in the company's annual report).

➤ 10-K: Companies must file this report after the end of each fiscal year.

➤ Schedule 14A: Better known as a "proxy statement," companies must send this report to shareholders whenever a vote is required, usually before an annual meeting. These reports are identified as "DEF 14A" (definitive) or "PRE 14A" (preliminary) in the EDGAR system.

➤ 8-K: Companies sometimes file Form 8-K to provide an update of important events and financial changes that affect shareholders.

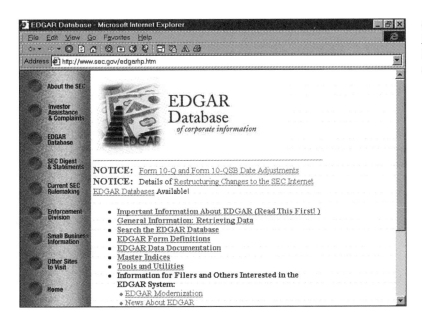

Get acquainted with EDGAR, and you can learn plenty about nearly any stock.

On the EDGAR site, just click the "Edgar Form Definitions" link and you can find lists and descriptions of the different types of reports that companies make using the EDGAR system.

To find a company's filings in the EDGAR system, just enter part of the company's name in the search box on the EDGAR main page. You'll get a list of EDGAR reports that concern your company. (If you see the names of other companies in the list, it's probably because your search term appeared in those reports, too.)

Companies Don't Always Celebrate New Year's Eve on December 31st!

Many businesses don't operate on a calendar–year basis, but according to their own *fiscal year*. A fiscal year is 12 months long, just like a calendar year, but it can start and end in any 356–day period. Companies have fiscal years that end June 30th, September 30th, January 31st, or any other day of the year.

A search for EDGAR reports on a particular company is likely to turn up a number of different filings.

```
Search SEC EDGAR Archives - Microsoft Internet Explorer                    _ ☐ ✕
File   Edit   View   Go   Favorites   Help                                     e
←  →  ▼ ⊗ ☐ ⌂ ░ ⊡ ⊙ ♡ ⊟ ☑ ⚠ ⎙
Address ☐ http://www.sec.gov/cgi-bin/srch-edgar?APPLE+COMPUTER              ▼
```

You can search this index. Type the keyword(s) you want to search for: [   ]

Result(s) of EDGAR search

Query: **APPLE COMPUTER**
Number of matches: **107**

Company name	Form Type	Date Filed	File Size
AMERICA ONLINE INC	SC 13D/A	(04/17/1996)	7101 Bytes
AMERICA ONLINE INC	SC 13D/A	(12/14/1995)	51342 Bytes
AMERICA ONLINE INC	SC 13D/A	(12/14/1995)	51603 Bytes
AMERICA ONLINE INC	SC 13D/A	(11/13/1995)	14282 Bytes
AMERICA ONLINE INC	SC 13D/A	(02/07/1995)	53234 Bytes
AMERICA ONLINE INC	SC 13D/A	(01/10/1995)	54372 Bytes
APPLE COMPUTER INC/ FA	8-K	(07/28/1997)	8197 Bytes
APPLE COMPUTER INC	10-Q	(08/10/1998)	59543 Bytes
APPLE COMPUTER INC	SC 13G	(08/10/1998)	16133 Bytes
APPLE COMPUTER INC	S-8	(07/31/1998)	132146 Bytes
APPLE COMPUTER INC	10-Q	(05/11/1998)	129050 Bytes
APPLE COMPUTER INC	DEF 14A	(03/16/1998)	203172 Bytes
APPLE COMPUTER INC	10-Q	(02/09/1998)	139805 Bytes
APPLE COMPUTER INC	10-K/A	(01/23/1998)	51055 Bytes

To read a report, click on the company name. The first part of the report includes some codes and data fields, but then the actual report begins. A company's 10-K and 10-Q reports follow the same basic format, so you can learn to navigate through them with ease once you get the hang of it!

The first part of the report includes financial statements, which are divided into three components: the Income Statement, the Balance Sheet, and the Cash Flow Statement.

➤ The *Income Statement* is the report of the company's revenues and expenses for a particular period.

➤ The *Balance Sheet* outlines all the company's assets (the things it owns that have value) and liabilities (its debts).

➤ The *Cash Flow Statement* details all the ways the company used and received cash during the period.

Quarterly and annual reports also include a section where the company's leaders explain their business activities and any changes since the last report. This

A Good Online Search Starts with Good Terms

If you want to find anything on a Web site, including reports at sites like EDGAR, you'll have to learn to build a good search query. In EDGAR, a search for "Apple Computer" turns up "Apple South Inc.", a restaurant company, as well as the computer manufacturer. If you read the online help page for the search function, you can learn that you should type "ADJ" in between words that are adjacent in your search query. A search of "Apple ADJ Computer" therefore returns only filings that contain a reference to the computer company.

section is called "Management's Discussion of Operations," and is where a company is obliged to detail any problems that affect its profitability.

These reports also include a statement from the company's auditors, the accounting experts who have examined the company's books and found them to have been prepared according to acceptable practices.

While a single, current 10-Q or 10-K report can provide important information about a company's operations, you also might want to consider how a company fared in the past. FreeEDGAR (`http://www.freeedgar.com`) provides a company's financial statements for several years, and in an easier-to-read format, too. FreeEDGAR collects a company's EDGAR filings, and then lists a company's financial statements for many quarters or years in a single table. This enables you to see changes in profits, sales, and other figures over time.

Not All Public Companies File Reports on EDGAR.

Companies with fewer than 500 investors and less than $10 million in net assets are not required to file annual and quarterly reports with the SEC, so don't expect to find information about small companies in the EDGAR system.

![FreeEDGAR.com: Companies. - Netscape browser window showing APPLE COMPUTER INC Profile Index]

APPLE COMPUTER INC **Profile Index**

NOTE: All numbers reported in company profiles are stated exactly as they are reported by the company. They do not reflect stock splits. Units also may display inconsistency due to variation in company reporting methods. FreeEDGAR Profile data is currently under development and may be subject to errors. Please click Legal Information for more details.

Annual Income Statement

	09/26/94	09/26/95	09/25/96	09/26/97
SALES	9188748	11062	9833	7081
TOTAL_REVENUES	9188748	11062	9833	7081
CCS	6844915	8204	8865	5713
TOTAL_COSTS	6844915	8204	8865	5713
OTHER_EXPENSES	1821559	2174	2321	2438
LOSS_PROVISION	0	0	0	0
INTEREST_EXPENSE	39653	48	60	-72
INCOME_PRETAX	500286	674	-1295	-1045
INCOME_TAX	190108	250	-479	0
INCOME_CONTINUING	310178	424	-816	-1045
DISCONTINUED	0	0	0	0

FreeEDGAR provides easy-to-read EDGAR reports, as well as an email alert service—all for free!

You can also retrieve complete EDGAR reports from FreeEDGAR, or you can sign up for a free email service that notifies you when a company makes a required filing with the SEC. One last thing to note is that FreeEDGAR publishes EDGAR reports as soon as they are filed, even before they are available from the SEC's own site! The

SEC delays the publication of reports on its site for 24 hours, selling a real-time feed to commercial publishers (like FreeEDGAR) who want to get their hands on the material sooner.

Annual Reports

Another terrific source for information about a company is its annual report. Often, this document is printed on glossy paper in full-color, and serves as more of a publicity vehicle than an information source. However, annual reports must present a company's financial statements, and they usually include plenty of material that can help you understand a company.

How Soon After a Company's Quarter Ends Are Its Quarterly Reports Available on EDGAR?

The SEC requires a company to file its quarterly reports (10-Q reports) within 45 days after the end of its quarter. Annual (10-K) reports must be filed within 90 days after the close of a company's fiscal year.

If you're a shareholder of a company, you should receive its annual report in the mail each year. If you're not a shareholder, you can contact the company and request a copy to be sent to you free of charge. Usually, the company sends other information as well, including recent press releases, quarterly reports, and brochures.

Glossy Four-Color Annual Reports Have Their Downside

Many companies go all out in creating their annual reports, filling the pages with color photographs, printed elegantly on expensive paper. While you might find a photograph of the board of directors interesting to look at, remember that all the money that's gone into creating a costly annual report comes straight from the profits that rightfully belong to investors. And what's the purpose of these fanciful reports, anyway? Is it to provide important information to investors? Or is it to sell investors on the idea that this company is well-established and worthy of your investment (in other words, an extended advertisement)? Many companies today are taking a more frugal route, by publishing a simple annual report or not publishing an annual report at all. For instance, in 1997, Apple Computer chose not to publish a glossy annual report, instead sending all shareholders a copy of their Form 10-K filed with the SEC.

But there's another convenient way to request a copy of a company's annual report—on the Web, of course! The Public Register's Annual Reports Service (http://www.prars.com) is an online clearinghouse for distribution of annual reports. Simply make your way to the site, and click on the link to search for corporate reports. (Or you can just click on the link **Order Annual Report** from the Invest-O-Rama! "Research a Stock" page, as long as it's available from PRARS.)

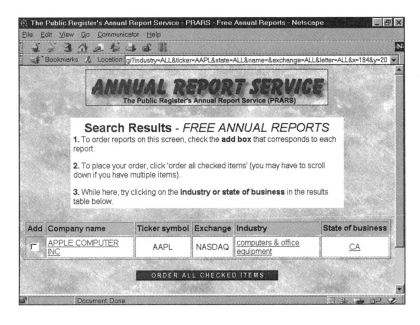

The Annual Reports Service provided by PRARS can have a company's printed report in your mailbox in a week or two.

You can search for reports by industry, as well as by ticker symbol, company name, or several other criteria. After you've found a report you want to order, check it off on the list, and click the order button. You can then continue to search for more reports. After you've found all companies you're researching, and fill in your name and address, the annual reports will be sent to you in the mail.

If you can't wait a couple of weeks for an annual report to arrive in the mail, there's another option. Many corporations are using the Internet as a tool to distribute information for investors and shareholders, and often this means that they'll publish their annual reports on their Web sites.

To help you find annual reports that have been published on the Web, PRARS maintains an "Online Annual Report Service" at http://www.annualreportservice.com. PRARS provides links to online annual reports of more than 1,444 companies—perfect for investors who seek instant gratification! Find your company, and then click a link to explore its annual report directly on the Web.

All the News (and How to Use It)

While you can learn plenty from a company's annual report or SEC filings, you should remember that sometimes things change over time. That goes for public companies, too. Any number of factors about a company's business can change, such as plant closings, increases in raw material costs, decreases in sales, changes in management, acquisitions of other companies, mergers, or any other unexpected events. Any of these could change your outlook about investing in a particular stock—as long as you know what's going on!

For that, you'll need to keep abreast of the news. One of the best places to find company-specific news on the Web is on the Yahoo! Finance site (http://quote.yahoo.com). Yahoo! Finance maintains an archive of news stories from various sources as well as press releases for publicly traded companies, going back at least 90 days for most companies.

To search for news at Yahoo! Finance, first get a quote for the stock by entering the ticker symbol on the main page of the site. Then click the "News" link from the quotes display screen, and you'll see a list of available stories.

Yahoo! Finance provides an archive of news stories and press releases for any publicly traded company.

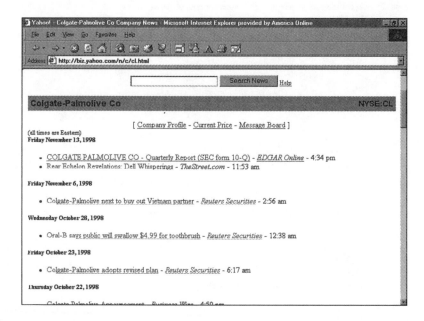

The news items are listed by date, and each headline is followed by the source of the news and the time it became available. Just click on the headline to read the article.

When you're researching a stock, these news articles and press releases can tip you off to important recent developments about a company. It might be an announcement of a new product, or a report from a financial analyst about the stock. It could be a statement about a lawsuit that's been filed against or by the company, or a pundit's commentary about a stock's future prospects. All this information can assist you in better understanding a stock's suitability for your own portfolio.

Bear in mind that there are two types of "news" that you'll find on the Web: press releases and news stories. There's a world of difference between them.

Press releases are issued by companies themselves. They are distributed to newspapers and other publications, and are intended to provide information that stimulates editors to assign the story to a reporter or summarize the release in their publication. Press releases are sometimes sent to shareholders, too, or are published on a company's Web site. They often make their way onto many online news services where other investors can find them. PR Newswire (http://www.prnewswire.com) and Business Wire (http://www.businesswire.com) are two of the biggest services that distribute company press releases, and you can search their sites for news about many public companies.

Press Release Information

A company's press release can give you the details of a company's quarterly or annual report before the company tells the SEC.

Many companies issue press releases that outline their performance in their most recently completed quarter or year, before they make the required filings with the Security and Exchange Commission. These releases can give you timely information about the company's operations. Just remember that the financial figures cited in the release may be labeled "preliminary" and be subject to change before the company files its official SEC report.

News stories are the actual articles that appear in a publication or newspaper. A news story can take many different forms. It might be a straight news story, a short reporting of a particular event, for instance. Or it could be a feature story, a more in-depth look at a company, individual, market trend, particular sector, or some other topic. Or it might be a commentary about a particular subject or company, infused with the opinion of the writer.

Whatever form a story might take, and regardless of whether the story is a more objective news item or a subjective commentary, it is written from the perspective of an outsider looking in at a company and its business. A press release, on the other hand, is written by a company's public relations staff, and is intended to cast the company's business in the best possible light. No matter how awful the news may be that's included in a press release, the company's executives will always be "optimistic about the future" or "disappointed, but taking positive steps." Press releases to a company's operations sound their rosiest, even when bad news is being announced.

That's not to say that press releases can't sometimes be helpful. You can learn a lot by reading what a company has to say about itself, or how it explains a particularly bad bit of news.

Top of the Charts

As the old saying goes, a picture is worth a thousand words. And a chart of a stock's prices over time can give you an indication of how a stock has performed during the period. BigCharts (http://www.bigcharts.com) is a provider of fast, easy to read charts of stocks, mutual funds, and indexes. Type in a ticker symbol or part of a company's name on the main page and choose to display a Quick Chart or Interactive Chart. The Quick Chart gives you the choice of time periods, from one day to a decade (or longer). The Interactive Chart gives you the capability to customize the time frame, style, or indicators that are also plotted on the chart. You can also compare two stocks on the same chart!

BigCharts offers clean and fast stock charts that you can customize or even have delivered via email.

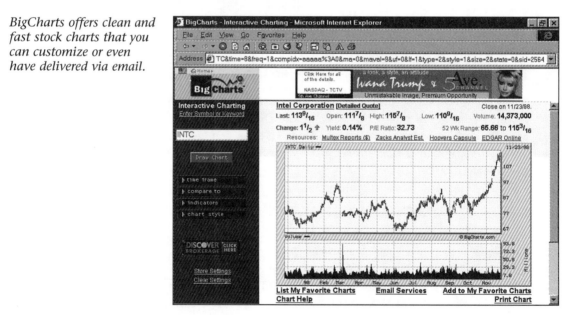

Once you've built the chart that's perfect for you, you can even choose to have it automatically emailed to you on any schedule you set, from once a day to once a week (click the "Email Services" link below the graph to enter your preferences). Or you can add the chart to your list of favorites that will appear whenever you arrive at the BigCharts site.

How to Send And Receive Pictures and Formatted Text In an Email Message

Email is usually plain text. You type some words into your email software, click send, and those words are delivered to the recipient with no formatting (no bold, italic, or underlined words), no colored text, and no fancy fonts. However, there is a way to dress up your email, as long as you have the right email software. Many email services, like BigCharts' chart delivery service, require the use of an email program that can handle HTML-formatted messages. HTML is the language of the Web, but it can also be used in email, as long as your software can interpret the codes. The advantage of HTML-enabled email is that you can send and receive graphics (such as a stock chart) and text that doesn't look like it was created on a typewriter. The most recent versions of Eudora Pro, Microsoft Outlook, and Netscape Messenger all support HTML mail.

There are lots of other sites on the Web where you can find stock charts. Some of them offer customizable date ranges, allow access to the underlying data, or have other features that you may find helpful. As you explore financial sites on the Web, you'll see plenty of price charts that you can try until you find your favorite.

Estimates and Guesstimates

One of the biggest games on Wall Street is the effort to predict a company's future earnings. Investment banks and full-service brokerage firms employ teams of financial analysts whose jobs are to follow particular companies and make recommendations to their clients. Much of the work of these analysts revolves around the practice of making regular estimates of a company's earnings for each of the upcoming quarters and years.

Based on these earnings estimates, an analyst can make a recommendation that an investor buy, sell, or hold a specific stock. These analyst recommendations are also the basis of the endless stream of "upgrades" and "downgrades" you'll hear or read about a stock, as these experts determine that it's the right time or wrong time to buy that stock.

What's a "Whisper Estimate?"

Today there's another number that's even more important than analysts' published estimates. It's the *whisper estimate,* which, as its name suggests, is an unpublished earnings estimate that investors are discussing before the release of the actual earnings. It's often higher than the more conservative published figures. If a company beats its consensus estimates, but doesn't beat the whisper numbers, the stock may fall dramatically in price. For the ultimate in rumormongering, check out EarningsWhispers.com (http://www.earningswhispers.com), a site devoted to tracking the whispers on the Street.

There may be dozens of analysts who follow a company's stock, so how do you know who to believe? One way is to look at what are known as the "consensus estimates." There are services that track the recommendations of all of the analysts who follow a stock, and then determine the average earnings estimate made by the group. Every quarter, investors look at a company's earnings report, and see how it compared to the consensus figure. If the company's actual earnings were higher than the estimate, the company is said to have "beat its estimate."

Zack's Investment Research is a leading provider of consensus earnings estimates and analyst ratings. On the Zack's Web site (http://www.zacks.com), you can look up a company report for a stock, and see how the experts view its future prospects. Enter a ticker on the main page of the Zack's site to get a free company report.

You'll Always Be Last In Line to Know about an Analyst's Recommendations

Typically, an analyst's recommendation about a stock is made available to the firm's institutional clients—the large pension funds, mutual funds, and other companies that buy and sell large blocks of stock at a time—and to its full-service clients before it's made available in other channels. If you're not a customer of that firm, you'll only get a crack at buying that stock after all the VIPs get theirs, at which point the price may have already gone up significantly.

Zacks Brokerage - Microsoft Internet Explorer provided by America Online

File Edit View Go Favorites Help

Address http://wwwo.zacks.com/ows-bin/owa/zbrc?tick=DIS&comp_id=main&search=5

ZACKS
Brokerage Research Center

$8 STOCK TRADE

DISNEY WALT
Snapshot

ZACKS FREE TRIAL | SYMBOL LOOKUP | NEW SEARCH [GO]

Last: 30.938   Net: 0.000   Open: N/A   Hi: N/A   Low: N/A   Vol: N/A

Industry : MEDIA CONGLOMERATES   Earnings Surprises   Earnings Calendar

Numbers of Brokers Recommending (11/23/98)		Earnings Estimates and Actuals	
Strong Buy	2	Actual Earnings Last Quarter	$.16
Moderate Buy	9		
Hold	11	EPS Surprise Last Quarter	7 %
Moderate Sell	0		
Strong Sell	0	Consensus Estimate for Current Quarter	$.27
Current Average Recommendation (1.0=Strong Buy, 5.0=Strong Sell)	2.4	Consensus Estimate for Current Fiscal Year	$.94
Last Weeks Average Recommendation	2.4	Consensus Estimate for Next Fiscal Year	$1.08
Change In Average Recommendation	0		

Industry Information	
Company Industry Group	MEDIA CONGLOMERATES
Rank Within Industry Group	4 of 6

Online Trading   Mutual Funds   Online Banking   Cyberstore

Zack's Investment Research provides clues to how the experts of Wall Street view a stock.

Zack's looks at the reports issued by more than 3,000 analysts employed by 230 brokerage firms in the United States, and then publishes the consensus earnings estimates of this group for the current and next fiscal years. Zack's also provides the number of analysts who rate a stock as a Strong Buy, Moderate Buy, Hold, Moderate Sell, or Strong Sell.

Zack's isn't the only provider of earnings estimates. Both First Call (`http://www.firstcall.com`) and I/B/E/S (`http://www.ibes.com`) also publish analyst information on their Web sites, mostly by subscription, however. You can often find reports of analyst reports included in sites that provide stock market news, too.

While it's easy enough to get consensus analyst estimates, it's much harder to get your hands on copies of an analyst's actual report about a stock. These reports and updates are between one and twenty pages long, with a careful examination of a company's business and operations, and explanation of the

The Truth Behind Analyst Ratings

While Zack's categorizes broker ratings into five categories (Strong Buy, Moderate Buy, Hold, Moderate Sell, or Strong Sell), each firm has its own system of appraising stocks. Some firms use the term "outperform" when they're most optimistic about a stock—this stock is set to "outperform" the overall market. Some firms say "neutral" when others say "hold." And "attractive" can mean "buy," but so can "accumulate." It can be confusing, and there's no universal system in place for stock ratings.

157

analyst's projections for the future. If you're a client of a full-service brokerage firm, you can get that firm's research from your broker.

If you don't have a relationship with a full-service firm, then you can still get these reports on the Web—for a fee. Multex Investor Network (`http://www.multexinvestor`) is a service that distributes analyst research reports for public companies. You can search for all available reports from the main page of its site, and then you'll have access to a list of reports available for purchase at costs ranging from a few dollars each up to $50 (for one report!). Occasionally, you'll find some free reports. All of these reports require the Adobe Acrobat reader.

When Is a Hold Really a Sell?

Many investment banks have two types of clients—the customers of the full-service brokerage side of the business, and the publicly traded companies who are clients on the investment banking side. Analysts may have more than the interest of individual investors in mind when they evaluate companies, because they may not want to offend a potential investment banking client. Or an investment bank might be a market maker and profit from sales of a specific stock. And because analysts are dependent on getting information directly from a company, they may refrain from being overly harsh in writing their evaluation. Taking all these factors into account, you'll rarely see a "sell" rating issued by an analyst, except in the direst of circumstances. That means that many "hold" ratings really mean that an analyst is recommending that investors "sell." Of course, there's no way to read the mind of an analyst, but you should consider this tendency to optimism whenever you look at analyst ratings.

The Price Is Right—Stock Quotes

There's one last thing you need to know about a stock before you make the decision to buy—its share price! Fortunately, you can find stock quotes at hundreds of financial Web sites. And with the results of your stock study in hand, you can determine if a stock's current price represents a good value for your portfolio, or if it might be more sensible to look elsewhere.

You'll learn more about current price quotes and historical price data in Chapter 18. For now, however, it's time to learn about how you can buy and sell stocks online.

The Least You Need to Know

➤ The SEC's EDGAR holds the key to understanding a company's business. FreeEDGAR also publishes the same reports found at the SEC site, but in an easier-to-read format. A company's annual report can expand on the information that's found in an official report filed with the SEC.

➤ News stories and press releases can inform you of recent developments in a particular company, though you should be wary of overly optimistic press releases written by the company itself. You can find a great company news archive on the Web at Yahoo! Finance.

➤ Price charts, like those at BigCharts.com, can tell you where a stock has been. Many online chart services can be customized, offering additional insights and comparisons.

➤ Analyst earnings estimates can shine the light on a company's future potential. Analyst ratings can also tell you if a stock is a buy, sell, or hold.

Buy, Sell, or Hold Begins with Buy

In This Chapter

➤ The difference between full-service and discount brokers

➤ How to select the best broker for you

➤ The ins and outs of online trading

After you've decided *which* stocks to buy, it's time to actually make the purchase. Unfortunately, you just can't walk into a McDonald's and order a Big Mac, fries, and 10 shares of stock! You also can't log on to a company's Web site and buy shares directly with a credit card. (At least not yet, anyway!)

If you want to be a shareholder of a company, you will need to use the services of a brokerage firm to buy shares of stock. This is where the Internet comes in—you can buy and sell stocks at more than 70 online brokerage firms after you've established an account. But how do you choose an online broker? And how do you know whether the firm is reputable?

Cost Versus Service—The Battle Between "Full-Service" and "Discount Commissions"

The brokerage business breaks down into two basic categories: "full-service" (sometimes known as "full-commission") and "discount-commission." As you can imagine, the battle lines are drawn around the level of service and the costs of the two types of brokerages.

When you think of a stockbroker, you probably think of someone who works for one of the big-name, traditional brokerage firms. You can recognize these firms because they're usually named after people: Dean Witter, Smith Barney, Salomon Brothers, Paine Webber, and Merrill Lynch. These companies have worked hard to build up an aura of authority and respectability about their businesses, usually with a lot of marble and granite logos and advertisements featuring attractive, older, successful-looking people who are meant to represent their clients.

Full-service brokers are the traditional way that Americans have invested in the stock market. Brokers have access to all sorts of information about the markets, and are trained and licensed to be able to give investment advice to the public. The companies have teams of analysts who research stocks, bonds, and mutual funds, and make recommendations for customers of the firm.

Of course, you will pay some fairly steep commissions whenever you buy a stock, bond, or mutual fund from a full-service broker. That's the price you pay for expert advice and for the privilege of working with a broker (at least, that's the theory).

Discount brokerage firms, on the other hand, charge commissions that are a fraction of what the full-service firms charge. However, the employees at a discount brokerage firm are not allowed to provide investment advice to customers. When you have an account at a discount firm, you get cut-rate commissions (especially on the Internet), but you won't get any handholding or recommendations from the company. That's the trade-off of saving on commissions.

So how do you know which is right for you? Are you better off with a full-service broker, or should you go it alone and work with a discounter?

Is a Full-Service Broker for You?

Full-service firms take pride in their ability to provide "full service" for all your financial needs. Besides helping you build an investment portfolio, most firms offer you the chance to meet with a planner to review your complete financial situation. Full-service firms can provide help or referrals to accountants and lawyers to deal with some of the more complicated components of personal finance.

You can get help with estate planning issues such as how to make sure your heirs are taken care of in the manner you desire after you pass away, for example. Your full-service firm can help you decide whether you need to set up some sort of trust or may suggest some other strategy to manage your estate. If you need assistance setting up your will, the firm can refer you to a lawyer, and can even work with you to make sure your will covers all the right financial concerns. If you would like to minimize your tax liabilities, your broker can offer you an array of municipal or government bonds for your portfolio.

If you decide that you just don't have the time to manage your own portfolio, you can give your broker the power to take over your accounts for you. Then, he or she can make sales and purchases on your behalf without getting your approval each time. If you travel abroad frequently, for instance, it might be a good idea to give your broker the ability to move quickly if something changes drastically with an investment you own, without making him or her track you down in the outback of Australia!

On top of all that, a full-service broker has the research of his firm's analysts at his fingertips. Your broker can give you the best picks of the firm and his own ideas about which stocks might be good for your portfolio.

The bottom line is that full-service brokers should emphasize *service*. If you think these services are helpful, you might want to consider working with a full-service broker.

Full-Service Brokerage Firms on the Web

If you decide that a full-service broker is for you, next you will need to find one! Because you will be working with your broker on a one-on-one basis, you will probably want to find someone who is near where you work or live. That way you can sit down with your broker periodically and review your portfolio.

What's the Difference Between a Broker, Financial Planner, and Investment Advisor?

All kinds of people work in the financial industry, and they all have different titles that can be confusing. Anyone who is in the business of offering specific investment advice to people must register with the SEC as a "registered investment advisor." There are no real requirements to receiving this designation, however, so you can't rely on this to figure out whether someone is really qualified to give advice. A *broker* is an individual who has been registered to sell securities and give advice to the public about investments. Brokers have to pass a test to receive what's known as a "Series 7" license. A *financial planner* is someone who has gone through a rigorous course of study about all areas of personal finance. Financial planners can offer help in dealing with estate planning, trusts, and other more complicated subjects going beyond mere investment advice. A broker might also be a financial planner (and vice versa), and both are considered investment advisors.

What's a Registered Representative?

Before anyone can sell securities, he or she must be licensed by the National Association of Securities Dealers, and registered with the Securities and Exchange Commission. A "registered representative" is a broker or account executive who has gone through the registration process and can therefore legally deal with the general public when it comes to financial matters.

One of the best ways to find a broker is to ask for referrals from people you know. Chances are that some of your friends, coworkers, and family members use a full-service broker, and they can offer a recommendation.

Another way to find a broker is to check out the Web sites of the full-service firms. You can find a complete listing of these companies on Invest-O-Rama! at (http://www.investorama.com/brokers_fullservice.html).

Most brokerage firms provide a search function on their sites to enable you to find the closest representatives to you. Just enter your telephone area code or state, and you will be presented with a list of the brokers in your area.

When you check out full-service brokerage sites on the Web, you will see, by and large, that full-service firms don't provide online trading functions, or a lot of interactive tools. In fact, full-service firms have been downright slow to embrace the Web. That's because they have concerns about how to maintain the personal relationships between brokers and their clients in an online atmosphere. If these firms allow customers to enter their own orders, how long will it take before they realize that they might be able to do without a full-service broker altogether (and then switch to a discounter)? Some brokerage firms do allow their representatives to communicate with clients using email, another step in the right direction.

The Prudential Securities Web site (http://www.prusec.com) features a searchable database of its advisors. Click on your state, or enter your area code, and you will learn the location of the closest Prudential office.

What you may find on the sites of many full-service firms is market news and commentary from their analysts and strategists, calculators, and educational materials, and maybe even some reports from their analysts about individual stocks, bonds, or mutual funds (although they may reserve the good stuff for clients only).

Some firms are even beginning to offer online account access for customers. Although you can't place orders, you can get your account balance and check the recent activity in your account.

You Can Get "Full Service" from a Smaller Brokerage

Although "full-service" is often used to describe the major, national investment banks and brokerage firms that charge full commissions, plenty of other smaller firms provide full service, but at much lower rates. Often, these firms are regional or local businesses that serve a community or part of the country, but their brokers can be just as knowledgeable as those at larger firms.

![Screenshot of Sample Portfolio Page in Microsoft Internet Explorer provided by America Online. Address: http://www.smithbarney.com/cgi-bin/client/viewdriver.cgi. Salomon Smith Barney "your portfolio" page with MARKETWATCH showing DJIA 8647.45 +152.42, NASDAQ 1777.15 +19.96.]

OUR SAMPLE PORTFOLIO allows you to view some of the features of Smith Barney Access℠ Premium Service with our selected stocks of the day. As a Smith Barney client you will have access to your personal accounts, including a portfolio summary, positions, account activities, company research, news, enhanced price and performance charts, as well as your Watch List...24 hours-a-day.

➤ Get more details on client access.

➤ Contact a Smith Barney Financial Consultant.

Track the stocks of your choice through your Watch List.

Sample Portfolio

The price and other data shown below is delayed for at least 20 minutes (while U.S. Securities markets are open) for stocks only. All other prices/NAVs reflect previous day's close.

Symbol	Description	Quantity	Price	Change	As of	Value	Charts	News	Research
CPQ	COMPAQ COMPUTER CORP	100	31 5/8	+1 13/16	1:19pm	$3,162.50		10/29/98	10/27/98
GLM	GLOBAL MARINE INC NEW	100	12 1/8	+3/16	1:18pm	$1,212.50		10/14/98	10/14/98

Smith Barney clients can access information about their accounts and portfolios on the Web (http://www.smithbarney.com).

Checking Out a Broker

After you've found a broker, you need to figure out whether he or she is right for you! Just like there are doctors who specialize in different ailments, brokers have expertise in some areas and know less about others.

You can do two things to check out a broker before you sign the paperwork to open an account. First, schedule a personal interview the broker. Use this appointment to try to get to know the broker, and be prepared to ask about the broker's background, licenses, work history, and approach to working with clients. Find out what kind of investments the broker is knowledgeable about, and what fees and commissions you will be charged. It can be helpful to bring along a notepad with some of these questions already jotted down so that you don't forget anything as the broker rattles off the advantages of working with his firm!

You should be prepared to meet with several brokers. Remember that you will be putting your financial future into the hands of your broker, so you need to find someone you trust, and someone who will answer your questions, no matter how "dumb" they might seem to you.

The second thing you can do to evaluate a broker is to find out whether any complaints have been filed against him or her. NASD Regulation, Inc., a subsidiary of the National Association of Securities Dealers (NASD) provides a database of brokers and others who work in the securities industry. You can access this database on its Web site (`http://www.nasdr.com`) to review a broker or firm and see whether they're registered and whether they have had complaints filed against them. (In Chapter 20, you will learn how to use this database to check up on a broker.)

Cheap, Easy, Convenient—Online Brokerage Firms

The allure of online trading is one of the biggest reasons that investors have flocked to the Web in the past few years. And why not? Now you can buy shares in any company in less than 60 seconds, and at a fraction of the cost of a full-commission firm.

Customers of Discount Brokerage Firms Can't Count on Personalized Service

If you open an account at a discount brokerage, you probably won't be assigned a particular representative at the firm with whom you will develop a relationship.

You can buy and sell stocks over the Internet at more than 100 discount brokerage firms that offer online trading. Some are well-established discount firms, like Charles Schwab, Waterhouse, and Quick & Reilly, that have launched online trading services. Others, such as Ameritrade, Datek, and Web Street Securities, are companies launched as Internet brokers. And some online brokers are subsidiaries of well-known investment banks, such as Discover Brokerage (owned by Morgan Stanley Dean Witter) and DLJ Direct (owned by Donaldson, Lufkin & Jenrette).

To find a broker, start with the directory of online brokers on Invest-O-Rama! at `http://www.investorama.com/brokers_online.html`.

Here you will find a listing of discount brokers that offer online trading, and you can click to explore the sites of those brokers who interest you most.

With so many brokers, however, how do you figure out which broker to choose? The key is to know which services and features you require from your broker. After you understand your own needs, you can whittle the list of candidates right down to a more manageable size.

Choosing the Online Broker That Is Right for You

All online brokers are not created equal. Some brokers cater to frequent traders, and some brokers offer a wide array of mutual funds that you can purchase with no transaction fees. Some brokers provide research, and some brokers offer customers the chance to get in on the ground floor of hot IPOs (initial public offerings). No matter what your approach to investing, you can find a broker that can provide services that save you money.

The first thing you need to do is figure out what's important to you. All online brokers can let you buy and sell shares of stock, but here's where the similarity ends. Here are some points to consider.

1. **How much do you need to open an account?** Some firms have no minimum requirement to open an account. Others can require a deposit of $1,000 or more before they will let you open an account. If you don't have enough to meet the minimum requirement, you can strike that firm off your list.

   Most firms offer a smaller minimum for IRA accounts or custodial accounts, however. You might consider transferring your IRA to a firm that offers great research and services, and then open a regular brokerage account (where you might be making more frequent trades) at a firm with a lower commission. That way, you can avail yourself of services and research through your IRA account, but still have the benefit of lower commissions.

2. **Do you want to include mutual funds in your portfolio?** Many online brokerages offer mutual fund "supermarkets," where you can buy and sell funds from many different fund families. The selection of funds varies from firm to firm, so make sure that a company offers the funds that you're interested in before you sign up. If you're not interested in funds, you don't need a brokerage that offers a large selection.

The Lowdown on Minimum Initial Balances

Many brokers require a certain amount, typically ranging from $1,000 to $10,000, to open an account. You may not be required to maintain a minimum balance after the account is opened, however. If you would like to open an account at a firm that demands a high minimum, but you don't necessarily want to keep all that money in the account indefinitely, just scrape together the cash and then withdraw part of it after the account is opened. Just watch for maintenance fees that some brokers charge if your balance falls below a certain amount.

3. **Do you want to buy or sell options, Canadian or foreign stocks, or penny stocks?** Not all online brokers offer options trading, stocks that trade on the OTC Bulletin Board or "pink sheets," or stocks that are listed on foreign exchanges.

A Discount Brokerage's Mutual Fund Marketplace May Not Be the Best Place to Buy a Fund

If your online broker advertises that it has several hundred funds in its "marketplace," make sure you find out how many of those can be purchased with no transaction fees (charges that you must pay when you buy or sell a fund). The broker's assortment of funds also contains funds for which you must pay a transaction fee to sell or purchase.

4. **Is it important to be able to talk to an actual person on the phone?** Some brokerages charge a higher commission if you place an order by telephone instead of using their Web site. If you think you might need some help, or don't always have access to your computer when you might like to make a trade, make sure you won't be penalized for it.

5. **Will you be able to make use of the research that the company provides?** Many online brokerages advertise the "research" that's available for their customers, but the truth is that much of this information is already available elsewhere for free. It may be more convenient to access research, quotes, and your account balance all in one place, but you shouldn't have to pay for the convenience!

Can Your Broker Handle Days When the Market Is Very Busy?

In the past, when the market has experienced very heavy trading volume, the customers at some online brokerage firms found that they could not log on to place orders. The online firms were just unprepared for the number of customers who were trying to place orders! Some online brokerage firms will automatically give you their online commission rate (when it's lower) anytime you are prevented from logging on to their site. Check out a firm's policies, or you might be left out in the cold on the market's hottest days.

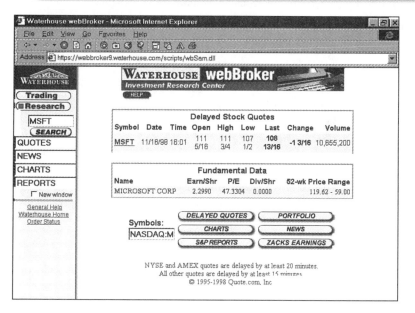

Waterhouse Securities (http:// www.waterhouse.com) offers its customers an array of research reports, quotes, news, charts, earnings estimates, and more about any stock.

6. **Are you interested in bonds?** Only a handful of online brokers offer bonds, and those that do usually only offer U.S. Treasury bonds. For instance, Discover Direct offers orders to be placed online for Treasury Bills, Notes, Bonds, and Zeros. Charles Schwab offers these as well as corporate bonds.

7. **Do you want to buy IPOs?** Some online brokers now hook up with investment banks to offer customers the chance to buy shares in current IPOs. Wit Capital, DLJ Direct, and Trade-Well are among the first to team with the IPO underwriters to provide this service. With IPOs formerly available only to the privileged clients of full-service firms, many investors are interested in having access to the same opportunity.

Buying an IPO from an Online Brokerage May Not Be All That Much to Get Excited About

Even if your online brokerage advertises access to IPOs for its customers, don't expect that you will be offered all the "hot" IPOs that come to market. Usually, this privilege is reserved for large accounts only. And even if you qualify, you will only have access to those offerings that your broker (or the investment bank that it's partnering with) are underwriting. Those may not be the most desirable IPOs, and the number of shares that you can buy will probably be very limited. Don't overlook the fact that investing in IPOs is risky business, and that many companies will fall in price within a year to be worth less than they were at the IPO!

8. **Do you want the ability to write checks from your account? Would you like a free credit, ATM, or debit card?** Brokerage firms are beginning to act more and more like banks, and many now provide free check writing or credit cards linked to your account.

9. **Would you like to buy stocks on margin?** Margin accounts enable you to buy stocks on credit, borrowing against the value of the securities already in your account. Of course, you will have to pay interest on the money you borrow, and you will find big differences in the interest rates that different firms charge. Also, some firms require a higher minimum to establish a margin account than a cash account.

Low Commission Brokers Aren't Always the Cheapest

It's easy to compare brokers solely on the basis of their advertised lowest commissions. After you read the fine print, however, you will see that comparing commissions from firm to firm can be like comparing apples to oranges. To effectively compare the commission rates at different brokers, you need to consider three things: whether you will be placing a "market" or a "limit" order, whether you will be buying "listed" or "OTC" securities, and how many shares you will be buying and selling at a time.

Margin Can Be Dangerous in the Wrong Hands

If you have a margin account, you can borrow up to 50% of your total account value to buy other shares. If the value of your account falls, however, the amount you can borrow on margin also falls! If that happens, you will get a "margin call" from your brokerage, and you will have to deposit more cash to bring you up to the required amount. That means that in a falling market, your account will drop in value but you will have to keep coming up with money—or sell shares—just to cover your margin loans. At the same time, you will be paying interest on the loan, so it's possible that buying on margin could drain you dry.

A *market order* is when you ask your broker to buy or sell shares at the best price available in the market at the time you place the order. A *limit order*, on the other hand, lets you specify the maximum price per share you will pay for a sale or purchase.

Some online brokers charge significantly higher rates for limit orders—even though they will probably advertise the low rate for market orders most prominently! At Ameritrade, for example, you pay a minimum of $8 for a market order, but $13 for a limit order.

If you like to specify your order price for all trades, or you frequently buy and sell fast-moving stocks, you will want to know how much a market order will cost you.

The second consideration is what types of securities you will be buying. *Listed* stocks are those shares that trade on a stock exchange, such as the American Stock Exchange or New York Stock Exchange. *OTC* is an abbreviation for *over-the-counter* and is often used to signify any shares that don't trade on the NYSE or AMEX. (Nasdaq claims that companies listed in its electronic market aren't really "OTC" stocks, but the distinction is still used broadly.)

The Advantage of Market Orders Over Limit Orders

When you place a market order, you are almost certainly guaranteed that your order will be filled. With limit orders, on the other hand, your order price may or may not ever be met, so it's possible that your purchase or sale will never be made. If you really want to buy or sell a stock, use a market order.

171

The Advantage of Limit Orders Over Market Orders

When you place a market order, your sale or purchase will be made at whatever price shares are trading for at that moment. That could be many dollars per share more or less than the price when you placed the order, even if it was just a few minutes earlier! With limit orders, you will know exactly how much a trade could cost you (and perhaps even less)—as long as the trade is executed. If you want to know exactly how much a trade could cost you, use a limit order.

Some online brokers charge higher commissions for trades of listed stocks than they do for OTC stocks, particularly if your order is larger than 5,000 or 10,000 shares. A market order for 10,000 shares of an OTC stock will cost you $19.95 at Trade4Less, for example. If it's a listed stock, however, the commission jumps to $100 for the same quantity.

Finally, many firms tout their low commissions, but those rates often change depending on the number of shares you're buying or selling. SureTrade's flat-rate $7.95 commission is only good on orders of 5,000 shares or less. After that, you pay an extra one-cent per share. It doesn't sound like much, but for an order of 10,000 shares, the commission rate is $107.95.

All online brokerage firms publish their commission schedules on their Web sites. Before you sign up, take a close look at the rates for various sizes of trades. Make sure that your brokerage fits the types and sizes of trades you're most likely to make.

How to Pay Zero Commissions!

Some firms, such as Web Street Securities, actually eliminate commissions altogether for orders of a particular size, and generally on trades of OTC stocks. That means that you can pay no commissions on some or all of your trades! How can brokers do this and stay in business? Part of the answer is "payment for order flow." When you purchase an OTC stock from your brokerage, they most likely fill your order by buying shares from a "market maker," the investment bank that serves as a dealer for that particular stock. Some market makers pack a little reward to brokerage firms who send business their way (what some call a kickback). Payment for order flow accounts for 20% of the revenues at some online brokers. Without it, a firm could not offer trades for free.

Hidden Fees Can Cost You Big Bucks

Unfortunately, commissions aren't the only costs involved with online trading. Some brokers charge dozens of other fees. Some of them may be obvious, like the annual account maintenance fee that may be charged on an IRA account. But you might overlook some other fees that might cause you to feel the pinch later on.

Some firms charge a fee of $15 to $25 for issuing and delivering a stock certificate, for example. Although you will probably want to hold most of your stocks in your account, there may be times when you want to have a certificate issued (for instance, to enroll in a dividend reinvestment plan—more on that in Chapter 15). Other firms may slam the door on your way out, and charge a fee of $50 if you close your account. You may be charged a fee if you request a copy of a statement, or if you wire funds into or out of your account.

The bottom line is that you should check out the fees, as well as the commissions, before you open an account at an online brokerage.

Online Trading Is Safe and Secure—Or Is It?

Many people are concerned about the security of the Internet. Before they put their personal financial information online somewhere, they worry about whether it's safe—or whether there's a risk that some hacker could find out their most personal financial secrets.

Never fear. All online brokers require the use of a secure Web browser, one that uses encryption to put your information into a secret code before it's sent out over the Internet. At the other end, the broker uses a special Web server that decodes the information. Although your data is out on the Internet, it's virtually impossible that anyone could crack the code and get access to the protected information. You will learn more about Internet security in Chapter 19.

Comparison of Commissions and Features

With 100 discount brokers now online, you could spend a couple of weeks surfing from site to site trying to compare all the details of each. For your convenience, here are two Web sites that can really help you narrow down the choices.

Gomez Advisors (http://www.gomez.com) is an independent consultant firm that reviews and rates online brokers. Several times a year, the company carefully evaluates the services of all the Internet brokerage firms, and ranks them from best to worst in a number of categories, such as Ease Of Use, Customer Confidence, and Overall Cost. Then, Gomez determines the company with the best overall score.

Because not all investors have the same needs, Gomez also rates the firms according to what criteria are most important to different types of investors. "Serious Investors" have different needs than "Hyper-active Traders" or "One-stop Shoppers," for instance.

The Gomez Advisors Web site can help you find the right online broker.

On the Gomez Advisors Web site, users can view tables of the scores of firms in each category. Click on the firm name to see Gomez's comments about the companies, too.

Another site to visit if you're researching brokers is the "Discount Stock Brokers Ranked Report" created by Don Johnson (http://www.sonic.net/donaldj). Twice a month, Johnson reviews more than 80 brokers, both those online and off, and compares them on the basis of commissions and services.

Opening an Account

After you have decided to open an account with a particular firm, the procedure is easy—and at some firms, it's even easier!

Nearly every firm provides an account application on its site that you can download. (Look for the big, bold link that says something like "OPEN AN ACCOUNT NOW" on the main page of the site.)

Some firms walk you through the application process right on their site, enabling you to complete the application while you're on the site by filling in the blanks, and then letting you print out the form. All you have to do then is sign the form, and send it back—along with your check, of course!

DLJ Direct (http://www.dljdirect.com) *enables customers to apply online and be trading with minutes!*

A few online brokerage firms, including DLJ Direct, have taken the process a step further. At DLJ Direct, you fill out the required information, read the account agreement, click a few buttons, and your account is opened for you almost immediately! You will have an account number and a password, and you can start trading right away.

Of course, you will have to send a check within three days of your first trade. Some firms who offer online applications also require a signed form to be sent to them to finalize the process and grant you online access to your account.

You can always open your account the old-fashioned way, by asking the firm to send you an application in the mail. Most firms have an email address or form on their site that you can use to request the paperwork. Then you will complete the entire form by hand and send it back to the brokerage with your check.

Why Do Brokerage Firms Ask So Many Personal Questions on Their Applications?

It's true, you can expect a brokerage firm's application form to require you to provide bank and credit card references, information about your salary and your employer, and other personal details. Much of this information is required by industry regulations, but they also want to try to find out whether you're likely to be a problem customer! Just answer truthfully and completely and you won't have any problem.

175

The Least You Need to Know

➤ Full-service brokers offer customized investment advice and financial services to account holders, but at a price. If you work with a full-service firm, you will work with a broker who will be your partner in building a portfolio.

➤ Discount brokers can't offer personalized investment advice, but their commissions are much lower than the full-service firms.

➤ More than 100 discount brokers offer online trading services. Choosing the right online broker depends on whether you're most interested in research, low commissions, other services, or a combination of all these.

Chapter 15

Skipping the Broker Altogether

If you've decided that the stock market is for you, but don't have thousands of dollars to open a brokerage account, there is a lower cost alternative to start building a portfolio of stocks without using the services of a broker. Did you know that you can buy stock in companies like Coca-Cola, Wendy's, Sara Lee, or Intel, one share at a time and without paying commissions to a broker? You can start building a portfolio of stocks with as little as $25!

What's the secret to becoming a shareholder without using a broker? It's buying shares of a stock directly from the company through its a Dividend Re-Investment Plan (commonly known as a DRIP). DRIPs are a great way to invest, and it takes as little as $25 to buy shares in some of the best companies in America. If this sounds appealing to you, you can get started as a DRIP investor with the help of a few sites on the Web.

Successful Investing, DRIP by DRIP

The first key to understanding how DRIP investing works is to know about *dividends*. *Dividends* are payments of a company's profit to its owners—the stockholders. Most blue-chip companies pay dividends to shareholders on a quarterly basis, sending a check to each owner of the company four times a year. If your shares are held in a brokerage account, your broker will credit your account each time a dividend is paid.

Some companies would rather not have to make these cash dividend payments each quarter. Instead, they give current shareholders the option to enroll in a special program and then receive their dividends in the form of additional shares of the company's stock—the dividends are automatically reinvested in purchases of additional shares. That's why these plans are known as Dividend Reinvestment Plans (DRIP).

Once you enroll in a DRIP, you no longer receive quarterly dividend checks. Instead, you receive a statement once a quarter showing the amount of the dividend and how many additional shares were purchased with those funds in your account. If your dividends didn't add up to an entire share, you would receive a fractional share (another nice touch—brokers only allow you to purchase whole shares). What's more, DRIPs charge little or no commissions on purchases made with these reinvested dividends.

DRIPs Can Be a Recordkeeping Nightmare

One of the downsides of DRIP investing is that each reinvested dividend and optional cash purchase must be carefully tracked to determine the cost basis of your investment for tax purposes. A good recordkeeping software program is a necessity when you're building a portfolio of DRIPs.

But the best part of DRIPs is not that your dividends are reinvested (although that's nice, and it certainly can add up to a lot over the course of many years), the real advantages of DRIPs are that most allow you to make additional purchases of stock free of commissions, and you can invest as little as $25 at a time. These are called Optional Cash Purchases (OCPs). If you tried to buy $25 of stocks at even the cheapest online broker, the broker would eat up nearly a third of your total investment. Now, you don't need hundreds or thousands of dollars to get started investing in stocks, and you don't have to worry about high commissions eating into your profits. You can build a portfolio of stock, DRIP by DRIP!

Because you can get started in DRIPs without a large amount of money, they make a great way to learn about investing. Instead of sticking your head in an investment book, you can buy a few shares and actually be a stockholder. As you gain knowledge, you can continue to invest, bit by bit, and eventually you'll find that you're the owner of a portfolio of blue-chip stocks.

To learn more about DRIPs, your first stop on the Web is DRIP Central (http://www.dripcentral.com). This site provides one-stop shopping for DRIP investors. To learn more about how DRIP investing works, select **Guide to DRIP Investing** to explore the ABC's of this low-cost method of investing.

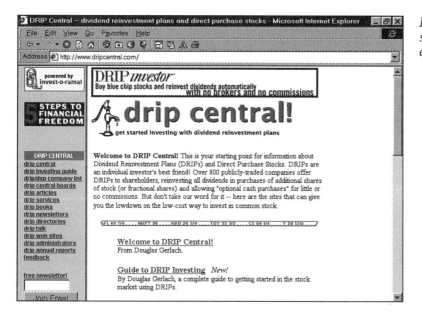

DRIP Central is your one-stop resource for DRIP education and research.

DRIP Central also offers links to articles about DRIP investing, a directory of companies that offer DRIPs, lists of DRIP books and newsletters, and a message board where you can ask any questions about DRIP investing. At DRIP Central, however, you will learn that there is one slight catch when you get started investing in DRIPs. To enroll in a company's DRIP and begin to buy shares of stock, you have to own at least one share of that company's stock. So how do you buy that first share of stock without going through a broker?

Click the **DRIP Services** link on DRIP Central and you'll get a list of companies that can assist you in buying that first share. The National Association of Investors Corporation's Low Cost Investment Plan and First Share are two popular ways that investors can get started in DRIPs.

NAIC's Low Cost Investment Plan (`http://www.better-investing.org/store/lcp.html`) is available only to members of the organization (membership is $39 a year). But after you're an NAIC member, the group will sell you a single share of any of 145 companies that offer DRIPs. Participating companies include AT&T, Colgate-Palmolive, Exxon, GTE, Intel, ITT, Kellogg Company, La-Z-Boy, Lucent Technologies, Maytag, Mobil, Motorola, Pepsico, Texaco, Volvo, Wendy's, and Whirlpool.

Select any of these companies in NAIC's Low Cost Investment Plan, and you can get started with your own DRIP portfolio.

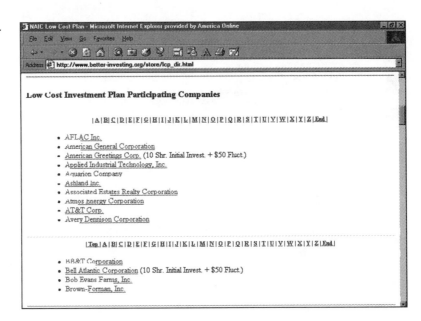

Low Cost Investment Plan Participating Companies

|A|B|C|D|E|F|G|H|I|J|K|L|M|N|O|P|Q|R|S|T|U|V|W|X|Y|Z| End |

- AFLAC Inc.
- American General Corporation
- American Greetings Corp. (10 Shr. Initial Invest. + $50 Fluct.)
- Applied Industrial Technology, Inc.
- Aquarion Company
- Ashland Inc.
- Associated Estates Realty Corporation
- Atmos Energy Corporation
- AT&T Corp.
- Avery Dennison Corporation

| Top |A|B|C|D|E|F|G|H|I|J|K|L|M|N|O|P|Q|R|S|T|U|V|W|X|Y|Z| End |

- BB&T Corporation
- Bell Atlantic Corporation (10 Shr. Initial Invest. + $50 Fluct.)
- Bob Evans Farms, Inc.
- Brown-Forman, Inc.

The cost is a one-time charge of just $7 per company, and you'll send NAIC the cost of one share plus an extra $10 in case there's any price fluctuation before the purchase is made (don't worry, you'll receive an extra $10 worth of stock when the purchase is made). After your initial share has been purchased, NAIC will set up your DRIP account directly with the company. Then, NAIC drops out of the picture, and you'll make all future purchases directly with the company's DRIP.

On the NAIC Web site, you can review the current list of available companies, along with details of their DRIP plan fees and minimums. You can also download an enrollment form from the site that you can complete and return to NAIC with your check.

First Share (http://www.firstshare.com) takes a more communal approach to helping investors get started in DRIPs. The company acts as a sort of clearinghouse to match up DRIP investors, helping them buy and sell the single shares needed to enroll in particular DRIPs.

Reinvested Dividends Are Taxable, Just Like Cash Dividends

Any dividends you receive from stocks you own are taxable. It doesn't matter if those dividends were reinvested in additional shares, or if you received them in cash—they still must be recorded on your tax return each year.

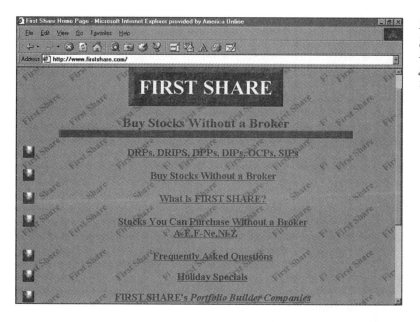

First Share offers a way for you to get started in DRIPs, and to help others get started at the same time.

Here's how it works. Membership in First Share is $24 a year. When you join the program, you agree to sell single shares in the DRIPs you already (or soon will) own to other investors in the program. In return, you can purchase shares from other investors in the program for the DRIPs in which you want to enroll.

Program members pay a one-time request fee to First Share of $5 or $10 for each company requested. First Share then searches its database and finds another member who is willing to sell a share of that company from his own DRIP account. Once the buyer and seller are matched up, First Share is out of the picture. The two investors sign an agreement that outlines the purchase price of the share and pay a transaction fee of $7.50 to cover any expenses. (Remember, you'll receive that $7.50 back when you sell one of your shares in the program.)

Next, the seller prepares a "stock power," a special form that authorizes the stock's transfer agent to register a single share in the name of the new owner. The transfer agent sends a stock certificate to the new owner along with enrollment forms for the company's DRIP. From now on, the new owner makes any purchases of shares directly through the company's DRIP.

You can enroll in First Share online, or download an enrollment form from the site that you can complete and return in the mail. First Share also offers a listing of companies available through the program and other information about DRIPs.

While it might seem to make sense to buy the initial shares of a DRIP stock through a discount broker, there's one small problem. In order to enroll in a DRIP, you have to hold the stock certificates yourself. Stock that you own in a brokerage account is referred to as being "held in street name," registered in the name of the broker for your benefit. Your broker can issue certificates to you, but many discount brokers charge about $25 for the service. That extra expense can quickly wipe out much of what you might save in the future by avoiding commissions.

There's one even easier way that you can get started in a DRIP. Many companies now offer Direct Stock Plans (DSPs) in which you can buy shares directly from the company.

With a DSP, you don't need a broker, or a service like NAIC or First Share. Instead, you get in touch with the company directly and make your initial purchase directly from them. Once you've bought your first shares of stock, you'll be enrolled in their DRIP and can then make additional purchases.

As more and more companies offer Direct Stock Plans, though, one trend has emerged. Companies are beginning to raise fees and minimums for these plans, requiring a $5 fee for every purchase you make. While this is still less than any discount online broker, it makes purchases impractical of any amount less than a few hundred dollars. Because DRIPs have traditionally been the way that investors could invest in stocks without hundreds of dollars, many investors may be shut out by these high fee DRIPs and DSPs.

However, there still are many plans that allow purchases of less than $100 and don't stick their DRIPholders with steep fees—you just need to search for them.

Beware "Synthetic DRIPs" Offered By Brokers

Many brokers offer their clients free "dividend reinvestment." While this is true, a broker's dividend reinvestment plan is missing the crucial piece that makes a company's DRIP so appealing—the capability to make additional purchases free of commissions. It's rare to find a broker that doesn't charge commissions.

More and More Companies Offer Direct Stock Plans

Nearly 500 companies now offer investors the chance to buy shares directly, a tenfold increase since 1995.

Some Companies That Offer Direct Stock Plans Don't Pay Dividends

While the overwhelming majority of companies who offer DSPs do pay dividends and allow dividend reinvestment, a handful of companies don't pay dividends. In these DSPs, you'll still get all the features of a DRIP, such as the capability to make additional purchases throughout the year, with the exception of dividend reinvestment.

Directory of DRIPs and Direct Purchase Stocks

If you like the idea of DRIP investing, the first thing you need to do is find a company that offers a DRIP. That's where NetStock Direct (`http://www.netstockdirect.com`) comes in. This firm hosts a Web site that is made up of a searchable directory of DRIPs and DSPs. Enter the name or ticker symbol of any company in the search box on the main page of the site, and NetStock Direct tells you if the company has a DRIP or DSP, as well as the details of the company's plan.

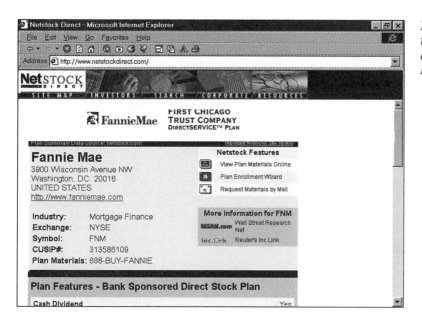

NetStock Direct gives you the essential details on any company's DRIP or DSP.

For many companies, NetStock Direct maintains all the forms and information on its Web site, so you can just download the paperwork you need to get started in a DSP. If you're interested in investing in a company's DRIP, NetStock Direct provides the telephone number of the DRIP administrator, where you can request plan materials. Just call and the enrollment package will be sent to you by mail.

Don't Invest In a Stock Just Because It Offers a DRIP

A company that doesn't perform for its shareholders is a bad investment, even if it has a DRIP. Make sure you base your decision to invest in a company on sound, fundamental qualities—not because it happens to offer a DRIP.

If you don't have a company in mind, but would like to explore the DRIPs and DSPs that are available, you can use NetStock Direct's advanced search function. Click the **Search** icon at the top of the Web page, and you can search for companies in a specific industry, companies that have low minimums, or companies that allow automatic transfers from your bank account into their plan.

One interesting glimpse into the future is NetStock Direct's electronic enrollment form. You can now enroll in a handful of DSPs just by completing an online registration form on the NetStock Web site. By streamlining the enrollment process, you can quickly and conveniently get started in a DSP. More and more companies will be offering this online access, so check back with the NetStock Direct site frequently to see what new companies have been added to their rosters.

There's no doubt about it—DRIPs and DSPs are a powerful way for the "little guy" to start on the path toward becoming a Wall Street tycoon!

NetStock Direct's advanced search function can help you find the right DRIP or DSP for you.

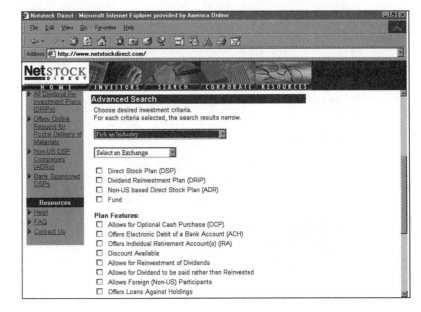

The Least You Need to Know

➤ Dividend reinvestment plans (DRIPs) and Direct Stock Plans (DSPs) are ways that you can invest in stocks without a broker. In addition, you can often invest with little or no commissions by using these plans.

➤ Hundreds of companies offer direct investment plans, making it even easier for you to purchase shares of their stock.

➤ You can research DRIPs and DSPs on the Web, and compare the fees and other features of their plans.

Part 4
Managing a Portfolio

Good job. You've built a market-savvy portfolio, but while you are patting yourself on the back and waiting for your ship to come in, don't let your investments just sit there! When you work hard at managing your portfolio, you will be able to anticipate changes in the financial climate and to adjust your investments for maximum growth. There are many online tools to make successful portfolio management achievable even for the novice investor.

Chapter 16

Recordkeeping Versus Portfolio Management

In This Chapter

➤ Learn how the Internet can help you maintain your investment records

➤ Understand how your investment decisions can affect your taxes

➤ Calculate the return of your portfolio

Sure, it is a snap to get updated prices for your stocks and mutual funds from the Web. But is looking at the quotes for your portfolio six times a day the same thing as managing your portfolio? Absolutely not!

In fact, you need to manage two completely different tasks if you really want to be a successful online investor.

The first is to keep track of all the important records related to the stocks and funds you buy and sell, and all the other activity in your portfolio. This is called *record-keeping*.

The second is to make sure that your portfolio is performing well and meeting all your objectives. This is called *portfolio management*.

The problem is that too many people confuse these two responsibilities. You should make sure that you don't. Although checking on the prices of the stocks that you own is part of the process of both recordkeeping and portfolio management, being a good portfolio manager requires much more than just looking at quotes on a computer screen.

Good Recordkeeping Is a Good Thing

After you start down the path to investing, one thing that you will notice is that the paperwork sure piles up fast! You will get a confirmation form every time you buy or sell a stock or mutual fund, and every time you move money into or out of an account. Each of your investment accounts will send you a statement every month, or at least every quarter. And each of those account statements will probably include a couple of transactions, such as dividends you have received or interest that has been credited to your account.

If you invest using dividend reinvestment plans, you will have another set of statements to deal with for each DRIP and for each transaction. Every time you buy a mutual fund, you will receive a prospectus in the mail. Stocks you own will send you quarterly and annual reports and proxy statements, too.

You Can't Avoid the Paperwork

One reason for the vast amounts of paperwork involved with investing is that regulatory agencies in the securities industry still require that certain information be sent to investors in printed format. Some of these regulations are slowly changing in the face of the cyber revolution to allow electronic communication, but for now, you can still expect to receive stacks of documents and statements in the mail from your investment accounts.

The bottom line is that you will be swimming in paper if you don't get organized! Besides the advantage of keeping your desk or dining room table clutter-free, being organized provides two other important benefits:

➤ You will be better equipped to know how much of your investing profits you will owe to the IRS, and you can make better decisions regarding the tax implications of any investment decision.

➤ You will be better equipped to figure out how well your portfolio has been performing and what problem areas you might need to address.

Nothing Is Certain but Taxes and More Taxes

You probably won't be surprised to hear that someone is interested in how well your portfolio is doing (besides your spouse, children, and any other potential heirs!).

If you are making money in the stock market, you can bet that Uncle Sam wants his fair share, too.

That's where good recordkeeping comes in. If you have kept good records and can document all your transactions, you will protect yourself from one day overpaying any taxes due to the IRS. As a general rule, the IRS doesn't accept statements such as, "Well, I think I bought those shares for about $8 or $9, but then it split once or twice, so I guess I owe you about $1,000 or so in capital gains taxes."

On the other hand, won't your accountant be ecstatic when you waltz into her office next February or March with a neatly printed report of all your transactions for the year, with summaries of all your income from dividends and interest, capital gains, and losses in your portfolio?

It's time to briefly review how investing affects your taxes in the first place. First, your investment accounts come under two categories: taxable and nontaxable.

That's a Lot of Capital Gains!

Individual taxpayers in the United States paid taxes on $251.9 billion in capital gains in 1996.

Source: Internal Revenue Service

Nontaxable accounts are retirement plans such as IRAs, 401(k)s, Roth IRAs, 403(b)s, Keoghs, and other accounts; as long as you don't withdraw money from these accounts, you don't have to worry about taxes. The taxes in these accounts are postponed (or *deferred*) until you start taking your money out of the accounts (probably after you retire). In some cases, you can even skip the taxes altogether! In the meantime, you don't have to worry about paying any taxes on the money you make in these accounts. Taxable accounts are any investments that aren't part of an official retirement plan. This could include a brokerage account, mutual fund accounts, or a dividend reinvestment plan. If you make money on these investments, the IRS wants to know about it so that they can collect the appropriate taxes.

Commissions and Fees Are Not Investment Expenses

Any commissions or fees that you have to pay to buy (or sell) a security are added to the cost (or subtracted from the proceeds) of those investments. They are not considered "investment expenses."

Let's say you bought 100 shares of stock in Associated Worldwide at $10 per share. You paid a $10 commission to buy the shares, which you added that to your initial investment of $1,000, making your total investment $1,010. This is the *cost basis* or *tax basis* or just plain *basis* of your investment, and it includes the cost of the investment plus any commissions or fees.

If the shares increase in price from $10 to $15 for the year, you have earned $490, and your portfolio is a bit richer for your investing skill! But do you owe any taxes on that increase? No, because these are *unrealized gains*.

Sure, your shares are worth a lot more, but no tax consequences come from having unrealized gains in your portfolio—that is, until you *realize the gains*. How do you do

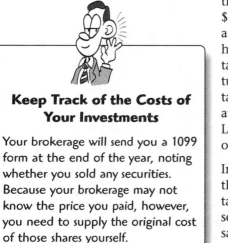

Keep Track of the Costs of Your Investments

Your brokerage will send you a 1099 form at the end of the year, noting whether you sold any securities. Because your brokerage may not know the price you paid, however, you need to supply the original cost of those shares yourself.

that? Just sell those shares. If you sell your shares at $15, paying another $10 commission, you will realize a $480 *capital gain*. Capital gains, you will be sorry to hear, are taxable. Even a set of special capital gains taxes exists just so that you can share your good fortune with the federal government. The capital gains tax rate is currently 28%. That means you would attach a Schedule D form, "Capital Gains and Losses," to your tax return, and pay the IRS $134.40 of your $480 profit. Ouch!

In 1997 and 1998, Congress made some changes to the tax laws and implemented a new capital gains tax rate of 20% that kicks in after you have owned a security for 12 months. This long-term rate on your sale would still cost you $96.

Unless you are a superhuman investor, chances are good that some of your investing decisions won't work out quite as planned. You may end up selling some shares at a loss. Maybe those 100 shares of American National, Inc. didn't do so well, falling from $10 to $8 after you bought them. The future of American National doesn't look so good, you think, so you sell the shares. You end up with $780, $220 less than your original investment of $1,000.

An Annual Portfolio Checkup Can Save You on Taxes

As the end of the year comes around, many investors review their portfolio to see how many capital gains they have received throughout the year. They also check to see whether any of their holdings have turned out to be dogs and whether they might be a candidate for selling to take the tax loss and wipe out some of the capital gains. It is important to do this before the end of the year—you can't sell a holding at a loss and apply it to the preceding year's gains.

This $220 is a *capital loss*. The good news is that you don't have to pay taxes on a loss—not even the IRS has figured out how to do that! The not-so-good news is that this loss will do you good in only one way: You can apply the amount of any capital losses toward any capital gains, and reduce the amount of capital gains taxes you have to pay.

In your case, you had a $220 loss from American National and a $480 gain from Associated Worldwide, leaving you with a net capital gain of $260. Your tax bill drops to $72.80 or $52 (depending on how long you have owned the Associated Worldwide stock).

When it comes to taxes, dividends are another matter. Associated National pays a regular quarterly dividend of five cents a share, and you are liable for paying taxes on that money, too. Dividends, as well as interest, are taxable as *ordinary income* at the same rate as your weekly paycheck.

You Can't Get Rich Selling at a Loss

At the end of each year, you are likely to hear news reports about "tax selling" as investors dump their losers so that they can write off the losses against their gains. But don't get too excited about building up capital losses. After all, you will never get rich selling at a loss.

The Internal Revenue Service publishes a guide that explains all you need to know about capital gains and losses. It is called "Investment Income and Expenses," but it is better known as "Publication 550." You can read the publication on the IRS Web site (`http://www.irs.gov`); just look in the "Forms & Pubs" section.

The Internal Revenue Service publishes several publications on its site that can help you understand capital gains, capital losses, and record-keeping.

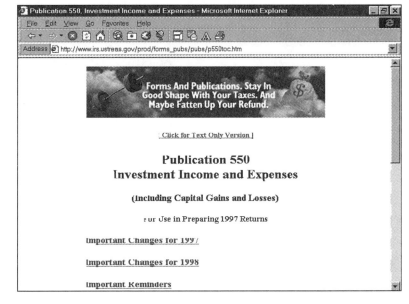

You can also download a copy of Schedule D, the form used to tell the IRS about your capital gains and losses. Publication 552 is another helpful publication, titled "Recordkeeping for Individuals." This booklet outlines the importance of keeping good records and provides guidelines for how long you should keep records.

Although the previous examples are pretty simple, what happens when you own a stock for 25 years? Chances are the shares have split along the way, or it may have spun off another company and issued new shares to you, or you may have made additional purchases of the same stock? All these factors can make it a bit harder to figure out the cost basis of your shares so that you will know what you will owe to the IRS if you need to sell.

Don't Get Tripped Up by the Wash Sale Rule

If you sell shares of a security that generate a capital loss, you can't buy back that same security for 30 days. If you do, it is considered a *wash sale* by the IRS, and your capital loss is cancelled out!

Each batch of shares that you purchase is called a *tax lot*. If you have made a number of purchases of its stock over the years, your American National shares could possibly be made up of dozens of tax lots. If you want to sell all your shares in the company, figuring your cost basis is easy. Just add up all the money that you have invested in the stock.

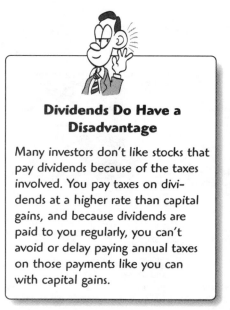

Dividends Do Have a Disadvantage

Many investors don't like stocks that pay dividends because of the taxes involved. You pay taxes on dividends at a higher rate than capital gains, and because dividends are paid to you regularly, you can't avoid or delay paying annual taxes on those payments like you can with capital gains.

What if you wanted to sell only part of your holdings? Then things get a bit more complicated. According to IRS rules, unless you specify another method, the shares you buy first are the shares you must sell first. This is called *first-in, first-out*, or *FIFO* for short.

After you have figured out the cost basis of your American National shares, you might discover that the tax bill you are facing is more than you really wanted to have to deal with right now. If you sold some shares that you purchased later, those with a higher cost basis, you would get to pay lower taxes.

You can avoid using FIFO by electing to sell specific shares and lots. To do this, you need to send your request in writing to your broker *before* you sell. If by chance you hold the actual stock certificates, you can just take the specific shares you would like to sell to the broker.

The advantage of this approach is that you can control (to some degree) the capital gains taxes you will have to pay on your profits. If you can sell your most expensive shares first, you will postpone the lion's share of your tax bill until a later date.

Unless you have all the facts at your fingertips, however, it is hard to figure the best selling decision to make. You might be very organized, carefully filing all your statements and confirmations in a filing cabinet, but it wouldn't help. It would be extremely tedious to sift through years of brokerage statements to find all the times you bought and sold a particular stock and then retroactively determine the cost basis of each lot.

You Can't Change How You Calculate Your Tax Basis in Midstream

After you begin using a particular method of determining your tax basis for a particular security, you have to stick with it!

You Can Use Any of Three Methods to Calculate Your Cost Basis in a Mutual Fund

If you sell a portion of your holdings in a mutual fund, you can use the FIFO or specific share method of computing your cost basis, or you can use the *average share price method,* a method unique to mutual funds. To use the average share price method, figure your cost basis by dividing the total dollar amount of shares you own by the number of shares. That's all!

In olden days (anytime before the 1980s), investors recorded all their investment transactions in big ledger books, using devices called "pencils." Today, this is a job that computers are much better equipped to handle. It is far simpler to use your computer and a software program that keeps track of all your investment records than to resort to the old-fashioned ways. You still need to file away the paperwork, of course, but you should also enter all your investment transactions into your computer as you make them. Then, with a few keystrokes, you can figure out the cost basis of any shares, as well as the overall return of your portfolio.

How Are You Doing? Calculating Your Portfolio's Return

Not so long ago, New York City had a colorful mayor named Ed Koch, better known by some by his nickname, "Hizzoner." One of Hizzoner's particular habits as he traveled throughout his expansive domain was to greet crowd of citizens with the question, "How'm I doin'?" The question was almost always certain to elicit either enthusiastic cheers from the gathered crowds—at least until a block of voters decided that the real answer to the question was "not so good" and booted him out of office. You should be able to ask the same question of your portfolio at any time—"How am I doing?"—and have a pretty good idea of the answer. This is one of the reasons that recordkeeping is essential to successful investing.

How to Measure Your Profits

ROI is the abbreviation for *return on investment*, the profit you could make from a security if you sold your shares in it today.

On the surface, it is not too hard to figure out the return that you have made on any investment. An investment's return is expressed as a percentage. If your 100 shares of Associated Worldwide increased in price to $15 per share from $10, what is your return? (Go ahead and leave the commissions out just to keep the math simple.) You can figure it out pretty easily with a calculator or a spreadsheet:

100 shares × $10 per share = $1,000 (the beginning value of your investment)

100 shares × $15 per share = $1,500 (the current value of your investment)

$1,500 (the current value) – $1,000 (the beginning value) = $500 (your unrealized gain)

$500 (your gain) ÷ $1,000 (the beginning value) = 0.50 (which is another way of saying 50%; this is your return)

You might be impressed to find out that your shares of American National increased 50%, but there's another very important variable that's missing: *time*.

It is one thing if your investment increased 50% in a month (yowza, that stock is moving!), but it is quite another thing if your shares took 10 years to grow by that amount (um, a bank savings account might be a better investment than that!).

And can you tell which mutual fund is growing faster: the one that's increased in price by 30% in 2 years or one that's increased by 22% in 30 months?

To get around that problem, returns are usually expressed on an *annualized* basis. An annualized rate of return is a percentage adjusted to a yearly figure. A 5% return on a stock in three months is equal to a 20% annualized return, for instance (if we temporarily forget about the effects of compounding):

12 months ÷ 3 months × 5% = 20%

A 20% return over two years is equal to 10% on an annualized basis:

12 months ÷ 24 months × 20% = 10%

These examples work fine—until you consider that many stocks pay dividends, and that the income from these dividends must also be considered when you want to figure out how well a stock is performing. When you include dividends or interest or other income, along with the changes in price, in calculating the returns of any security or an entire portfolio, it is called the *total return* of the investment.

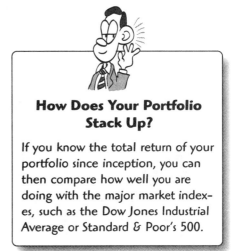

How Does Your Portfolio Stack Up?

If you know the total return of your portfolio since inception, you can then compare how well you are doing with the major market indexes, such as the Dow Jones Industrial Average or Standard & Poor's 500.

If your American National stock pays a dividend of $0.10 each quarter, you would receive $0.40 a year per share in dividends. (By the way, because you purchased the shares for $10, your *dividend yield* is 4.0%.)

$0.40 annual dividend / $10 cost per share = 0.040 (or 4.0%, the dividend yield)

If your American National stock jumps to $15 a share, your total return in a year is 54%:

50% change in price + 4% dividend yield = 54%

Total return is usually expressed as an annualized figure.

Things are beginning to get a little more complicated, aren't they?

Here's another twist: How do you figure out the total return of a stock or bond or mutual fund when you have made several purchases of that same security over a period of months or years? Maybe you are dollar cost averaging into a mutual fund, making monthly purchases. Or maybe you have enrolled in a dividend reinvestment plan, and your dividends are used to buy new shares each quarter.

And what if you want to determine the total return of your entire portfolio? You probably own more than one security—are you going to do these calculations for every holding? Remember, you won't have invested equal amounts in each of the different holdings in your portfolio, either, or have owned each for the same amount of time.

If you are a glutton for punishment, you can figure out the return of your entire portfolio by weighting the total returns of the various holdings by time, like this: Multiply the return percentage of each investment by the length time you have owned it, in years or months. Then multiply that figure by the percentage of your entire portfolio made up of that holding. Repeat for each investment, and then add all the figures together. This will give you a good idea of your portfolio's total return. But there's a much easier way, so keep reading. As you can see, you would need to perform dozens and dozens of calculations just to get to the magic total return number for a single investment or your complete portfolio. As long as you try to do these calculations by hand, this isn't going to get any easier.

Fortunately, this is exactly why computers were invented many years ago—to prevent mere mortals from having to agonize over mathematical calculations. It's time to get familiar with some recordkeeping software.

Software Is Your Friend

Although no place on the Web currently enables you to keep track of your investment transactions, a number of software programs can help you with recordkeeping, and many of these can interact with online services to help make the chores even easier. Check out these more popular programs:

➤ Capital Gainz (`http://localweb.com/alleycatsw`)

➤ Captool for Windows (`http://www.captools.com`)

➤ Microsoft Money (`http://www.microsoft.com/money`)

➤ NAIC Personal Record Keeper (`http://www.better-investing.org/computer/prk.html`)

➤ Quicken (`http://www.quicken.com`)

➤ Portfolio Logic (`http://www.blogicnyc.com/portfolio.shtml`)

Microsoft Money and Quicken are full-featured personal finance programs, and they can balance your checkbook, track your mortgage, and keep your investment records. Either of these programs can help you keep accurate investment records.

The other programs are specifically designed for investment tasks. That means they probably won't be much use with your checking account, but they have additional features that will make your investing job a bit easier.

You can download free trial versions of all these programs from their Web sites, so the best thing to do is to check the descriptions and other information on their Web sites. Then, try out one or two of them and see how you like them!

All these programs feature wizards or interactive screens to walk you through the process of entering a transaction. If you buy shares, for instance, the program will prompt you to enter the number of shares, the commission, and the price per share. The same goes for sales, reinvestments, dividend payments, and any other type of transaction.

Entering investment transactions is easy in Quicken.

NAIC Personal Record Keeper takes a slightly different approach from Quicken when it comes to entering a sale, but the basics are the same.

Every time you sell or purchase a security, you should enter the transaction in your software program. Some people prefer to enter all the transactions as they occur; others will enter all of a month's transactions at the end of the month when a printed statement arrives in the mail. Either way, make it a habit to keep your records up to date.

To make recordkeeping even easier, Money and Quicken have established partnerships with banks and brokers to enable you to download account information directly to your computer. The only catch (and a big catch it is) is that your bank or broker must support the software that you use. Some firms support Quicken; others support Money.

Don't Toss Those Investment Records!

According to IRS guidelines, you need to keep records relating to your tax returns for up to seven years, depending on the circumstances. Check Publication 552 for details.

After you have determined that your bank or broker or credit card supports the software you use, you will have to get on the phone with them to sign up for the service. The institution will assign you a username, PIN, and the other identification numbers that you will need to get started.

Next, you need to tell your Quicken or Money software that you want to use electronic services. This is as easy as editing the account name and checking a box that says you want the account to be linked online, and then entering your account number and user information (the same numbers that your bank or broker gave you).

Now you are ready to go online! Go to the online center in your software and connect! The first time you connect to your institution, you will have to change your trial PIN to a permanent one of your choice. Log on again, and then your transactions and balance will be downloaded to your computer.

If your bank, brokerage, or credit card company is one of Quicken's partners, you can automatically download transactions into the software.

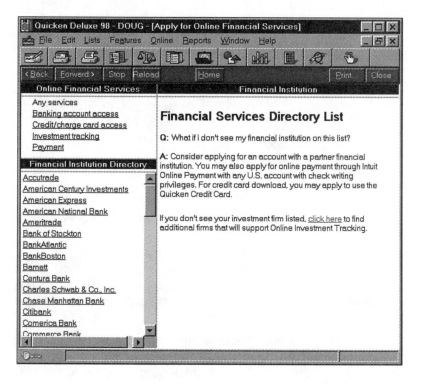

Quicken Deluxe 98 - DOUG

File Edit Lists Features Online Reports Window Help

Online Financial Services Center

Contact Info   Trade Print Close

Financial Institution: Update/Send...
Charles Schwab & Co., Inc.

Transactions Balances Holdings

Downloaded transactions as of 7/17/98 7:00:00 PM   Compare to Register...

Account	Transactions
Education IRA	0
IRA-Douglas	11

Date	Activity	Description	Price	Quantity	Amount
6/3/98	Shares In	SIGMA ALDRICH CORP	$0	100.0000	
6/3/98	Shares In	ATMEL CORP	$0	75.0000	
6/15/98	Dividend	SCHWAB MONEY MARKET FUND			$14.00
6/29/98	Sell	TOYS R US INC HOLDING CO	$24.25	-100.0000	$2394.98
7/15/98	Dividend	SCHWAB MONEY MARKET FUND			$40.00

With online banking, just click a button in Quicken, and all your trades or credit card charges are delivered to your computer.

Every week or so, you can download your transactions. You will always know exactly how much you have (or don't have) in the bank!

Besides transactions, good recordkeeping means that you will also need to update the prices of all your holdings on a regular basis. This is where the Internet can really make your life a lot easier. All these software programs interact with the online world, although in different ways. All these programs can either import quotes that you have downloaded from the Web or an online service. Some will even log on to the Web for you and update the prices of all your holdings automatically. These save you time, particularly if you own a lot of stocks and funds. Instead of updating your prices manually, security by security, you can update them all simultaneously!

In Quicken 97, for instance, go to the Portfolio View screen, and click the **Update Prices** button in the upper-left corner. If you are already connected to the Internet, Quicken will automatically retrieve quotes and news from their

Software Can't Replace All Your Recordkeeping Needs

Although software can help you to be organized, you still need to keep the paper versions of your account statements around. A good, old-fashioned filing system will help—but if your software recordkeeping is good, you will never need to consult the paper copies!

Internet server, and then update the prices of all your holdings in the program. If you are not connected, Quicken will dial your Internet service provider first. You do need to configure the Quicken software to let it know the details of your Internet connection, but that's a one-time chore. After that, updating prices is a snap!

A click of a button in Quicken will automatically update your portfolio quotes from the Internet.

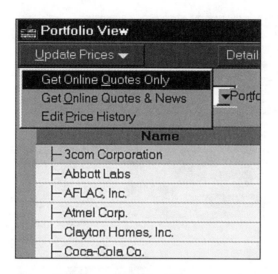

What's most important about all these programs is that each will produce reports about the performance of your portfolio, particular holdings, or specific accounts, for many time frames. Some of them will even generate colorful graphs and charts to give you a visual clue about your portfolio's performance.

In Quicken, for example, you can create graphs of your investment performance or asset allocation. You can use preset dates, such as last year, this year to date, or last month, or you can enter custom dates. You can chart the performance of your portfolio since you started investing (as long as you have entered all your transactions into the software). You can look at charts that only include specific accounts or securities or asset classes—the possibilities are limitless!

The Least You Need to Know

➤ You need to keep records of all your investment transactions, primarily to determine how much you might owe in taxes. Software makes the job easier.

➤ To determine how successful you are with your portfolio, you need to be able to calculate the returns you earn on your investment dollars. Computers can handle these complex calculations in seconds.

➤ Many banks, brokers, and credit card companies now offer online access to make the task of recordkeeping even easier. You may be able to download transactions and account information for your accounts directly to your computer.

Chapter 17

Keeping Tabs on Your Portfolio

In This Chapter

➤ Discover services that help you keep up to date on your investments

➤ Track your investment portfolio using the Web and email

You might be surprised to learn that the biggest part of investing is not figuring out what stocks or funds to buy. After you have built up your portfolio, the most important job is still ahead of you.

Now you need to manage your portfolio to make sure that all your investments are performing about as you expected when you first purchased them. Here is the point where most investors fail to follow through.

By far the biggest mistake investors make is confusing "stockwatching" (or its close cousin "fundwatching") with portfolio management. Stockwatching and fundwatching are addictive habits. The primary symptom is logging on and checking the prices of a portfolio several times a day. "Microsoft is up $2!" "IBM is down 2%!"

These hapless investors love the Internet because it keeps them in touch with their investments (or so they believe). They also think that by just looking at the prices of their holdings, they are being successful portfolio managers.

It's your choice: You can be a real portfolio manager, or you can just look like one. Checking your quotes every 20 minutes might make you feel like a pro, but portfolio management is a lot more than that. And although the changes in price of your stocks are a sign that something may be amiss in your portfolio, you may be able to uncover the warning signals before a stock falls 15% in price in one day. How?

To keep tabs on your holdings, do these two things:

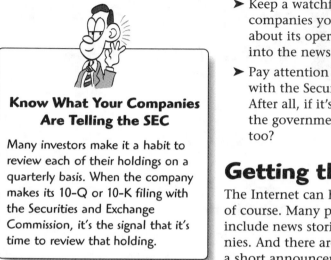

Know What Your Companies Are Telling the SEC

Many investors make it a habit to review each of their holdings on a quarterly basis. When the company makes its 10–Q or 10–K filing with the Securities and Exchange Commission, it's the signal that it's time to review that holding.

➤ Keep a watchful eye on the news. If one of the companies you own makes an announcement about its operations, or if its business makes it into the news-paper, you should know about it.

➤ Pay attention to the filings the company makes with the Securities and Exchange Commission. After all, if it's important enough to report to the government, shouldn't you know about it too?

Getting the Right Info

The Internet can help you with both of these jobs, of course. Many portfolio trackers on the Web include news stories and press releases about companies. And there are email services that will send you a short announcement whenever a company files a report with the SEC.

There's plenty of information on the Web, but how much of it is really meaningful?

A Press Release Usually Tries to Portray the Company in a Good Light

There can be a world of difference between a company press release and a news story. Remember that a press release is written and issued by a company, and can be less than totally objective. A press release may put a positive spin on a problem, for instance. On the other hand, news stories, although aiming to be fair, often can't tell you the whole picture because of space constraints. In other cases, a company release may have more data, such as a complete financial statement. The bottom line is that you should know the source of any "news" that you come across and be able to identify the source of the information.

"Noise" is all the completely useless information about a topic that's floating around in cyberspace. One of the disadvantages of using the Internet is that you can quickly be the victim of information overload, as you are bombarded with information from all kinds of sources.

Here's the key to avoiding this problem. You have to learn to figure out what information is useful, and what information is next to worthless.

When you hear bad news about a company, you need to figure out the impact on your investment. Here are some questions you should ask about any information that you come across, good or bad:

➤ How is this news likely to affect the profitability of the stock in the future, both in the short-term and the long-term? Even great companies occasionally stumble, but many often recover quickly.

➤ Is this a problem that's specific to this company, or does it affect the entire industry? A company could be the subject of "bad news," but still be a standout among its competitors.

➤ How is this news likely to affect the performance of this investment in your time frame? Or is the worst already over? In many cases, "bad" news is temporary and may have little impact on a long-term investment.

➤ If the company has announced changes in management, such as the resignation of the CEO or retirement of the Chairman of the Board, are these unexpected events? Or has the company properly prepared for the succession of management, with a seamless transition period as the new executives take over control of the company? A sudden management change can be a bad sign that a company is desperately seeking solutions for its floundering business.

Is the First Sign of Bad News a Sign of Impending Doom?

On Wall Street, there's a saying that "the first bad news is often the tip of the iceberg." Many times, investors sell at the first sign of trouble so that they don't have to worry about being sunk by larger problems later on. Many times there is no iceberg, however, just a chunk of ice that floated on by with very little impact.

Another way that a company might make the news is because an analyst has "downgraded" or "upgraded" its stock. Before you decide to take action based on an analyst's recommendation, consider this: Do you know the time frame that the analyst used in making the recommendation? Many analysts are only interested in stocks that increase in price in a relatively short period. If you have a long-term goal, this action may be only a tiny ripple in the stock's otherwise steady performance.

Think First!

If you hear bad news about your portfolio, above all else, *don't panic!* It's likely that by the time you hear any news, the price has already dropped significantly. So waiting until you can figure out the real impact of the news on your holdings won't result in too much further damage.

Remember that institutional traders and other professionals who have real-time newsfeeds can act much more quickly than you ever could. Don't try to beat them at their game. Take your time, and make a careful analysis of the situation before you take action.

Maintaining the Right Balance

If you build a portfolio of stocks according to the principles laid out in Chapter 11, you will invest pretty equal amounts in 10 or so companies, all from different industries and spread out in small, mid-sized, and large companies.

Some of the stocks you buy will go up in price, and some will go down in price. As they rise and fall, the percentage of each stock in your portfolio changes. After holding those stocks for a while, however, you will probably find what was initially a nice, neat basket of stocks, with each holding making up about the same percentage, is now wildly out of whack!

Ironically, one of the problems that comes with being a successful investor is that the big winners in your portfolio usually end up turning your asset allocation plan upside down and your diversification scheme completely lopsided! Remember this: If a stock you own outpaces the rest of your portfolio, perhaps by tripling or quadrupling in price, that stock may become a dominant part of your portfolio. That's great if the stock is rising in price. If the price falls, however, your portfolio could take a big hit. That's one of the big reasons you will need to rebalance your portfolio.

As your portfolio grows, you need to keep a watchful eye to ensure that your plans remain consistently on track. Good portfolio management is a perpetual rebalancing job.

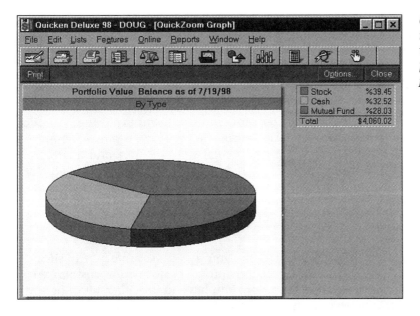

Quicken provides graphs to give you an instant visual picture of your portfolio's balance, growth, or performance.

Your recordkeeping software, such as Quicken or Microsoft Investor, can help with the task of watching the balance of your portfolio. With a few clicks of your mouse, you can see graphs and charts of your portfolio holdings that indicate whether some of your holdings make up too much of your portfolio. You should periodically review the balance of your portfolio, perhaps twice a year or once a quarter.

If you see that your portfolio has fallen out of balance, you have two choices: You can direct future investments into those areas where your portfolio is underrepresented. Or, you can sell some of your current holdings in the overweighted part of your portfolio, and reinvest those funds in your areas that you have targeted. In either case, good recordkeeping or portfolio management tools can provide the information you need to make an informed decision.

Tracking Your Portfolio Online

Lots of investors hang out on the Web at their favorite portfolio trackers. You probably will, too! It's easy to see the attraction of these online tools. Just enter the tickers once for all the stocks and funds you own, and then you can see the updated prices of those securities every time you visit the portfolio tracker. You can check up on your portfolio once a week, once a day, or once every 20 minutes. It's fast, easy, and convenient.

Some trackers go beyond the basics, and enable you to enter the date of your first purchase, price per share, number of shares you own, and other details. Then they will add up the value of your entire portfolio every time you visit.

With most trackers, you can create more than one portfolio. You can separate your 401 from your regular brokerage account, or set up a portfolio just for your investment club, or organize your holdings in whatever way works best for you.

Some trackers enable you to enter other assets, such as real estate or automobiles. Of course, they don't have a clue how much the assets are worth, so the trackers won't update their values for you! But this can be a convenient way of keeping track of other possessions. One important point to remember as you begin exploring portfolio trackers on the Web is that they are not designed for use as recordkeeping systems. You can enter only individual purchases for a particular stock or fund, and the tracker then displays the total number of shares of that holding. You can't enter individual purchases of a stock or fund and have them automatically "roll up" into a total number of shares for that particular holding. (The only exception to this rule is Microsoft Investor, although you can expect to see other sites adding this capability in the future.)

As you begin using these online portfolio trackers, you should be protective of the personal information you provide. Because trackers provide information customized just for you, all these services require registration. You have to provide a bit of personal information and create a username and password. Besides the details of your portfolios, you probably need to tell them your name and email address, at the very least.

Fortunately, many quality portfolio trackers provided by reputable firms take steps to protect the personal information they do collect and don't use it for any disreputable purpose. A few of these tracking sites are covered later in this chapter.

Some of the trackers offer you the ability to save your logon information on your computer. If you are the only person who uses (or has access to) your computer, this can be a useful feature. If you work in an office where others occasionally sit down at your desk and borrow your computer (even for just a few minutes), however, another user could pull up your portfolio just by surfing to one of the sites in your hotlist. You might soon learn that your personal net worth is the subject of office gossip! If that's the case, you had better avoid this timesaver.

On a practical level, the information that will likely never make its way to an online portfolio tracker is the information that would be most useful to someone bent on fiscal tomfoolery. You should never use account numbers or even the names of the brokerage firms and mutual fund companies where you hold your accounts when setting up your portfolios online, for example. The number of shares of Microsoft that you own, or even the total value of your portfolio, just isn't that interesting to a hacker bent on destruction. There are much bigger fish to catch!

Finally, no one can verify that the information you enter in a portfolio tracker is accurate. You could sign up with a phony name and build a portfolio that consists of a million shares of Microsoft, a million shares of Intel, and 10,000 shares of Berkshire Hathaway. According to the portfolio tracker, you would sure be one wealthy investor! But that doesn't make it true. That's one reason that few online portfolio trackers are set up on secure Web servers that would require the use of a secure browser.

Be Careful If You Check Your Portfolio on a Computer That's Not Your Own

If you check your portfolio in a public place, such as a public library, shared office terminal, or Internet cafe, you should take some extra steps to keep your information private. If the tracker has the option, log off after you finish checking your information. Then shut down the browser and restart it. In most cases, this ought to keep others from seeing your information.

The bottom line is that you really don't have much choice in the matter: If you want the convenience of using an online tracker, you have to put up with the minimal risks of providing some personal information.

To use any of these portfolio trackers, you need to follow these steps:

1. Register to use the service, usually by giving your name, email address, and creating a password. (As always, remember your username and password!)
2. Create a portfolio, giving it a name that helps you identify it at glance.
3. Enter the ticker symbols of the stocks and funds in your portfolio. If you don't know the ticker symbol, the tracker will help you to look it up.
4. Optionally, enter the number of shares, cost per share, purchase date, and other information. You can always come back and enter this information later.

Don't Use the Exact Same Password for Every Site or Service

When registering for services on the Web, don't use the same password as the one you use for your account with your Internet service provider or online broker. If someone were to learn the password you use at a low-security site, like a portfolio tracker, you wouldn't want him to have access to your brokerage account or be able to run up charges with your ISP.

That's it! Now you can take your pick of any of the following portfolio trackers. They all offer slightly different functions, and some are easier to use than others. But you can try them all out by starting a portfolio with just a few ticker symbols, and see which one you like best. They are all free, too!

Yahoo! Finance (`http://quote.yahoo.com`) is one of the fastest and easiest to use portfolio trackers on the Web. Yahoo! also supports advanced features that provide you with customized views of your portfolios, and plenty of research. Getting started is easy. You will have to register first, but then you just create a portfolio, give it a name (like "IRA" or "Brokerage Account" or "Doug's Stocks"), and enter a list of ticker symbols. If you want, you can enter the number of shares you own, the purchase price, and other details. Then click the **Finished** button and your portfolio is displayed for you.

Yahoo!'s portfolio tracker offers links to plenty of other information about each of your stocks or funds.

Whenever you visit your portfolio on Yahoo!, you can just click the links in the right column to see current news, analyst reports, company profile, and charts. Or, scan the listing of recent news stories at the bottom of the page. The newest stories are listed first, so you can discover at a glance what's affecting your holdings.

And here's another tip: If you use Yahoo!'s personalized My Yahoo! service, your portfolio will be displayed there in an abbreviated format. Just go to `http://my.yahoo.com` and configure your preferences. You can even download a ticker program that will continuously update your portfolio prices and deliver them via tickertape to your computer screen.

FYI	PR	News	Sym.	Name	Last	Change	Today	Quantity	Mkt. Val.	Gain
			ABT	Abbott Laboratories	44⁷/₈	⁵/₁₆ ↑	2.58 ↑	8.3	371.12	232.23
			AFL	AFLAC Incorporated	37⁷/₈	⁹/₁₆ ↑	5.45 ↑	9.7	367.01	262.00
			CMH	Clayton Homes, Inc.	19¹⁵/₁₆	³/₁₆ ↑	5.22 ↑	27.9	555.32	98.32
			KO	Coca-Cola Company	86¹/₈	-1¹/₁₆ ↓	-4.18 ↓	3.9	338.90	238.37
			INTC	Intel Corporation	83¹/₈	-1¹/₈ ↓	-3.04 ↓	2.7	224.48	137.48
			MRK	Merck & Co., Inc.	138	-³/₈ ↓	-2.19 ↓	5.9	807.71	564.68
			MOT	Motorola, Inc.	53¹¹/₁₆	-³/₄ ↓	-3.95 ↓	5.3	282.60	0.61
			RPO...	RPM, Inc.	15¹⁵/₁₆	-¹/₈ ↓	-2.03 ↓	16.3	258.99	89.42
			RBD	Rubbermaid Incorporat...	31¹¹/₁₆	-⁵/₁₆ ↓	-0.31 ↓	1.0	31.69	31.11
			SLE	Sara Lee Corporation	57¹/₈	-³/₁₆ ↓	-0.97 ↓	5.2	294.28	163.03
			WEN	Wendy's International, I...	22¹¹/₁₆	⁷/₁₆ ↑	7.79 ↑	17.8	403.94	129.15
				Cash					-0.01	
				Total Account Value			4.38 ↑		3,936.03	1,946.40

The portfolio tracker provided by Microsoft Investor includes some advanced tools, but it's a little more complicated to use than some of the others.

Some users will shy away from Microsoft Investor's portfolio tracker (http://www.investor.com), but it's worth taking a look at. It shouldn't come as a surprise that the Microsoft Investor site works best with the Microsoft Internet Explorer Web browser; if you use Netscape Navigator, however, you should do just fine.

First of all, the Microsoft Investor site is partly subscription based, and partly free. The tracker is free, but some of the research links contained within it are available only if you are a subscriber.

Using the Microsoft Investor site also requires that you download a small plug-in—a piece of software that is then integrated into your browser. (After it's installed, you will never even know it's there.) But then whenever you visit the Investor site, it asks you to verify that you have installed the software—and that becomes annoying quickly.

After you are set up, however, the upside is that Investor offers the only transaction-based portfolio tracker on the Web. Enter all your buys, sells, and dividends and the program keeps track of your balances and total number of shares. You can even import all your transactions from Quicken or Microsoft Money automatically, too, or download all the quotes to your computer in a CSV file.

Build a Stock Watch List of Your Very Own

Some portfolio trackers come with a built-in *watch list*. This is where you can watch stocks that you might be thinking about buying. If the tracker you are using doesn't provide a special watch list, just create a portfolio called "Watch List" and enter the symbols of the stocks you are following.

The portfolio tracker provided by Quicken (http://www.quicken.com/investments/portfolio) works nicely, providing the option to enter the details of your holdings or just the ticker symbols.

Quicken's Portfolio Analysis takes an x-ray of your portfolio, and lets you know how your assets are allocated.

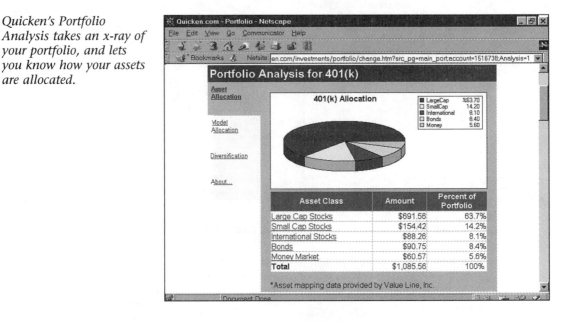

The real bonus, however, is its Portfolio Analysis tool. Quicken looks at the holdings in your portfolio, and then displays a chart of your portfolio's asset allocation, dividing your stocks and funds (and the holdings of your funds) into categories such as large cap stocks, small cap stocks, international stocks, bonds, and cash. Quicken then calculates the returns that a portfolio with the same asset allocation would have earned historically and can even suggest a new asset allocation model that might improve your return. This tool is especially useful in x-raying a portfolio of mutual funds to see whether you hold too many funds that invest in the same asset classes.

With the Invest-O-Rama! portfolio tracker (http://www.investorama.com/markets), you can manage a number of portfolios. Invest-O-Rama! enables you to customize how the portfolios are displayed and sends you email updates on a regular basis. This tracker accepts assets such as real estate and cars, and has a desktop ticker that you can launch to send quotes scrolling across your computer screen. You can also use currencies other than U.S. dollars.

Finally, a service for the forgetful type: Many people don't want to have to remember to check their portfolio. InfoBeat Finance (http://www.infobeat.com) is an email service that enables you to set up three portfolios and then delivers daily or weekly messages that include the recent prices of your stocks and funds. You can also receive news summaries for your holdings, or an attached file that can be imported into Quicken or NAIC Personal Record Keeper.

InfoBeat Finance delivers email each day with your portfolio's closing quotes.

To sign up for the service, just enter your email address and the ticker symbols of your holdings, and then select from the many options for delivery. You can receive a message at the end of the day or once a week, and you can choose to receive daily summaries of market activity. What's even better is that the service is free, supported by unobtrusive advertisements at the top of each message.

Finally, you can always know what your investments are reporting to the Securities and Exchange Commission if you set up a free watchlist with FreeEDGAR (http://www.freeedgar.com). Register with the site, and then enter the names of companies or ticker symbols of the companies or funds you are following. When any of those companies files a report with the SEC's EDGAR, FreeEDGAR will send you an email message notifying you of the filing. Then you can go to the FreeEDGAR site and review the filing directly.

The Least You Need to Know

➤ You need to keep records of all your investment transactions, primarily to determine how much you might owe in taxes. Software makes the job easier, and your bank, broker, or credit card company may offer online access to make the task of recordkeeping even easier.

➤ Portfolio management is more than just checking the prices of your investments. You need to watch for signs that your investments may be headed in the wrong direction. Portfolio trackers and email services that can help you keep tabs on your portfolio are available.

➤ Online portfolio trackers provide an easy and convenient way to check up on your portfolio. Besides providing prices, however, these services also provide easy access to news, charts, and research about your investments.

Chapter 18

Getting Price Quotes Online

In This Chapter

➤ Getting price quotes on the Internet for the stocks, options, commodities, bonds, and mutual funds you own or are studying

➤ Downloading quotes to your computer and importing them into recordkeeping and analysis software programs

➤ Discovering Web sites that offer free real-time stock quotes

---

Serving Up a Slew of Quotes

One of the easiest things to find on the World Wide Web is a price quote for a stock or mutual fund. In fact, if you haven't yet found a place to get price quotes on the Web, you're just not looking!

On the Web, sites that maintain databases of the prices of stocks, funds, and other securities are called *quote servers*. Some of the busiest quote servers serve up prices to interested investors millions of times each day!

Quote servers get their prices directly from the stock exchanges (or from other quote servers). The stock exchanges charge expensive prices for these continuous data feeds, and the quote servers package up the prices to display on Web sites for individual investors like you.

Several companies specialize in delivering security price quotes on the Web. The Data Broadcasting Corporation (`http://www.dbc.com`) is a leading provider of market data to investors. Not only does it serve free quotes on its Web site, you can subscribe to your choice of services that deliver real-time quotes on the Web or through a wireless receiver.

Why Are They Called "Quotes"?

The word *quotes* comes from *quotations*, the term used to describe a statement of the price for which a security is currently selling.

Besides the current price of a stock or fund, online quote servers often provide a lot of other information. Here's how you can retrieve and interpret the quotes and all the related data you get from DBC or from any other quote server on the Web.

On DBC's main page, you can request a quote by entering the ticker symbol of a stock. This is the single most important bit of information you need to know when you're looking up a stock or mutual fund quote. The ticker symbol is made up of one to five unique characters that represent a particular stock or fund, or sometimes a particular class of stock.

Let's Go to the Tickertape

The phrase *ticker symbol* comes from the old, mechanical quote machines that ticked as they delivered stock prices to brokers by printing them on narrow, continuous rolls of paper, called *tickertape*. Even though the computer age has made ticker tape machines obsolete, electronic versions of tickers still deliver an uninterrupted stream of quotes in broker's offices, on television, on the Web, and even on the side of a building in New York City's Times Square!

If you don't know a security's ticker symbol, just look it up! All quote servers provide a lookup feature where you can search for ticker symbols. You may be able enter a part of the company's name into a search box, or you can look through an alphabetic list of stocks to find the one you're looking for.

You can search for ticker symbols using the alphabetic listings on the DBC Web site.

Stock Symbols Make Life Easier for Telegraph Operators—and Investors!

The practice of using symbols to represent stocks goes back to the 1800s, when telegraph operators needed a fast way to deliver quotes. Symbols were assigned to all stocks on the exchanges; the most active stocks received one-letter symbols, and the rest were given symbols of two and three letters. Back then, railroads were the biggest businesses of the country, and so they received one-letter symbols.

Besides the price of the most recent trade of a stock, quote servers can tell you a lot of other useful information about a stock. Different quote servers provide different amounts of information, but you can see the basic components of a stock quote in this example.

Newspapers Don't Include the Ticker Symbols of Stocks

The abbreviations that newspapers use in the tables of stock prices are not the same thing as a stock's ticker symbol. Newspaper abbreviations are created to use as few letters as possible while still letting you figure out the name of the company. Ticker symbols are made up of one to five characters, and you probably won't be able to guess the name of a company from its symbol.

This quote from Data Broadcasting Corporation shows the most recent price of Intel Corporation's stock, as well as other information about the security.

Whenever a stock quote is displayed, the first bit of information you will see is the name of the stock, or the ticker symbol, or sometimes both. In this case, INTC is the ticker symbol for Intel Corporation.

You will also see an abbreviation for the stock exchange on which shares of the stock are bought and sold. NYSE is the New York Stock Exchange, AMEX is the American Stock Exchange, and Nasdaq is the National Association of Securities Dealers Automated Quotations System, the leading market for over-the-counter stocks. Intel's shares trade on Nasdaq. The fifth letter of a ticker symbol of a Nasdaq listed stock has special significance. Here's a guide that can help you decipher the meaning of the fifth letter of a ticker symbol.

Symbol	Meaning
A	Class A shares
B	Class B shares
C	Exempt from Nasdaq listing qualifications for a limited period
D	New issue
E	Delinquent in making required SEC filings
F	Foreign company
G	First convertible bond
H	Second convertible bond (same company)
I	Third convertible bond (same company)
J	Voting shares
K	Non-voting shares
L	Miscellaneous situations, including second class units, third class warrants, or sixth class preferred stock
M	Fourth class preferred (same company)
N	Third class preferred (same company)
O	Second class preferred (same company)
P	First class preferred (same company)
Q	Company is in bankruptcy proceedings
R	Rights
S	Shares of beneficial interest
T	Shares with warrants or rights
U	Units
V	When issued and when distributed
W	Warrants
X	Mutual fund
Y	American Depositary Receipts
Z	Miscellaneous situations, including second class of warrants, fifth class preferred stock or any unit, receipt or certificate representing a limited partnership interest

Give Me an A

Want to know how you can tell whether a stock trades in the over-the-counter market (such as on Nasdaq) or on a stock exchange? Just count the number of letters in its ticker symbol! A ticker symbol with three letters is a stock that trades on the New York or American Stock Exchange. If the ticker has four or five letters, it's an OTC or Nasdaq stock.

In the case of the stock quote for Intel, DBC also provides the country (USA) where the exchange is located. DBC's quote servers deliver prices from exchanges all around the world.

The date and time of the quote is also displayed, usually along with the time that you requested the quote. U.S. stock markets close each day at 4:00 p.m. Eastern time.

You will also notice that stock prices are always 15 or 20 minutes old by the time you get them. That's because the exchanges charge steep fees for real-time prices. Because brokerage firms and investment banks can't do business without knowing the prices of securities at every second, they pay for the privilege! A broker has to know how much a client must pay for shares—quotes that are a few minutes old are useless to them.

This also means that stock quotes that are a few minutes old have so little value to professionals that they can be given away for free by the quote servers. Most of the time, it's not a problem for individual investors to get their prices a little bit later, so everyone's happy.

As a result, you will find that NYSE stock prices are always delayed by 20 minutes; AMEX and Nasdaq stocks are delayed by 15 minutes. (You can pay for real-time quotes, or even get them for free from some new Web sites—but more about that later in this chapter.)

Different Classes of Stock Are Represented by Slightly Different Ticker Symbols

If a company has more than one share of stock, such as Class A and Class B, the letter of the class is usually appended to the end of the ticker symbol, sometimes by itself and other times following a period. Therefore, Brown Forman Class A shares are known as BF.A, and Class B shares are BF.B.

The next piece of information in the quote is the *last price*. This is just what it sounds like—the price of the last trade of that stock. Stocks are bought and sold in prices based on fractions, such as eighths, quarters, sixteenths, or even sixty-fourths! Intel's last price was $81 5/8, and in this case that was the closing price for the day.

Change is the amount that the security's price has changed from the previous day's closing price to the latest price. This is sometimes expressed as a percentage, as well. In Wall Street–speak, you would say, "Intel is down an eighth today," which is 0.15% lower than the yesterday's closing price.

The *opening price* is the price of the stock's first trade at the beginning of the day. An investor bought shares of Intel for $81 3/8 in the first trade of this day.

A *tick* is the change in the price of a security, and ticks come in two varieties. An *uptick* happens when the last trade in a security takes place at a higher price than the prior trade. A *downtick* happens when the last trade in a security takes place at a lower price than the prior trade.

In DBC's quote server, a plus sign represents an uptick, and a minus sign represents a downtick. In this case, you can see the direction of the prices (compared to the prior trade) of the previous four trades. The first of those four trades was higher than the last trade, the next was lower than that, the next was higher than that, and the last trade price was down from that.

Your Browser's Cache Enables You to Surf the Web More Quickly

To speed up how fast Web pages load to your computer, browsers automatically save pages to your hard drive in what's known as a *cache*. If you access a page that you have already visited, your browser can load it from the cache much faster than it can load it from the Web server.

Reload Browser Pages with Timely Data to Make Sure You're Seeing the Latest Information

When you're accessing quotes online, you will want to see the most current information available. Unfortunately, after you have viewed a page of quotes, pressing the Reload or Refresh button may load the page from the browser's cache instead of updating the prices from the Web site. If this happens in Internet Explorer, press the Ctrl (Control) key and Refresh button at the same time. This forces the browser to reload the page from the Web server, not from the cache. To do the same thing in Netscape Navigator, press the Shift key plus the Reload button.

Why Stocks Trade in Eighths of a Dollar

What do "pieces of eight" have to do with the stock market? Legend has it that the reason that stocks are priced in fractions is that Spanish traders 400 years ago used to quote prices in fractions of gold doubloons. A doubloon could be cut into two, four, or eight pieces, so four "pieces of eight" equaled half a doubloon. The earliest stock traders used this practice, and the habit has continued until modern times with stocks trading in eighths on the major exchanges.

Because Intel is a stock that isn't listed on a stock exchange, but trades instead in the over-the-counter market (in this case, the Nasdaq market), the price quote includes information on the *bid* and *ask* prices for the stock.

A Stock's Opening Price Doesn't Have to Be the Same as the Prior Day's Closing Price

Usually, the opening price of a stock is close to the preceding day's closing price. If important news is announced before the market opens, however, the opening price could be much higher or lower than the prior day's closing price. Remember that a stock is only worth what someone is willing to pay for it. Therefore the first price of Tuesday is not necessarily the last price from Monday!

The *bid* is the highest price any investor is willing to pay for a stock at a particular time. You make your bid, just like at an auction.

The *ask* is the lowest price that any investor is willing to accept to sell a stock at that particular time. If you were selling your used car, for example, you would establish your *asking price*. That's the price you would ask a potential buyer to meet if he or she wanted to buy your car.

Buying a stock is really no different from buying a car! If you have a stock that you want to sell, you can establish your asking price. If you want to buy shares in a stock, you can make a bid. Unless you're one of the big players on the Street, however, you will usually have to resolve yourself to buying your shares at "the ask" and selling them at "the bid." If you placed an order with your broker to buy shares at a price lower than the current asking price of a stock, it's unlikely that any other investor would take you up on the offer. Why should they, when they can buy shares elsewhere at a cheaper price? Likewise, you could tell your broker to only sell your shares at a price higher than the current price that other investors are paying, but no one would jump at an offer like that! In the case of Intel, the bid was

$81 5/8, the price you could have sold shares at. The bid was $81 11/16, the price you could have purchased shares for.

The *bid size* and *ask size* tell you how many shares are available for buyers and for sellers. Size is reported in blocks of 1,000 shares; so a bid size of 270 means that bids have been made to buy 270,000 shares of Intel's stock. The ask size of 10 indicates that sellers have offered 10 blocks of 1,000 shares (or 10,000 shares) of stock at the ask price.

Sometimes, trade size is reported in this format: 270×10. If you wanted to sound really cool, you could say the current quote for Intel as "bid 81 5/8, ask 81 1/16, size 270 by 10" and any Wall Street pro would know what you mean (although your friends might look at you funny!).

The *day high* and *day low* are the highest and lowest prices that investors have paid for that security today. Some investors purchased shares of Intel at 81 3/16 today; others paid 84 13/16.

The *previous* price is the share price of the trade right before the last trade.

Finally, *volume* has nothing to do with how loud a stock is. This is the total number of shares of the stock that were bought and sold on that day. A total of 19,987,000 Intel shares traded on this day.

In addition to stocks, DBC can deliver quotes for commodities, options, mutual funds, and indexes.

DBC's database isn't limited to U.S. securities, either. You can get quotes for stocks listed on exchanges in nearly 30 cities around the world, including Prague, Sao Paulo, Bangladesh, Istanbul, Toronto, and Shanghai.

Ticks That Keep Check

The *uptick rule* prevents investors from selling a stock short unless the last tick was up or even. This rule helps maintain order in the market and keep short sellers from shorting a stock that's falling in price and driving the price down even further.

You Can't Fight the Tape

On Wall Street, professionals often repeat the adage, "You can't fight the tape." This word of advice is a reminder that there's nothing you can do to stop the momentum of a stock that's moving up or down in price on the tickertape.

Market Makers Make Money on the Spread

The *spread* is the difference between the bid and the ask prices of an over-the-counter traded stock. It's sometimes called the *markup*, which may be more appropriate because the spread is kept by the market maker in return for facilitating the transaction between the buyer and seller of the stock.

One problem with getting quotes on international stocks is that ticker symbols aren't always standardized. That means all quote servers may not use the same symbol. Another problem is that the same ticker symbol may be used on more than one exchange. SLM is the symbol of SLM Holdings, commonly known as Sallie Mae, whose shares trade on the New York Stock Exchange. But the Santa Cantalina Mining Co. also uses the ticker symbol SLM. That's okay, because its shares trade on the Vancouver Stock Exchange.

DBC works around this by using an extension on the ticker symbols of non-U.S. stocks. "-VC" is the extension that represents the Vancouver exchange, so "SLM-VC" is the symbol of Santa Cantalina Mining. "-NZ" is used for stocks on the New Zealand Stock Exchange, "-SN" represents the Shenzhen Stock Exchange in China, and so on.

Bid and Ask Prices Aren't Reported for Listed Stocks

Don't look for bid and ask prices for quotes on stocks listed on a stock exchange. Typically, quotes on exchange-listed stocks include the daily high and low prices rather than the bid and ask prices.

Fortunately, DBC provides a symbol lookup feature that makes it easy to find the tickers you need. Click on the link beneath its quote request box and you can see a list of all the stock exchanges around the world for which the site can offer quotes.

If you are interested in penny stocks, DBC provides quotes on over-the-counter Bulletin Board stocks, too, one of the few quote servers on the Web that provides prices for these stocks.

DBC provides a variety of free reports in addition to price quotes, such as charts, news stories, company profile, earnings reports, and links to SEC filings. After you have requested a quote from the site, a small button bar is displayed above the prices, offering quick links to a lot of other free information about that stock.

This feature is common to most quote servers on the Web. In addition to prices, you can quickly review other information about a stock or mutual fund. Although you are not likely to find extensive research on these sites, you can get a good snapshot of a particular stock, especially if it's one you're not familiar with.

Navigating for NAVs

It's just as easy to get prices of mutual funds as it is to get stock quotes. You have to remember, however, that fund managers figure the net asset value (NAV) of their funds just once a day, after the market closes when they have the closing prices of all the stocks and bonds in their portfolio. Generally, you can get the NAV of a fund a few hours after the markets close each day.

It Can Be Hard to Find Quotes for OTC Bulletin Board Stocks

Not all quote servers provide prices for over-the-counter Bulletin Board stocks. And there is no online source of prices for stocks that trade on the "Pink Sheets"—stocks that aren't listed on an exchange or traded on the Nasdaq system.

Just about every stock quote server will provide prices of mutual funds. PC Quote (http://www.pcquote.com) is another major provider of quotes to individual investors, and they offer prices of stocks, options, currencies, and indexes, as well as mutual funds.

Mutual funds have tickers just like stocks. If you know the ticker symbol for your fund, you can use the QuickQuote box on PC Quote's main page. Enter the symbol and click the Submit button to find out the most recent NAV of your fund.

PC Quote's mutual fund quotes tell you the closing net asset value of the fund, as well as the prior day's NAV and the net change from the prior day in both dollars and as a percent. They also provide the annual dividend and the dividend yield, and the 52-week high and low NAVs for the fund.

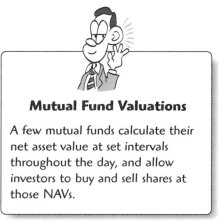

Mutual Fund Valuations

A few mutual funds calculate their net asset value at set intervals throughout the day, and allow investors to buy and sell shares at those NAVs.

PC Quote also provides a figure that represents the volatility of the fund. This number is figured by comparing the weekly returns of all funds over the past six months; the higher the number (the more volatile the fund).

X Marks the Spot

Ticker symbols for mutual funds are always five characters long and always end with the letter *X*. Money market fund symbols are also five characters long and always end with the letters *XX*.

If you don't know the ticker symbol of your fund, you can ask the fund company, or you can look it up on the PC Quote Web site. Whenever you display a quote, you have access to a navigation toolbar with a symbol lookup feature. Enter the name of the fund (or part of the name) and PC Quote will tell you the funds that match your entry.

You can find the net asset value of your mutual funds by using a quote server like PC Quote.

PC Quote Micro Watch - Microsoft Internet Explorer		
File Edit View Go Favorites Help		
Address http://www.pcquote.com/cgi-bin/getquote.dll?ticker=vfinx		

VANGUARD INDEX TRUST 500 (vfinx)   106.02   + 0.09 ▲

Price Data Table
Jul 24, 1998 @ 9:30 (All data 20 minutes delayed.)

Closing Value	**106.02**	Net Change	+ 0.09
Net Asset Value	105.93	Percent Change	+ 0.08
Yield	2.60	Dividend Amount	0.270
52 Week High	110.28	52 Week Low	82.09
Volatility	7.47		

DOW	8937.33 + 4.35
NASDAQ	1930.99 - 4.23
S&P 500	1140.80 + 1.05
S&P 100	558.22 + 2.12
DJ Util	286.08 - 1.44

Trade here
Trade here
Trade here

Yet More Options for Quotes (Or Quotes for Options)

Every stock has a unique ticker symbol that never changes. But a stock can have dozens of options available at any one time. Some options expire in different months, and at different strike prices in those months. Then there are call options and put options. All those variables make it a bit harder to find prices of options, not to mention trying to figure out the ticker symbol of a particular option!

For that reason, most quote servers that provide prices on options also provide a way for
you to find all the options connected to a particular security. A list of all the options linked
to a security is called, quite sensibly, an *options
chain.*

On the Invest-O-Rama! quote server
(`http://www.investorama.com/markets`),
provided by Reality Online, you can select
Option Chains from the menu on the left side
of the screen. From there, you can enter a
stock ticker symbol, the month in which the
options contract expires, a strike price range (if
you wish), and whether you're looking for put options or call options.

**Your Fund May Provide NAVs
on Its Site**

Many mutual funds have Web sites
where you can also find the fund's
latest NAV.

*Option chains, like this
one on Invest-O-Rama!,
enable you to find prices
and symbols for stock
options.*

Click **Get Chain** and you will get a list of all the options available in the period you
selected.

The option chain gives you some details about the recent activity in each option,
including the last trade, volume, open interest, daily high and low, and the date of
the last trade. (Some contracts may not be traded frequently; so it's not uncommon
that date may be a few days old.)

You will see that each option in the chain is identified with some symbols and codes.
Here's how to decipher "IBM Sep8 120.0 C," for example. "IBM" is the ticker symbol
of the underlying stock. "Sep8" is the expiration date of the contract. (You don't have

The Open Interest of a Stock Option Can Tell You How Active That Option Is

Open interest is the number of contracts for a particular future or option outstanding at a particular time. An option with a lot of open interest has more contracts available for trading, and will be a more actively traded option.

to worry about the year because options don't have contracts that extend that far into the future.) "120.0" is the strike price, $120.00, of the option on the expiration date. And "C" means that this is a call option; "P" would indicate a put.

From the option chain, you can see more information about an option by clicking on it. One final tip: The Invest-O-Rama! Portfolio Tracker enables you to enter options, one of the few Web services to provide this capability. When entering option symbols, use the symbol listed in the option chain but omit the numeric day: "IBM Sep8 120.0 C" should be entered as "IBM Sep 120.0 C" in the portfolio. You can also just use the Lookup feature when you want to enter a new option in your portfolio and let the server find the right symbol, and that may be an easier method.

This option chain provides all the call options for IBM available in the months of September and October.

Symbol	Strike	Last Trade	Net Change	Vol	Open Interest	Daily High	Daily Low	Date
IBM Sep8 95.0 C	95	30	0	0	0	0	0	07/23
IBM Sep8 100.0 C	100	23	0	14	14	23	23	07/20
IBM Sep8 105.0 C	105	$20\,^3/_8$	0	0	0	0	0	07/23
IBM Sep8 110. C	110	21	$+6\,^5/_8$	5	5	0	0	07/21
IBM Sep8 115. C	115	15	0	10	23	15	15	07/23
IBM Sep8 120.0 C	120	$8\,^1/_4$	$-^1/_8$	91	342	$9\,^1/_4$	$7\,^3/_8$	07/24
IBM Sep8 125.0 C	125	$5\,^1/_2$	$-^1/_8$	1437	1030	$6\,^1/_4$	$4\,^3/_4$	07/24
IBM Sep8 130.0 C	130	$3\,^1/_2$	0	369	1948	4	$2\,^7/_8$	07/24

OPTION CHAINS

INTL BUS MACHINE — IBM — New York Composite
PRICE: 124 $^1/_4$ — ↑ $+^3/_8$ +0.30% — US DOLLAR
VOLUME: 2.8746M — *Quotes are delayed at least 20 minutes*

SEP-OCT 1998 CALLS

Where to Find Historical and Daily Data

Although it's easy enough to find stock, commodity, and fund prices today, it's another matter altogether to find prices for a specific date (whether it's last week, last month, or years ago).

If you are Marty McFly, you can see whether Doc has enough plutonium pellets for the flux capacitor, hop in the DeLorean, and travel back in time to find the prices of those commodity contracts. (That's from the movie *Back to the Future*, of course!)

But for the rest of you, what do you do when you need to establish the price of shares on a particular date, or you want to know the highest and lowest prices of a stock in a particular year?

You turn to the Web, of course! A few sites are perfect for digging up the past.

The first site you need to know is BigCharts (http://www.bigcharts.com). BigChart's database goes back to 1985. So if you're looking for a price from a date older than that, you're out of luck. But, it is still one of the best resources for information on past prices.

It is easy to use. Just click on the **Historical Quotes** link at the top of the page, and then you can enter the ticker symbol of *any* stock or fund. And they do mean *any* stock or fund—BigCharts claims to have prices for 50,000 stocks, funds, and indexes. That's one reason they call them BigCharts!

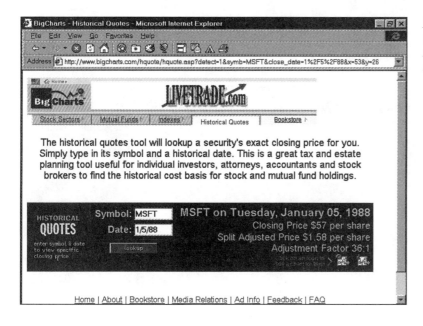

BigCharts can give you the price per share of any stock or mutual fund for any date since 1985.

Microsoft Investor (http://www.investor.com) is another place to turn to if you are looking for historical price quotes. Investor will give you prices for a whole range of dates.

When you go to the Investor site, enter a ticker symbol in the entry box at the top of the main page. This will display a price quote for the security you entered. Next, click on the Historical Charts item on the menu on the left side of your screen. This will display a chart for your stock or fund. If you move your mouse cursor over the line on the graph, you will see that the price is displayed in a box right on your screen.

Microsoft Investor's stock and mutual funds charts can be created for a period that you select.

Move your mouse over a price chart at Microsoft Investor and this box appears, telling you the date and price.

If you click on the price line, a vertical line appears on the graph. You can drag this line from left to right, and the price and date appear at the top of the chart.

If you are looking for prices for a period not displayed on the chart, click the **Period** button and select the dates that you're looking for, anywhere from the most recent trading day's intraday quotes to the past 10 years.

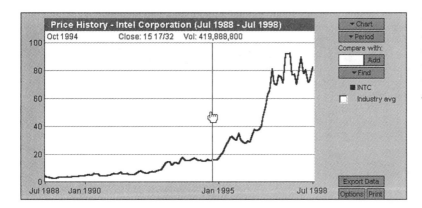

Click and drag on a Microsoft Investor price chart, and this bar appears, along with more details at the top of the graph.

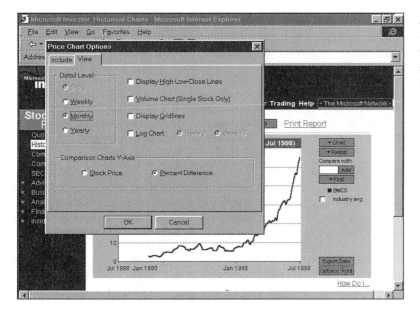

Do you want daily, monthly, or yearly high and low prices? Microsoft Investor gives you the choice.

One of the advantages of Microsoft Investor's price database is that you can access monthly or yearly prices, as well as prices for a single day. Click the **Options** button at the bottom of the screen. This enables you to set the chart's view to daily, weekly, monthly or yearly high and low prices for the dates you selected. Now, one of more of these options may be unavailable, depending on the period you chose. Investor won't give you daily quotes for a 10-year period, for instance, only monthly or yearly.

Now, click the **Export Data** button. Investor delivers a file that you can open in a spreadsheet or a text editor. The file may automatically be downloaded into Microsoft Excel or another spreadsheet program if you have one loaded on your computer.

Besides graphing the prices on a chart, Microsoft Investor delivers the underlying data in spreadsheet format.

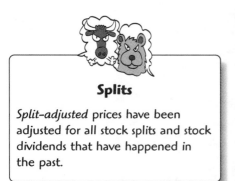

Another destination worth mentioning if you're looking for historical stock prices is the Web site of Dreyfus Brokerage Services (http://www.tradepbs.com), an online discount brokerage firm. Dreyfus Brokerage maintains a historical pricing database on their Web site and makes it available for all to use at no charge. Click the **Historical Prices** link on their main page, and then enter the ticker symbol of a stock and the number of days of prices that you require, from 5 to 360.

Dreyfus delivers the quotes in a plain text format, so they're not too easily imported into another software program. (It is possible to cut and paste the price tables from Dreyfus into a spreadsheet program such as Microsoft Excel, and then separate the data into columns.) And the prices here are not adjusted for previous splits, as are most data sources; so be aware that any sudden price changes might be due to a split.

Splits

Split-adjusted prices have been adjusted for all stock splits and stock dividends that have happened in the past.

Microsoft Investor, BigCharts, and Dreyfus Brokerage are great sites for accessing a limited range of historical prices. But many investing software programs require large databases of prices and other data. These include technical analysis and screening software programs, such as MetaStock, Window on WallStreet, SuperCharts, or Wall Street Analyst. Besides needing a large historical database, these programs also require daily updates of the prices for thousands of stocks or mutual funds.

In the days before the Internet became popular, computerized investors needed to subscribe to services that provided data, usually through computer bulletin boards or private networks. But the Internet is a convenient way to update these databases on a regular basis.

The downside is that there is no comprehensive source of historical and daily data available for free. This area is still ruled by commercial data providers. On the upside, prices have fallen so that it's possible to maintain your own private database of security prices for as little as $15 a month.

If you need extensive historical prices for just about any security, here are some services that can help you. The details of how you download the data and import it into your program will vary among the services and software. You will have to figure out how to retrieve the data from your chosen service and plug it into your program. (The tips in the next section will help you learn more about the procedure, however.)

Stock Splits Can Trip Up Your Data Collection

You need to watch out if your data source does not adjust for stock splits, or if you maintain your own prices. Until the data is adjusted for splits, you can't make valid comparisons between current and past prices.

HISTORICAL PRICING - Microsoft Internet Explorer

File   Edit   View   Go   Favorites   Help

Address http://www.tradepbs.com/pbscgi/hstqtetd

Dreyfus Brokerage Services, Inc. Member New York Stock Exchange	**Dreyfus Investment Center** online trading & market data

Prices are maintained for one year. Enter a symbol and the number of days (5-360) to display.

Symbol: [   ]   Number of Days [30]   [Process]   [Clear]   [Fraction]

Home | Client Access | Mkt Watch | Mkt Stats | News & Links
Quotations | Order Entry | Fast Quote/Order Entry | Download

SYMBOL	DESCRIPTION	LAST	CHG	HIGH	LOW	VOLUME
INTC	INTEL CORP	83 1/16	+1/2	84	81 5/8	14,746,200

DATE	CLOSING PRICE	OPEN	HIGH	LOW	VOLUME
7/24/98	83 1/16	82 3/4	84	81 5/8	14,746,200
7/23/98	82 9/16	81 11/16	84 15/16	81 7/16	21,351,000
7/22/98	82 3/8	80 5/8	83 13/32	80 5/8	164,550
7/21/98	81 5/8	81 3/8	84 13/16	81 3/16	19,987,000
7/20/98	81 3/4	82 3/8	83 1/16	81 9/16	9,385,400
7/17/98	83 1/8	83 7/8	83 15/16	82 7/16	125,282
7/16/98	84 1/4	84	84 7/8	83	16,826,800

Dreyfus Brokerage Services provides historical prices for stocks going back 360 days.

233

Prophet Direct (http://www.prophetdirect.com) is one source of historical price data for stocks, funds, options, and commodities. Prophet has data going back for decades, and their Internet data delivery service works with the built-in downloading functions of most charting software. This approach may be the easiest way to maintain your price database—just fire up your analysis software, connect to the Internet, and download the data right into the software. Prophet Direct subscriptions start at $15 a month, but you can try them free for 31 days.

Primate Software (http://www.primate.com) requires that its subscribers use their Quote Monkey software to retrieve data using a toll-free telephone number, not over the Internet. They also offer a free charting program: Chart Monkey. (Have you noticed a theme in these titles?) Primate's charges start at $25 a month to download historical and end-of-day quotes. Their database includes Canadian and over-the-counter bulletin board stocks as well as stocks on the major U.S. exchanges, mutual funds, indices, and futures.

If the convenience of having your daily data emailed to you sounds appealing, check out Stock Data (http://www.stockdata.com). Rather than manually retrieving a file each day, Stock Data will send a file to your email Inbox. The file includes quotes on 11,000 securities. The service costs between $20 and $30 a month, depending on whether you want bulletin board stocks, Canadian stocks, and mutual funds in addition to stocks on the major U.S. exchanges. You also can download prices from the Internet if you prefer.

Downloading Quotes into Spreadsheets or Software

When you're working with financial information, sometimes you just can't avoid getting your hands a little dirty and working with chunks of raw data. Data is often essential to both recordkeeping and analysis, but getting the data from the Internet onto your computer and into your software can sometimes be a frustrating experience.

In NAIC Personal Record Keeper and many other programs, you need to import a file that contains prices in a particular format known as *comma-separated values*, or CSV. A CSV file is just a text file that contains values (particular pieces of data such as prices or dates or tickers) separated by commas. The comma is known as the *delimiter*, but other characters could be used, such as a tab character. If you come across a *tab-delimited* file, it's the same thing as a CSV file—just with tabs rather than commas indicating the start of a new data field.

The price file that you got from Microsoft Investor in the last section is a CSV file, in fact. If you opened a CSV file in your computer (you can do that using the Windows Notepad), it might look something like this:

```
MSFT,125.125,07/17/98
```

NAIC Personal Record Keeper enables you to import a price file in CSV format that will update your portfolio prices.

In this case, the three values in the file are ticker, closing price, and date. A CSV quote file can contain hundreds of lines like these, with quotes for hundreds of stocks or funds.

Often, some of the specific values in a CSV file are surrounded by quotation marks, like this:

    "MSFT",125.125,"07/17/98"

You can safely ignore the quotation marks—your software will know how to handle them. They are used to indicate that a certain value is not numeric, like the ticker symbol and date.

A CSV quote file doesn't have to include just the ticker, closing price, and date. Other fields that you might find in a CSV file are the day's opening, high, and low prices; time of the last trade; daily price change; and volume of shares traded.

Here is an example of a CSV downloaded from the Yahoo! Finance Web site, for example:

    "MSFT",125.125,"7/17/1998","4:08PM",+1.25,123.875,125.125,123.875,
    10685800

Whew! Fortunately, you can just select a few commands in your software to import a file and update the prices of all your holdings. In NAIC Personal Record Keeper, click on the **File** menu option, and then select **Import Prodigy CSV File**. (Even though the program refers to the Prodigy online service, a CSV quote file from most any source will work just as well.)

NAIC Personal Record Keeper interprets the CSV file and then imports it, updating all your portfolio prices.

IMPORT PRODIGY CSV FILE

Contents of Prodigy import file

Symbol	Mkt Price	Date
COMS	29.563	07/17/98
AFL	37.875	07/17/98
ABT	44.875	07/17/98
ATML	13.875	07/17/98
KO	86.125	07/17/98
INTC	83.125	07/17/98
MCD	73.250	07/17/98
MRK	138.000	07/17/98
MSFT	117.938	07/17/98
MOT	53.688	07/17/98
NVLS	36.875	07/17/98
RPM	15.938	07/17/98
RCOT	36.938	07/17/98
RBD	31.688	07/17/98

[Import]   [Print]   [Cancel]   [Help]

There are two easy-to-use sources for CSV files on the Internet. The first is Yahoo! Finance (http://quote.yahoo.com). This site's free portfolio tracking also gives you the ability to download the prices of a portfolio to your computer in a CSV file.

To do this, you first need to enter your portfolio in the Yahoo! service. You can create dozens of portfolios on the site, with a limit of 200 stocks or funds in each. There's no way you can automatically import a portfolio, so you will have to do this manually. You can enter as little or as much information as you like, including your cost per share and purchase date.

After you have created a portfolio, it will have a link at the bottom of the page that says, "Download Spreadsheet Format." This "spreadsheet format" file is really a CSV file in disguise! If you click this file, it will quickly download to your computer.

Depending on your computer setup, you may run into trouble when you try to download a CSV file. Many spreadsheet programs, such as Microsoft Excel, are set up to handle CSV files. When you try to download a CSV file, Excel might start up and display the file, or an Excel window might open in your browser (if you're using Internet Explorer) with the file. You should just save the file to your hard drive, probably in a directory where your recordkeeping software can easily find it. (At any rate, remember the directory and name of the file!)

When you try to download the file, your browser might pop up a warning that says it doesn't know how to handle a CSV file. In that case, tell your browser to save the file to your hard drive. (Again, remember where you save the file!)

d quote. Quotes delayed 15 minutes for Nasdaq, 20 minutes other

Finance - COOL JOBS @ YAHOO - Yahoo! Finance Home

ables Version - Download Spreadsheet Format

Open
Open in New Window
Save Target As...
Print Target
Copy Shortcut
Add to Favorites...
Properties

st Update: As earnings explode, th

to announce patent cross-licensin

If you right-click with your mouse on any link in your Web browser, this menu appears.

The easiest way to save the file may be to use the "right-click mouse trick." Position the mouse cursor over the link, but instead of clicking the left button on your mouse (as you would if you were trying to click a link regularly), click on the right mouse button. This pops up a small menu in your browser, and one of the options is to Save Target As (if you're using Internet Explorer) or Save Link As (if you're using Netscape Navigator). Now, switch back to the left mouse button and click on the Save option. Now you can quickly save the file to your hard drive.

The other source of price files for your portfolio is InfoBeat Finance (http://www.infobeat.com). This free email service delivers customized quotes and news right to your Inbox. The service gives you the option of receiving stock price data in either Quicken or Lotus/Excel format, as either an "attached" file or an "appended" file.

This attached price quote file was delivered via email by InfoBeat.

237

You Can Send and Receive Files of All Kinds Using Your Email Program

Email programs usually include an option that enables you to send and receive files to and from others on the Internet. These files could be any file that you can save on your computer: a text file, word processing document, spreadsheet, program, or sound file. To view the file, however, you need to have the appropriate software program on your computer first. Some email programs have built-in file viewers that can read many types of files, or you can download viewers for Excel and Word from the Microsoft Web site (`http://www.microsoft.com/msdownload`).

An attached file arrives along with the email message as a separate file. Some email programs have trouble with attachments, so InfoBeat provides the option of receiving files in an appended format. This just means the CSV file is actually included in the email message, right at the bottom. If you receive the file this way, you would need to copy the quotes and paste them into a text file using Windows Notepad, and then save the file to your hard drive.

What's the Difference Between "Streaming Quotes" and "Snap Quotes?"

If you look up the price of a single stock on the Web, you have used a method of delivering price data known as "snap quotes." On the other hand, "streaming quotes" are a continuously delivered flow of prices automatically updated on your computer screen, usually on a real-time basis.

Now Available Live!—Real-Time Quote Servers

If you have ever seen the terminal on a broker's desk, you will notice right away that the numbers and letters on the screen are in nonstop motion. The letters are the ticker symbols of stocks, and the flashing numbers are the prices of trades that have just happened in those stocks, continuously changing as a result of each trade.

Brokers and other investment pros pay a lot of money to have instantaneous access all the action in the market. The prices are delivered to the broker's terminal in real-time (or as close to real-time as possible).

Now, you can turn your desktop computer into a machine that resembles a broker's trading terminal, delivering real-time quotes and providing you with an instantaneous picture of the action in the market. All it takes is some special software, a link to the Internet, and a subscription to a data delivery service.

Several services can transport you to the trading floors of the exchanges (at least electronically!). PC Quote (http://www.pcquote.com) is a leader in the delivery of real-time quotes to individual investors. For $75 a month, you can have real-time quotes delivered to your computer using PC Quote's software, along with news headlines and fundamental data. If you're really serious about real-time data, you can spend hundreds of additional dollars for additional features like full news stories, charts, and more-detailed quotes.

> ### The Software May Be Free, but the Service Costs Money!
>
> Don't be fooled by quote providers who offer "free software" on their Web sites. Although these programs often *are* free, they won't even run unless you have a subscription to the site's services!

InterQuote (http://www.interquote.com) is the oldest provider of real-time market data on the Web. Real-time "tick-by-tick" quotes are available for $69.95 a month using InterQuote's software; unlimited real-time snapshot quotes on the Web cost $29.95 a month.

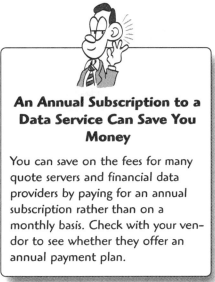

For most investors, however, these real-time quote services will be overkill. Do you really need a direct line into the stock exchanges to make your investment strategy work? Unless you're a day trader, the answer is probably no.

Still, there are times when it might be handy to be able to check the price of a stock and know that what you're seeing is the exact, current price per share. And that's why *free* real-time quote services have just recently starting making their debut on the Web. These sites only allow you to look up a single price at a time, but the prices you see are absolutely timely—and you can't beat the price!

> ### An Annual Subscription to a Data Service Can Save You Money
>
> You can save on the fees for many quote servers and financial data providers by paying for an annual subscription rather than on a monthly basis. Check with your vendor to see whether they offer an annual payment plan.

You can take your pick of any (or all) of the half dozen or so free real-time quote servers now on the Web.

InterQuote's software will turn your PC into something very close to a broker's trading terminal.

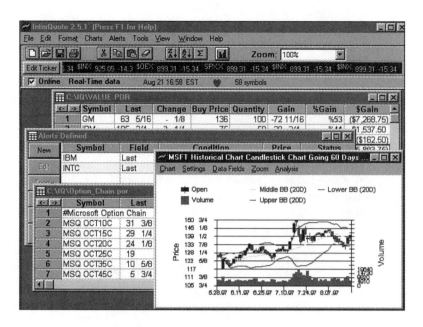

See All the Information a Broker Sees

Real-time quote providers also give you the option (*if you subscribe and pay for the service*) to see *Nasdaq Level II quotes*. These are the actual bid and ask prices supplied by each individual market maker in a particular Nasdaq stock.

Free Realtime.com (http://www.freerealtime.com) and Wall Street City (http://www.wallstreetcity.com/) both offer unlimited access to free real-time stock prices. You can look up as many prices as you want to each day. Wall Street City also lets you see the previous 10 trades made in a stock (look for the link to register for free real-time quotes on their site).

Thomson RTQ (http://rtq.thomsoninvest.net) was the first online provider of free real-time quotes. Thomson also provides the quotes for two other free real-time services, Money (http://www.money.com/rtq) and Fox Marketwire (http://www.foxmarketwire.com). All three of these services allow you to retrieve only 50 quotes per day.

You must register before you use each service, and the registration process is pretty extensive. You need to provide your name and address and other contact information, and then pick out a username and password. Then, you need to answer a series of questions to signify that you agree with the terms of the stock exchanges. These legal documents go on and on, but the exchanges require them of all investors who have access to real-time quotes.

Get Free Real-Time Quotes from Your Online Broker

Another source of real-time quotes may be your brokerage. Online discount brokers usually give free real-time quotes to clients, typically in blocks of, say, 250 quotes for each trade made by the customer. When you're placing an order, for instance, you would definitely want to know the absolute most-current price of that stock.

After you register, you must log on before you access quotes from any of these sites. From there, the only thing that's different about these quotes is that they're not delayed—the same information is provided just as with prices that you would get from a delayed quote server.

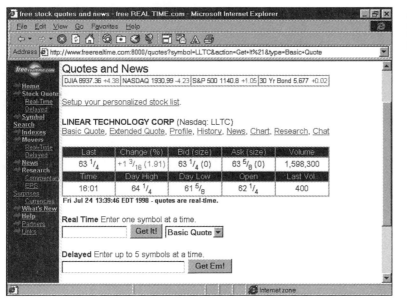

Free Realtime.com gives you stock quotes without a delay.

The Least You Need to Know

➤ You can retrieve price quotes for stocks, mutual funds, options, and commodities on a delayed basis during the day. You can find many quote servers on the Web, and many provide additional research, news, and charts as well as prices.

➤ It can be a real timesaver to download prices from the Internet and import them into your analysis or recordkeeping software.

➤ Several free real-time quote servers are available on the Web. Although registration is required, these services connect your computer to the stock markets so that you can see the most recent price of a stock.

Part 5

The Dark Side of the Web

When you've found a terrific deal, is there always a catch? Probably. On the Internet you've got to be alert to crooked deals and disreputable advisors. They are both out there in cyberspace waiting for you, but you've got good common sense and plenty of tips from this guide to help you avoid the danger.

Chapter 19

Hazards and Pitfalls of the Online World

In This Chapter

➤ Learn how to be a safe, secure, and private Web surfer

➤ Understand how cookies work and whether you should avoid them

➤ Realize the dangers of viruses and how to protect yourself from harm

---

"Is it safe?" "Are the private details of my financial accounts protected from prying eyes?" "How can I tell whether a tip I hear on the Internet is to be believed?"

As you begin to explore the Internet in search of investment information, you may be wondering about the answers to these questions. Or you may have your own questions about privacy, security, and investment fraud on the Internet. Now it's time to dispel the rumors and provide you with some straight talk about using the Internet and how to avoid get tangled up in the process of navigating the Web.

This chapter provides some basic explanations of technical details, and also offers some practical advice to help protect yourself.

Security on the Internet

When the Internet (or at least, the network that eventually became the Internet) was first designed, the creators never imagined that so many people would use their system or use it in the ways it is used today. A little history lesson would probably be helpful.

Back in the late 1960s, the ARPAnet was built by the Department of Defense to provide a way for the nation's military complexes to communicate in the event of a catastrophic attack on the United States. The ARPAnet was designed so that if any link in the network were to become disrupted, traffic would be automatically redirected to routes that were undamaged. As a result, communications among sites connected to the network would be able to continue.

Over the years, the ARPAnet expanded and was eventually replaced, but today's Internet was built on the framework forged by ARPAnet.

Archie and Veronica Are Popular No More

You have probably heard of email and File Transfer Protocol (FTP), two common ways of sending data across the Internet. But maybe you haven't heard of Gopher, Archie, Veronica, or WAIS. These were once common methods of finding and retrieving information on the Internet, but have by now fallen by the wayside.

In the mid-1990s, a whole new crowd discovered the Internet. This was largely due to the development of a new method of sending information across the Internet called the *Hypertext Transfer Protocol*. You are probably familiar with the abbreviation for this protocol, *http*, since it's used in every address on the World Wide Web.

The Web, with its capability to deliver formatted documents—and then images, and then music, and then movies, and then complete programs—has changed the way that people use the Internet. The developers of ARPAnet probably never imagined that users would listen to the radio or watch news broadcast over their network!

More importantly, despite the military beginnings of the Internet, it was never designed to be a "secure" network. The Internet is designed to work a bit like the old party-line system used by telephone companies. A number of customers would share the same line, and anyone who picked up the phone could listen in on any conversation that might be going on.

On the Internet, it is *possible* that someone could "listen in" on any information being sent across the network, whether it's sent by email or to and from a Web site. Where your personal and financial information is concerned, that's a potential problem.

Fortunately, technology has come to the rescue with some solutions to this security problem. The makers of Web server and browser software have created versions of their products that use *encryption* to protect information as it is delivered from your computer, across the Internet, and to a Web server at the other end. Encryption is the process of scrambling information into a secret code and then unscrambling it after it arrives at a secured Web server. Encryption turns the Internet party line into a private line!

The encryption technology used on the Web is called the *Secure Sockets Layer* protocol (or SSL). Web browsers that use it are often called *secure browsers*. Currently, two levels of encryption are in use in the SSL protocol: *low* or *40-bit* encryption, and *high* or *128-bit* encryption. (The number of bits refers to the strength of the encryption; the higher the number, the longer it would take any hacker to crack the code and read your information.)

To take advantage of SSL, all you have to do is use a secure browser. The site you connect to must also be a secure site. Versions of Microsoft Internet Explorer and Netscape Navigator higher than 3.0 can support secure transactions.

It is easy to know if you are connected to a secure Web site. First, the address of a secure Web server will always begin with `https://` rather than `http://`, letting you know that the server will accept a private connection with your browser. Then, after you arrive at a secure site, your browser will give you a sign that it's properly connected. Have you ever noticed a small lock or key at the bottom of your Web browser's screen? When you connect to a secure Web site using Netscape Navigator 4.0, for instance, you will see a small, unlatched padlock in the lower-left corner of the screen and in the toolbar at the top of the screen. After you make a secure connection to the site, both these padlocks become latched and are highlighted with yellow backgrounds.

Keep That Credit Card Number Private

To be safe, you should never send a credit card number, bank or brokerage account number, Social Security number, usernames, passwords, or other personal information via email. This information could be intercepted on the Internet by a *sniffer*—a software program that scans traffic on the Internet looking for series of numbers that match a certain pattern, such as the series of numbers on a credit card.

In Microsoft Internet Explorer 4.0, the locked padlock appears in the center of the status bar at the bottom of the screen only when you connect to a secure Web site. Whenever you see this padlock, you know that your information is protected while it travels across the Internet.

Beware of Hacker Attacks

Hackers are individuals who try to secretly invade computer systems, and then steal private information.

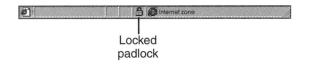

Locked
padlock

The locked padlock in the status bar of Microsoft Internet Explorer indicates that you have connected to a secure Web site.

247

Your online brokerage firm will require that you use a secure Web browser to access your account on its site. This makes it impossible for anyone to steal your password or account number when you log on to your broker's Web site, or to track your activity when you're on its site.

It's Browser Giveaway!

It's easy to get a copy of the latest Web browsers from Netscape or Microsoft. Just go to their Web sites, http://www.netscape.com or http://www.microsoft.com, and look for the browser downloading area. Both browsers are free!

On the other hand, most of the portfolio trackers on the Web *don't* support secure Web browsers. That's because there usually isn't any significant personal information entered in these trackers, like your name or brokerage account number. Sure, some hacker might be able to find out that you own 500 shares of some stock, but it would be hard to trace that information back to you personally. So what if someone did? Most hackers would likely be interested in finding much larger fish to catch in the Internet ocean.

To be completely safe, any time you're asked to provide highly personal information on the Internet, such as a credit card number, account number, or your Social Security number, you should make sure that the site requesting that information is using a secure server.

Your Browser Needs to Handle the Highest Level of Encryption

Some online brokerage firms require that you use 128-bit encryption rather than 40-bit. If your browser doesn't support 128-bit encryption, you will have to upgrade your browser; otherwise, you won't be able to access your account information on your broker's Web site! Check on the firm's site to see which encryption level your browser must support.

Protecting Your Privacy

Software does a great job in providing the security that makes it possible for investors to safely use an online broker or make a purchase from a catalog on the Internet. When it comes to protecting your privacy online, however, it takes more than technology to do the job. After all, ultimately you are in control of the personal information you reveal to anyone, whether it's your name or more intimate details of your stock portfolio.

If you have surfed around the Web for any amount of time whatsoever, chances are you've come across a site that asked you to "register," or that has special areas for "registered members only." Web sites ask users to register for many reasons, and registration could be voluntary or mandatory.

Your Office Computer Network May Prevent You from Connecting to Secure Web Sites

If you connect from the Web at work, your office network may be protected by a firewall—a system of software that is designed to protect the network from intruders. If that's the case, you probably won't be able to connect to a secure site from your office computer.

For sites that are available only to subscribers who pay for the privilege, registration is the way they collect payment. Before they will process your credit card, you must provide your name, address, and telephone number.

On some sites, registration is used to make sure that you agree to some particular terms before you access certain information (protecting the site publisher from being sued, for instance). Other sites make you register so that you can be issued a unique username and password that you can use on a message board.

Another common reason for registration is for a site to collect demographic information about all its users. The site may ask such questions as your income range, your age, your gender, your employment status, and your education level. These sites aren't really interested in you personally. Their goal is to collect information about their user population as a whole. Then they can tell advertisers that "65% of our users are college graduates, 73% are women, and 87% have salaries above $50,000."

Keep Personal Information to Yourself

The only people or organizations that need to know your mother's maiden name are you, your mother, your bank, your broker, and other trusted financial institutions. The same goes with your Social Security number. If anyone else on the Web requests these personal details, politely refuse.

Just Because They Ask Doesn't Mean You Have to Answer

Many sites that require registration don't necessarily *require* that you provide all the information they ask for. On some sites, required fields on a signup form will be indicated with an asterisk; the remaining fields are voluntary.

Other Web sites are interested in finding out as much about you as possible, however, so that they can target you with other services, promotions, or products. They want to know your interests so that they can target you with specific ad pitches.

It's not always easy to know whether a Web site's intentions are honorable. In 1998, the Federal Trade Commission got involved in the issues surrounding privacy on the Internet. The Commission learned that many Web sites were not disclosing the types of information they collect from their site visitors, or the ways that they use that data.

As a result of the FTC's interest in the subject of online privacy, many sites that require registration or otherwise collect data on their users now publish a privacy statement outlining their policies. You should look for this statement on any Web site if you are concerned about how the personal information you provide could be used. If you don't like what you read, don't provide personal facts about yourself!

For more about online privacy, see the "Consumer Protection" section of the Federal Trade Commission's Web site (`http://www.ftc.gov/ftc/consumer.htm`). You will find tips and guidelines for protecting your privacy on the Internet, and who to contact if you have problems or concerns.

Try Skipping over Questions That Seem Too Personal

You might be able to circumvent a site's request for personal information by filling in only a few of the blanks on the form it supplies. If the site absolutely requires more information, you can just use your browser's Back button to return to the form and provide the additional answers.

Many users are also concerned with keeping their email addresses private. An unfortunate problem with the Internet is that your email address can end up on a list that's used to send "junk mail" over the Internet. This unsolicited commercial email is called "spam," and it can quickly fill up your mailbox with offers for various products and services.

Companies that spam collect email addresses from a number of places: Web pages, Usenet groups, or mailing lists. They use these sources to compile their giant databases of all those who will soon receive the spam. One way to keep your identity a bit more private is to use a free email service. You can sign up for a free email account from a number of services. Just go to a free service's Web site and create your account. You will get an email address that you can use. When you want to check your mail, just return to the site and log on.

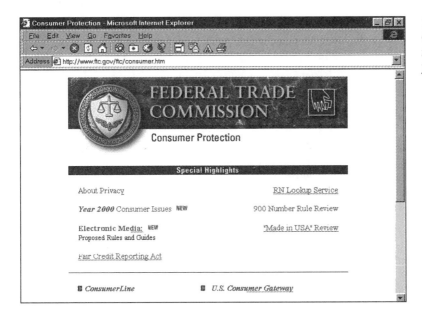

The Federal Trade Commission offers information about protecting your privacy on the Web.

After you sign up, rather than give out your main email address to sites when you register or post to Web message boards, you can use an alternative address from one of these services. If you do begin to get an overwhelming amount of spam, you will know that your email address was compromised.

Here are some popular free email providers:

> Yahoo! Mail (http://mail.yahoo.com)
>
> HotMail (http://www.hotmail.com)
>
> MailExcite (http://mailexcite.com)
>
> WhoWhere? Mail
> (http://www.whowhere.com/MailCity)
>
> RocketMail
> (http://www.rocketmail.com)

One last note: Even though these services provide you with anonymity on the Internet, you should still strive to be a good Internet citizen. Unscrupulous Web surfers hide behind these services so that they can act rudely, indecently, or illegally; don't stoop to their level just because your true identity is hidden.

Uncheck the Check Boxes

When completing registration forms on a Web site, beware of check boxes that are already checked by default. Often, these give the site permission to email you or even share your email address with other sites. If you don't want to receive email, uncheck the box before submitting the form.

Dealing with the Cookie Monster

Would you like a cookie to go with your Web surfing? You may have heard talk about "cookies" on the Web, and are wondering whether this is something you should be worried about.

Web Sites May Not Tell All

As of June 1998, only 14% of commercial Web sites provided users with any disclosure about their information collection practices.

Source: Federal Trade Commission

The answer is probably not. Here's the recipe for a Web cookie. Cookies are small text files sent to your browser from a Web site. Some of these cookie files are saved on your computer's hard drive, and other cookies are stored only temporarily in your computer's memory until you shut down your browser.

Cookies are generally good things. With cookies, a site could be customized according to your particular preferences. Cookies could indicate which parts of a site you've already visited, or which ad banners you've already seen.

Another helpful use for cookies is to streamline your visits to a particular site. A cookie could be used to indicate that you've read a disclosure statement so that you don't have to read it each time you visit the site. Your personal logon information could also be saved in a cookie on your computer, making it easier for you to access a site.

If You Log On in Public, Make Sure to Log Off, Too

If you use a shared computer, at a library, for instance, or if coworkers occasionally borrow your computer, you should take a little extra care when accessing a portfolio tracker or other site that stores log-on information on your computer. Choose not to have log-on information saved to your computer, or else make it a habit to log off the site after each use. Otherwise, your private portfolio may become a little too public.

You don't have to worry about any security issues with cookies. They can't be used to get your email address, find data on your hard drive, or access other personal information. Only the site that originally sent a cookie can access or alter the information in that cookie; no other site or user can view or change it.

Reject Those Cookies!

You can set your browser to reject all cookies, or to warn you when a site wants to deliver a cookie. Look for the cookie settings in your browser's options or preferences area. If you do, you may be surprised at how common cookies are!

If you are an active surfer, you might build up quite a collection of cookies. You don't have to worry about them clogging up your hard drive, however, because cookies are very small (only 255 characters). Cookies sent from secure Web sites are encrypted, so there's an additional bit of protection there.

If you're wondering just how common the use of cookies is on the Web, you can try a little experiment. Tell your browser to reject all cookies or just to warn you whenever a site tries to give you a cookie. After your browser has warned you a dozen times about attempted cookie deliveries, you'll see that refusing cookies just isn't worth the frustration caused by the interruption to your surfing session.

Cookies are a way of life on the Web now, so the most practical way to deal with them is just to ignore them! But if you just have to know more about them, check out Cookie Central (`http://www.cookiecentral.com`), a Web site devoted exclusively to cookies! It's a great resource from which to learn more about cookies and how they work.

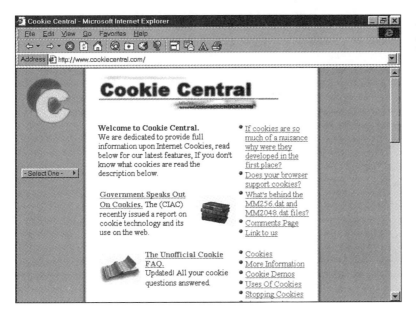

For answers to all your burning cookie questions, visit Cookie Central.

Warning: The Internet Can Be Contagious!

Another hazard that you must be prepared for when you venture on to the Internet is the risk of downloading a *virus*. A computer virus is a tiny program that hides itself in another file. After that file is on your computer, the virus can run without your knowledge, and possibly wreak havoc on your system.

The damage can range from displaying a silly message on your computer screen to wiping out your hard drive. Recently, viruses have been created that hide in Microsoft Word documents and Excel spreadsheets. These are called *macro viruses*. They execute automatically when you open the document, can damage your document template, and then spread to any other documents you save or create.

On the Internet hazard scale, viruses are high on the list. You must do three basic things to protect yourself from a virus attack:

1. Install anti-virus software. There are a number of well-known programs, including Norton AntiVirus (http://www.symantec.com), McAfee VirusScan (http://www.mcafee.com), and Dr. Solomon's Anti-Virus Toolkit (http://www.drsolomon.com). All three of these products are easy to use and are effective at protecting your system. Chances are that one of these programs is already on your computer.

2. Make sure the software is running. Although this seems obvious, users sometimes have to temporarily turn off their virus checkers, for instance, to install another software program. If you don't remember to turn the anti-virus software back on, it doesn't do you any good. You've got to use it if you don't want to lose it!

3. Update the software's "virus definition file" regularly. This is a list of all known computer viruses and how the antivirus program can vaccinate your system against those strains. The problem is that hackers create new viruses nearly every day, so your antivirus program needs to know about all those new viruses.

Don't Open Files Sent to You by Someone You Don't Know

If you ever receive an email message from an unknown source that contains an attached program, avoid downloading the program if possible. If you have already downloaded the program to your computer, don't run it until after a virus checker has cleared it. Even then, it wouldn't be a bad idea to throw out the program altogether and notify whoever sent it that the file was corrupt.

Viruses Can't Be Spread by an Email Message Alone

You can't get a virus from an email message or a text file. However, an email message could arrive in your mailbox with an attached file that could contain a virus.

Periodically you should check the Web site of your anti-virus software and download the latest updates. (There may be a small charge or subscription fee.) After your anti-virus software is up and running, you can sleep comfortably knowing that you have greatly reduced the risk of a virus penetrating your computer.

Before You Spread a Virus Alert, Make Sure It's True

One problem that may be bigger than viruses is the spread of virus hoaxes. Dozens of well-known fake "virus alerts" are constantly traveling around the world by email, with names like "Irina," "Good Times," and "Join the Crew." If you get messages warning you about these "viruses," ignore them—*do not send them to others!* Check with an authority such as the U.S. Department of Energy's Computer Incident Advisory Capability (http://www.ciac.org) to determine the accuracy of any virus warning.

The Least You Need to Know

➤ Online brokerage firms require that clients use a secure Web browser. This protects your private account information from prying eyes on the Internet.

➤ You need to take steps to protect your privacy online just as you would offline. Don't give out personal information unless it is unavoidable, and be sure to check a site's privacy policy to see how they use the information they do collect from users.

➤ Many sites use cookies to store information on your computer, usually for demographic studies or to track which parts of a site or ads that you've visited or seen. In most cases, you don't have to worry about cookies. Often, they can make your Web surfing more convenient.

➤ You can download viruses from the Internet without your knowledge. These viruses can damage your computer—unless you use anti-virus software. Exercise extreme caution before running a program sent to you by a stranger, and check any new file for viruses before opening it on your computer.

255

Chapter 20

Online Schemes and Ploys to Get Your Money

In This Chapter

➤ Uncover some of the tactics used to promote stocks to gullible individual investors

➤ Learn how to protect yourself from scams and frauds

➤ Find out how to check a broker or firm's disciplinary record on the Web

---

Newspapers and magazines love a sensational story, and the Internet seems to provide plenty of fodder for stories about the "dark side of the Web," murky tales of deception and blatant fraud. In reality, not much has changed since the days that quack doctors in traveling medicine shows hawked snake oil to gullible folks all across the country. The tools of the trade of the hucksters have merely evolved with the times, as scoundrels have discovered that many investors are all too willing to abandon any shred of common sense after they log on to the Internet.

But is the Internet really the problem? How many people are swindled out of money each year over the telephone? When photocopiers became popular, con men quickly put them to use in coming up with schemes to defraud investors. Fax machines ensured that a rogue could send "urgent" (but phony) messages to thousands of people in a single day. When personal computers and laser printers arrived, anyone could create a professional-looking logo and letterhead.

It's a good bet that the medicine show quack of the 1800s would have embraced—had he had them—all these new tools and would have used them to come up with new schemes to prey on unsuspecting citizens.

The point is this: Nothing has changed in the history of scams and schemes except the addition of a new set of tools in the con man's handbook. You can now be swindled on a street corner, over the telephone, or on the Internet. Here's the practical advice that will alert you to the warning signs and help protect you and your nest egg when you're on the Internet.

Fraud Is as Popular as Ever

Every week, the National Fraud Information Center and Internet Fraud Watch programs receive an average of 1,500 calls and an equal number of emails from consumers seeking help about offers they have received or help with filing complaints about frauds they have discovered.

Source: National Consumers League

First, you need to learn to identify some of the common ways that you can be deceived when it comes to investment "advice." Begin with the National Fraud Information Center (http://www.fraud.org). The NFIC is a watchdog organization that works to educate consumers about fraud, both on the Internet and off. Founded by the National Consumers League, NFIC maintains an "Internet Fraud Watch" with tips, news, and alerts to help protect consumers from online fraud. If you think you've been a victim of fraud, the Center can direct you to places where you can get help.

The "Pump and Dump"

One common ploy used to generate interest in a stock is the "pump and dump." A company or an individual can use this tactic to drive up a stock's price to new highs (the "pump"). After the stock's price has increased, the "pumpers" then sell their shares at the peak (the "dump").

Anyone Can Create a Fancy Web Site—Even a Crook

Just because a company has a flashy Web site doesn't mean that it is a legitimate business. Anyone can create a Web site in a few days without a lot of money, so don't be fooled by appearances.

The National Fraud Information Center can educate you about fraud on the Internet or provide help if you need to file a complaint.

This tactic works only with shares of very small companies. These are typically shares that trade on the over-the-counter bulletin board—the market for stocks that don't qualify for listing in the NASDAQ market. These stocks usually don't have a lot of trading activity, their shares have low prices, and they may not have a large number of outstanding shares. This combination of factors means that it's possible for a person or a company to drum up enough interest in the stock among individual investors to have a significant impact on the price.

On the Internet, it is relatively easy to promote a stock by posting messages on bulletin boards, or by sending out email messages, or by publishing a "research report" on the stock, or by using many other methods. Today, it's possible to reach thousands of investors in a matter of minutes.

Don't Try to "Make Money Fast"

Trying to "make money fast" in any investment or business opportunity is a sure way to lose it faster.

259

Don't Let Greed Get in the Way of Making Good Investment Decisions

There's a saying on Wall Street that goes like this: Pigs get fat; hogs get slaughtered. It means that it's okay to try to make money on your investments, but if you get too greedy, you're bound to make mistakes that can turn profits into losses.

Investors who are anxious to make a quick profit are usually susceptible to buying stocks on the basis of hot tips. When they do purchase shares in the company, the stock price goes up and up. The more that investors buy, the more the price increases, and a vicious circle is begun.

That is, the circle continues until the touting stops. After the price of shares increases, sometimes by as much as four or five times, all the activity that has gone into promoting the stock ends—but not before the promoters dump all their shares at an enormous profit.

With all the fanfare ended, the stock has no where to go but down. Because the increase in price was based on purely superficial "hot tips" and exaggerated claims, there's no way the price can remain at those inflated levels. And as the price falls, so does the value of the investments made by individuals, particularly if they got in at the end of the pump. If prices go back to the level they were at before the frenzy began, investors could lose up to 75% or 80% of their investment if they aren't able to sell in time.

The Securities and Exchange Commission's Office of Investor Education and Assistance wants to help you avoid fraud and can help if you have been a victim.

> Investor Assistance & Complaints - Microsoft Internet Explorer
>
> File Edit View Go Favorites Help
>
> Address http://www.sec.gov/invkhome.htm
>
> About the SEC
> Investor Assistance & Complaints
> EDGAR Database
> SEC Digest & Statements
> Current SEC Rulemaking
> Enforcement Division
> Small Business Information
> Other Sites to Visit
> Home
>
> Investor Assistance & Complaints
>
> "The SEC has been a beacon for investors since 1934."
> - Chairman Arthur Levitt
>
> Brought to you by the SEC's Office of Investor Education and Assistance, providing investors with the information they need to invest wisely and avoid securities fraud and abuse.
>
> • "Facts on Saving and Investing Campaign"
>
> • SEC, State Securities Administrators Warn Consumers About "Cold Calling"
>
> • About the Office of Investor Education and Assistance

For more on various schemes and investment fraud that have been used to victimize investors, visit the Web site of the SEC's Office of Investor Education and Assistance (`http://www.sec.gov/invkhome.htm`). Besides providing educational information to help you avoid investment fraud on the Internet, as well as offline, the Office also provides a form and instructions for filing a complaint if you have been a victim.

Hot Tips and Sad Stories

It's time for a little pop quiz. (Your answer will be used to determine your suitability as a future investment maven.) Here goes:

> You're reading messages about technology stocks on a Web discussion board. You come across a well-written message by someone you've never heard of before. The message lays out an ironclad case for why investors should "jump all over" shares of a small-cap stock you've never heard of before, Mini-Micro-Macro Technology, Inc. This stock is "poised for a breakout" and "could be the next Microsoft." The author of the message urges investors to "back up the truck" before they lose the opportunity to "make some serious money" fast.

What do you do?

> A) Log on to your brokerage account and buy several hundred shares of Mini-Micro-Macro Technology, Inc. What the heck! If it takes off, you could make a nice quick profit, even if you don't know what the company even does.

> B) Put the stock on your watch list and make a note to do some of your own research.

Don't Be Afraid to Report a Case of Fraud

Too many times, investors are too embarrassed to speak up after they have been swindled. If you think you've been taken in by fraud, it's important to put your shame behind you and report it to the authorities. You might prevent someone else from being conned, as well.

The correct answer is B, unless you're determined to retire a pauper. It's surprising how many investors seem to believe that any "hot tip" they read on the Web *must* be true. A good dose of healthy skepticism can go a long way toward protecting your nest egg. Remember the adage "Do your homework" before you make any investment.

It's probably safe to assume that anyone who posts a message to a discussion group on the Web about a stock has a vested interest in that stock. If you had a great stock idea, you would probably want to share it with the rest of the world, too. There's nothing wrong with that. The problem is that you have no way of knowing whether a message was written by an honest individual investor like yourself or by a promoter hiding behind a pseudonym.

Laws Regulate What Company Insiders Can Say to Outsiders

It's illegal for insiders to publicly talk about the nonpublic details of a company's operation. Insiders are people who own the stock of a company that also employs them, or on whose board they sit, or who otherwise have some formal connection that gives them access to privileged details about a company's operations. If someone claims to have "insider information," they're probably either breaking the law or spreading unfounded rumors.

Financial message boards, mailing lists, and newsgroups can be great ways to learn about new investing ideas. The best discussion areas are really small communities where ideas are openly shared and where the participants are respectful of the opinions of others. The advantage of these communities is that members get to know each other, and are naturally wary of outsiders. If someone swaggers into town with a "hot tip" in each holster and starts shooting off his mouth down at the local watering hole, the other citizens will probably stand back and take in the spectacle for a bit.

Automatically Sign All Your Email Messages

Most email programs enable you to set up a "sig" file. That's short for "signature," and it is a common practice on the Internet to have a sig automatically appear at the bottom of each email message you send. Your sig could include your real name, your company, your home page address, or any other information that can help others know more about you.

Like any small town, you will eventually find out who you can trust on a particular message board—as well as who is merely blowing hot air. The key is that it takes time for you to learn about the people in a new neighborhood. So look for an online community where you're comfortable, one that fits your investing style.

"Newsletters" Aren't Always What They Seem

When is a newsletter not a newsletter? When it's purely an advertisement that's trying to sell you a stock.

Many Web and email newsletters or research services promote stocks. But these are usually not independent publications. Usually, the company whose stock is being promoted is also paying for the newsletter!

Here's how these ventures usually work. A publicly traded company hires a promoter to help increase awareness of its stock among investors. The promoter will issue press releases, write research reports, publish a newsletter, create a Web site, or use any other method to stir up interest in the stock. In return, the promoter may be paid in cash, stock, stock options, or some combination of all three.

According to the Securities Act of 1933, anyone who receives compensation for publishing or circulating information about a security, even if it is *not* a sales pitch, must disclose the fact of their compensation to investors.

The problem is, the disclosure on many sites is nonexistent or difficult to find. In one well-publicized case, the Security and Exchange Commission settled a 1997 case with online stock promoter, George Chelekis, the publisher of several popular Internet newsletters. The SEC charged that Chelekis improperly disclosed to subscribers that he received substantial payments in return for promoting several stocks. Chelekis paid $163,000 to the SEC to settle the civil case, without admitting or denying the commission's charges. He also agreed to a permanent injunction barring him from violating securities laws (an oxymoron if there ever was one!).

Since 1997, the Securities and Exchange Commission has stepped up enforcement. But this isn't enough. You should make it a practice to read the fine print on any investment newsletter you come across—on the Web, in your email Inbox, or in the postal mail. Even though there's nothing that says a report on a stock is completely invalid if written by someone paid to do the analysis, you have the right to know before you invest.

If you have questions about a small-cap Web site, pay a visit to the Stock Detective (http://www.stockdetective.com). The Stock Detective uncovers the truth about stock "newsletters" that provide analyses of small-cap stocks and whether those services are providing adequate disclosure about any compensation that they have received.

Watching You Step: How to Protect Yourself and Your Money

Now that you know some of the ways that investing could fool you, how do you protect yourself from falling victim? You can start by sticking to a consistent investment methodology and avoid making decisions on the basis of tips altogether. In addition, here are a few simple rules to make sure you won't lose money in an investment for all the wrong reasons:

1. The first rule is to be especially wary of "penny stocks," those low-priced, small-cap stocks that trade on the Over-The-Counter (OTC) Bulletin Board. These stocks are particularly susceptible to pump-and-dump schemes, and you should always view these investments on a speculative basis.

2. If you read messages on a discussion board or mailing list recommending an OTC Bulletin Board stock, ask yourself what do you know about the author of the message? Is he or she someone you know, or whose past advice you know to be reliable? Is the message signed with a real name, or does the writer use a nickname? Does the message sound "too good to be true?" Is the person using a free email service such as HotMail, Yahoo! Mail, Juno, or RocketMail? Although many people use these services as their primary email accounts, these services also offer anonymous ways of posting messages on boards.

3. Does the tip you heard just sound too good to be true? Don't be lured by promises of big returns in a short period—that's the route to a sure money-losing proposition.

4. What's your hurry? Take your time; there's no investment opportunity that's so great you have to take advantage of it right now. Even if you do miss your chance to invest in a stock that subsequently increases in value significantly, there will be other stocks to buy; it's guaranteed!

5. Read the fine print. If a Web site is promoting stocks, read the fine print to see whether they are an independent analysis firm or whether the companies that they are touting are paying them.

6. Finally, there's no replacement for doing your homework when it comes to investing. Can you substantiate the claims that have been made about a stock that's been recommended to you? Remember that the best defense is a good offense. Do your homework before acting on any tip.

Check Before You Send That Check

There's no doubt about it: The online brokerage business is exploding. And trying to tell the new companies apart can be a dizzying experience in itself. There's Accutrade, E*Trade, InvesTrade, Pro-Trade, SureTrade, TruTrade, Trade-well, Tradefast, TradeStar, Trading Direct, and Trade4Less. Who can you trust? Who's a fly-by-night operator? How can you measure the integrity of all these firms? Would you open an account with Mr. Stock (the real name of a new online brokerage firm)?

First, you should verify that a brokerage firm is a member of the National Association of Securities Dealers (NASD) and is registered with the Securities and Exchange Commission (SEC). Brokers must also be licensed in each state in which they do business with clients. A brokerage will usually tell you this information on its Web site.

Next, check the record of any broker or brokerage firm on the Web site of NASD Regulation (http://www.nasdr.com), the regulatory arm of NASD. NASD Regulation's Public Disclosure Program will tell you whether the firm has had any significant disciplinary actions taken against it by NASD and will also provide other information.

To use the NASDR service, click the **About Your Broker** link on the main page of the site, and click the Perform an **Online Search** button. You will have to agree to their terms, and click the Agree button at the bottom. Then you need to identify why you are interested in a firm's record. Choose **General Public/Individual Investor**, and then click either the **Firm** or **Broker** button.

Next you enter the first part of a company's name. You can enter a company's CRD (Central Registration Depository) number assigned by NASD, if you know it; but the name is enough to run the search. Next, find your firm in the search results page and click on its name.

NASD Regulation offers an online way to verify the legitimacy of a broker or other securities firm.

In the left navigation bar, NASD Regulation provides links to the address of the firm, the types of business it can legally be involved in, and its legal status (for instance, where and when it was incorporated). The "Registration Information" link will tell you the states in which the firm is registered to be in the securities business, and what kinds of securities it is licensed to handle.

Disclosure events are what you really want to know about, however. These are criminal charges and convictions, regulatory actions, customer complaints, and other activities that might influence your decision to use a particular firm. Unfortunately, NASD Regulation isn't delivering these on the Web right now; they will send a report to you in the mail, however. Just click the **Deliver Report** icon at the top of the screen, and a full report should arrive in the mail within two weeks.

One other item to check is the account protection that the firm offers. Brokerage firms are required to carry coverage for their clients from the Securities Investor Protection Corporation (SIPC) of $500,000 per account, and many provide additional protection from a private insurer as well, sometimes up to $100 million and more! This coverage is similar to the FDIC insurance that guarantees bank losses. It protects you from having your assets disappear if the brokerage firm fails. It *doesn't* protect you from losing money on bad investments!

The Least You Need to Know

➤ Don't be a "hot tips" investor. Take the time to do your homework before you take the plunge.

➤ Don't believe everything you read, particularly in small-cap "newsletters"— these may be nothing more than paid advertisements.

➤ You can check the disciplinary record of any online brokerage firm or individual broker on the NASD Regulation Web site.

Part 6
Putting It Together

Everyone has big goals in life: buying a home, paying for your kids' education, and on top of all that we want to retire wealthy—not an easy feat. But, with sound, long-term investment strategies these goals—your goals—are within reach.

Chapter 21

How to Retire a Millionaire

In This Chapter

➤ Learn about the various types of retirement plans, and figure out which is best for you

➤ See how important it is to take advantage of your company's 401(k) retirement plan

➤ Find the IRA that's right for you

➤ Request an estimate of the Social Security benefits you will receive when you retire

➤ Build a plan to save and invest for your retirement

One of the most common reasons that people get started investing is because they are worried about their retirement. Today, fewer and fewer companies offer pension plans that guarantee retirement payments to workers. Now, employees often must fund their own retirement in a 401(k) plan. Maybe you have also heard the bleak news about the future of Social Security and have decided to take matters into your own hand.

At any rate, the thought of becoming a millionaire is deeply ingrained into the American dream. But it doesn't have to be just a "dream." Many people are actually surprised to find out that it's really not so hard to put together a retirement plan that will make them millionaires by the time they retire.

You don't need to be an investing genius to reach your million-dollar goal, either. You just need to invest regularly in the stock market and let the power of time do its trick. As your returns compound over the course of 20 or 30 years, your nest egg will grow considerably.

You don't have any time to waste, however. You have to get started *today* if you want to have a fighting chance of retiring a millionaire. Fortunately, the Web has tools that can help.

Understanding the Alphabet Soup of Retirement Plans

Too many investors put off starting their retirement plans because they're befuddled by the options. Just figuring out the abbreviations of the many available retirement plans can be a chore. You can save and invest using an IRA, Roth IRA, SEP IRA, SIMPLE IRA, 401(k), 403(b), or other types of plans. Your eligibility to participate in these various plans depends on whether you can join a retirement plan sponsored by your employer, your income, whether you are self-employed, and many other factors.

Too Many People Pass This Opportunity By

Only 75% of eligible employees participate in their companies' 401(k) retirement plans.

Source: USA Today

A *retirement plan* is a special type of account that you can establish at a bank, brokerage, or any other financial institution, either on your own or through your employer. Then, you or your company (or both!) can deposit money that's earmarked for retirement. But retirement plans are more than just a place to save—you can invest in stocks, bonds, or mutual funds inside your retirement accounts. In fact, if you want to ever reach that million dollars, you must *invest* in your retirement plans. The U.S. government wants you to save for your own retirement, so they're willing to give you some pretty nice tax breaks to encourage you to save in these retirement accounts, as long as you agree not to take out the money before you retire. After you put money into a retirement fund, the funds grow on a *tax-deferred* basis. That just means you won't be liable for paying taxes on any of the profits earned in your retirement account, generally until you retire and start withdrawing money.

Did you catch that? You don't have to pay taxes on the profits that you earn in a retirement account, at least until you retire—when (presumably) you will be in a lower tax bracket. Because you don't have to worry about taxes in the meantime, all your earnings will compound in the account and lead to higher returns. The end result is that your retirement account can grow and grow and grow!

But wait, it gets better. You can even get a tax break in every year that you make a contribution to a retirement plan. Want a way to cut your taxes? The government will give you a tax break right now if you contribute to your retirement plan!

What could be better than postponing taxes on your future profits and lowering your current taxes at the same time? Well, how about not paying taxes at all? Yes, some retirement accounts now allow you to forget about paying taxes on the profits you earn in the account—now or after you retire!

Some Retirement Plans Get Special Tax Treatment

A *qualified retirement plan* is a plan sponsored by a company for its employees, and that has been given special tax treatment by the IRS. A 401(k) plan is a qualified retirement plan, for instance.

Never mind all the tax savings, however, because the real purpose of a retirement plan is to let you slowly build wealth. During all your working years, you make contributions to your plan. When you retire, you can enjoy your golden years free from financial worries. *That* is what investing is really all about!

IRAs, 401(k)s, SEP IRAs, 403(b)s, and So On

Which retirement plan is right for you? Here's a brief guide to the different types of retirement plans that may be available to you. Your employer provides some, and some others are available from just about any brokerage firm, bank, or mutual fund company.

401(k) Plan

For most people, a 401(k) plan is the first retirement plan option to consider. Many companies offer 401(k) plans to their employees. Check with the human resources department in your company to see whether they have a 401(k) plan that you can join.

If You Withdraw Too Soon, You Will Pay the Penalty

In most retirement plans, you will have to pay a penalty and taxes if you withdraw money before retirement.

Here's how it works. You can contribute up to 15% of your salary each year to your 401(k), up to a limit of $10,000 in 1998. If you make $500 a week, you can contribute up to $75 a week to your 401(k), for instance. The first step in your retirement plan is to contribute the maximum you can to your 401(k) plan. The money in your 401(k) plan grows on a tax-deferred basis until you retire; then you will pay taxes on your withdrawals at your regular income tax rate.

The Father of the 401(k)

R. Theodore Benna is known as the Father of the 401(k). In the early 1980s, the corporate benefits consultant studied the tax code and realized that employers could offer a savings plan to help employees save for retirement. Benna's clients were afraid the IRS would disallow the new plan, so Benna gave his own employees the first 401(k) in 1981.

You May Be Able to Fatten Your Retirement Plan with Additional Contributions

Some plans allow you to make after-tax contributions to your 401(k). You can pump up your savings plan by having more money sent to your 401(k) from each paycheck. Even though you don't get the tax deduction, the money still grows on a tax–deferred basis.

Many companies match employee 401(k) contributions. If your employer puts in 50 cents for every dollar you put in the plan, you have earned an immediate 50% return on your actual out-of-pocket investment! If you contribute $50, and your employer throws in another $25, for example, you have a total of $75. Not bad. However, the total contributions of you and your employer can't be more than 25% of your adjusted salary (your salary minus your 401(k) contribution).

If your employer offers a 401(k) with a match, you are giving up free money if you decline to participate!

But that's not all that makes 401(k) plans so attractive. Your contribution comes out of your *pre-tax salary*—it's deducted from your gross salary before taxes and other deductions.

Here's how you save. Your $75 contribution is taken from your $500 paycheck, leaving $425. Instead of being taxed on a paycheck of $500, your taxes are based on $425. If your payroll taxes amount to 32% of your salary, you would have paid $160 to the taxman from your $500 paycheck. But 32% of $425 is $136, the taxes you would pay after your 401(k) contribution. You saved $24!

Of course, you still had to part with $75 in the first place. Not exactly. You are actually only out $51. Check the math: $75 – $24 = $51). That's an instant 33% return on your initial investment—there's no magician who can turn $51 into $75 like that! If your company matches your contributions, it just gets better and better.

403(b) Plan

If you work for a nonprofit organization, your employer might offer a 403(b) plan rather than a 401(k). These are quite similar to 401(k) plans, except that you can usually only invest in mutual funds and annuities in a 403(b) account. The same rule for 401(k) plans holds true: Put as much as you can afford into your 403(b) plan.

Some 401(k) Plans Offer Web Access

Some 401(k) providers now offer their account holders the opportunity to access their accounts on the Web. Check with your employer to see whether you have this option available in your 401(k).

Individual Retirement Account (IRA)

If your company doesn't offer a retirement plan for its employees, you will probably want to set up an IRA account. There are three types of IRAs: a traditional, deductible IRA; a non-deductible IRA; and a Roth IRA. Each has different eligibility requirements, depending on your income and other factors.

Traditional IRAs are tax-deductible, tax-deferred retirement plans. If your company doesn't offer a 401(k) or 403(b) plan, you can contribute up to $2,000 a year to a traditional IRA. You get a tax deduction when you file your income taxes, and the money in your IRA grows tax-free until retirement.

Don't Cash Out Your 401(k)—Roll It Over Instead

When you leave a job, your employer may give you the option to cash out your 401(k) plan. Although the cash may be attractive, don't ever cash out—roll it over instead! You can transfer (or *rollover*) your 401(k) account, either to your new job's 401(k) plan or to a Rollover IRA. Some companies will even continue to manage your 401(k) after you leave. If you withdraw the cash, you are liable for taxes and you undercut your long-term retirement planning.

Borrow from Your 401(k) Only as a Last Resort

Most 401(k) plans give you the option to borrow up to half of the savings in the account. You then repay the loan, with interest, into the account. Although it sounds like a good deal, you should rarely take a loan from your 401(k). Not only are you paying taxes twice (the loan is repaid with after-tax money—money you've already paid taxes on; then you pay taxes again when you withdraw the funds at retirement), you are also derailing your plan to accumulate wealth. And if you change jobs, you have 90 days to come up with the cash; otherwise, you will pay taxes *and* a 10% penalty to the IRS.

The Roth IRA was introduced in 1997 and offers an alternative for many retirement savers. Although you don't get a tax break from making a contribution to a Roth IRA, you can withdraw funds from the account on a tax-free basis after you retire. In addition, you can take out funds without paying taxes in several other situations, such as buying a first home or paying education expenses.

Don't Invest Too Heavily in Company Stock

Many 401(k) plans give you an option to invest in the stock of your employer. If you invest too much in shares of your company, however, you can throw your portfolio out of balance.

If you have questions about the Roth IRA, check out the Roth IRA Web site (http:// www.rothira.com). This site is devoted to one topic—the Roth IRA—and provides articles, news, and links to calculators and software. Although it might not answer all your detailed or highly specific questions, it is a good place to start (maybe even directing you to just the source your need to answer your query).

If you don't qualify for a Roth IRA or a traditional IRA, you can make a contribution of up to $2,000 to a nondeductible IRA. The account grows on a tax-deferred basis until retirement, but you will pay taxes only on the earnings, not the contributions (because you made them with after-tax dollars).

The decision whether to contribute to a Roth IRA, traditional IRA, or nondeductible IRA can be difficult to make. Each type of IRA has advantages. Depending on your personal situation, you may be unable to contribute to a particular kind of IRA. To help you figure out the best IRA choice for you, try one of the many IRA analyzers on the Web.

Strong Funds, a leading mutual fund company, offers an easy-to-use tool on their Web site (`http://www.strong-funds.com/strong/ Retirement/roth/analyzers.htm`) that can help you decide which IRA is right for you. You indicate your marital status, and then give some information:

April 15th Is the Deadline for IRA Contributions for the Preceding Year

You have until April 15th to make contributions to your IRA for the preceding tax year.

➤ Your tax return filing status.

➤ If you or your spouse have a 401(k) or other plan at work.

➤ If you have children, their ages and whether you would like to contribute to an Education IRA for them.

➤ Your adjusted gross income (AGI) from the preceding year. This is the amount on which you paid income taxes last year, taken from your tax return.

➤ Your expected income for the current year.

➤ How many years you expect to contribute to an IRA.

➤ The rate of return you expect in your portfolio.

➤ Your expected tax bracket in the years before and after you retire.

After you have answered these questions, click the Submit button. The program will determine which IRA you might be eligible to use, and how much you can contribute.

Self-Employed and Small Company Retirement Plans

If you own a small business, work for a small business, or work for yourself, your retirement plan options are a bit different. You might be able to invest in a Savings Incentive Match Plan for Employees (SIMPLE) IRA, a Simplified Employee Pension (SEP), an SEP IRA, or a Keogh plan.

After answering a few questions in the Strong Funds IRA Analyzer, you can see which IRA makes sense for you.

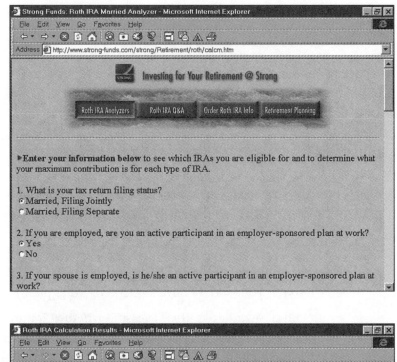

The Strong Funds IRA Analyzer tells you which IRA you're eligible for and how much you can contribute in the current year.

The details of all these plans vary considerably; just like a 401(k), however, you should max out your contributions to the plan now so that your retirement will be more secure.

Other Retirement Income Sources

Besides your actual retirement accounts, a successful plan for your retirement should take into consideration other sources of income that you might receive after you retire.

Pension Plan

Did you ever hold a job that provided employees with a *defined benefit plan*? You might know this better as a *pension plan*, in which a company funds a retirement plan for employees. The amount of your pension is determined by a fixed formula—that's why it's called a "defined benefit" plan. Most companies require that you work for them for five years before you *vest* (become eligible) in the pension plan.

The Pension Benefit Guaranty Corporation, an agency of the federal government, insures pension plans. The agency's Web site (`http://www.pbgc.gov`) provides information about corporate pension plans, as well as an online Pension Search Directory. The Directory is filled with the names of people who have worked long enough to earn a pension benefit, but could no longer be located by their companies. If you think a past employer may have lost touch with you, enter your name in the search field and see whether you have any money coming to you!

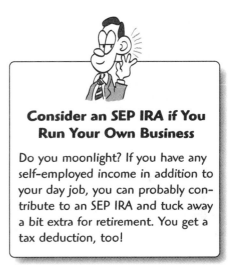

Consider an SEP IRA if You Run Your Own Business

Do you moonlight? If you have any self-employed income in addition to your day job, you can probably contribute to an SEP IRA and tuck away a bit extra for retirement. You get a tax deduction, too!

If you are now or have ever been covered by a pension plan, you can find out from the company's pension fund manager or human resources department how much you can expect to receive after you retire.

Social Security

It's possible that you might receive benefits from the Social Security Administration after you retire. Some experts, however, are dubious that the system will still exist in another 20 years. According to some experts, Social Security will begin paying out more in benefits than it collects in revenues in the year 2013. Anytime you pay out more than you have coming in, you will eventually go broke!

Don't Let Your Pension Fund Lose Track of You

If you have a pension due to be paid when you retire, it's important that your company can always find you. You should always keep your address updated in the company's records, even after you've stopped working for them.

Is Your Social Security Check in the Mail?

In 1996, 43,736,000 Americans received Social Security benefits.

Source: Social Security Administration

If you want to learn more about the debate over the future of Social Security, surf to the Cato Institute's Social Security Privatization Web site (http://www.socialsecurity.org). Also check in with Americans Discuss Social Security (http://www.americansdiscuss.org), a site produced by a nonpartisan organization that aims to bring together elected officials and citizens to try to fix Social Security.

Assuming that the politicians in Washington can fix the Social Security system, the payments you've made all the years that you worked will come back to you after you retire. You can find out how much you will probably receive by requesting a Personal Earnings and Benefit Estimate Statement (or PEBES) from the Social Security Administration. The Administration's Web site (http://www.ssa.gov) offers an online form that you can use to request your PEBES.

From the Social Security Administration site, select the link to "Request a Personal Earnings and Benefit Estimate Statement." You will be connected to the Administration's secure Web server, so all the information you provide in this process will remain safe.

Taxable Savings and Investments

The last ingredient in your retirement planning will be your taxable savings and investments. Even if you contribute the maximum to retirement plans like a 401(k) or IRA, chances are that they won't be enough to get you to your goal. If you want to retire a millionaire, you need to save and invest regularly, *in addition* to your retirement plans.

![SSA-7004 Personal Earnings and Benefit Estimate Statement (PEBES) - Netscape browser window showing a form]

**Personal Earnings and Benefit Estimate Statement
(SSA-7004 PEBES)**

Please indicate if you wish to receive your statement in English or Spanish:

⊙ English ○ Spanish

1.<u>Name</u> shown on your Social Security card:

First Name:
Middle Initial:
Last Name:

2. Your <u>Social Security Number</u> as shown on your Social Security card:

Find out how much you could receive from Social Security after you retire by requesting your personal earnings statement.

Build Your Retirement Plan Online

If you have been confused by all the choices, it's time to stop procrastinating and get started. But how are you going to make it all come together? You should head right to one of the many retirement planning programs on the Web. These interactive applications enable you to enter details of your current savings and investments, and plot how much you will need to save in the future to reach your retirement goal.

JavaScript Provides Many Web Sites with Additional Features

Many Web sites use a programming language called *JavaScript* to create calculators and handle other basic interactive functions. Despite its name, JavaScript has nothing to with the *Java* programming language that is also used to build full-featured applications. Microsoft Internet Explorer and Netscape Navigator provide different levels of support for JavaScript, so a particular browser may occasionally give you an error message that it can't run a script that's built in to some Web site. This is another reason that heavy-duty Web surfers install both Explorer and Navigator. With both installed, they can always be sure they can access any site.

One of the best retirement planners comes from Quicken.com. Its online retirement planner (http://www.quicken.com/retirement/planner) can help you to figure out the best way to reach your retirement goals. In about 10 minutes, you can work through a 12-step planner, answering questions about your current financial position and your goals for the future.

When you access the retirement planner, it may take a few minutes to download to your computer. Just be patient—it's worth the wait.

Answer the questions presented by Quicken.com's online retirement planner and you will see how much you need to save to retire comfortably.

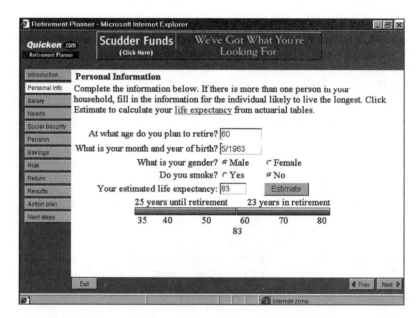

In a series of worksheets, you will enter the details of your current savings, your age, your expectations, when you would like to retire, and other information. After you finish with one screen, click the **Next** button at the bottom of the screen. If you want to change your answers, click the **Previous** button to return to the prior screen and then make your adjustments. You can go back and forth as often as you like, changing your answers and looking at different scenarios. What would it take to be able to retire at age 45? Just change the retirement age and see how much more you need to save to take an early retirement.

Along the way, if you have questions about terms that are used, you can click on them and get a more detailed explanation. After you have answered all the questions, you will learn where you can expect to find your financial situation during your retirement years. If there's a gap between the amount you expect to need each year and the amount your investments, Social Security, and your pension will provide, then you will either have to make do with less *then* or increase your savings *now*. For most people, increasing their savings now will have little (if any) impact on their lifestyle, but it can make a big difference in 25 years!

Retirement Planner - Microsoft Internet Explorer

Quicken .com
Retirement Planner

Scudder Funds
(Click Here)

We've Got What You're
Looking For.

Introduction
Personal Info
Salary
Needs
Social Security
Pension
Savings
Risk
Return
Results
Action plan
Next steps

Results
Change one or more values and click Recalculate to see how your plan changes.

Recalculate

Needs | Savings

Retirement age: 60
Life expectancy: 83
Salary: 45,000
Annual salary increase: 3 %
Annual inflation: 3 %
Retirement needs: 65,000

Your projected income, in today's dollars, is 63,868 during retirement, or 98 % of your goal of 65,000.

Needs Income

Gap
1,132

Investments
43,184

Pension
7,500

Soc. Security
13,184

Exit

◀ Prev   Next ▶

Downloading picture http://www.quicker

Internet zone

After you have finished the questionnaire, Quicken.com presents you with a projection of your projected annual income during retirement.

Don't Be Too Aggressive with Your Projections

When you make projections about the future growth of your portfolio, it can be tempting to plug in a high growth rate. But consider that as you get older and closer to retirement, you might not want to invest in aggressive, high-growth stocks. You will probably be more interested in bonds and other fixed-income investments so that you can protect all the wealth you have built up over the years from bounces in the market. That also means that your portfolio's growth will slow the closer you get to retirement. You can account for this slowdown by using a lower-average annual growth rate when you make future projections about your portfolio.

There's a big difference between having a goal and knowing how to get there, however. Quicken.com provides an action plan for you—an asset allocation plan that's been developed by a financial planner to match your desired rate of return in your portfolio.

Quicken.com offers an asset allocation plan that can help you reach your retirement goal, based on your personal situation.

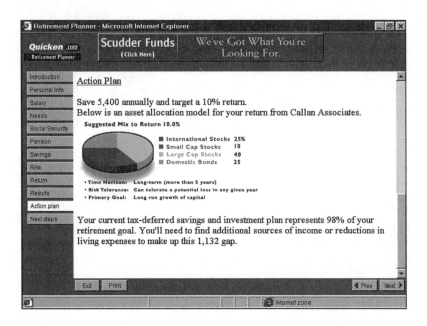

For another take on an asset allocation plan that you can use in your retirement accounts, the Armchair Millionaire (http://www.armchairmillionaire.com) has developed a simple approach to investing for retirement. The Armchair Millionaire's motto is "Common sense saving and investing," and its advice is geared to those who want a sensible, low-maintenance, and profitable way to build a portfolio.

The #1 Armchair Investing Strategy is a plan you can use in your own retirement accounts.

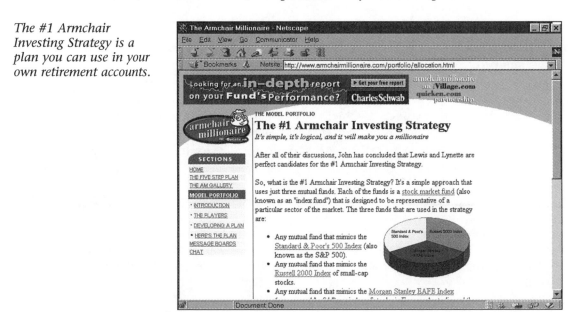

Its "Five Steps to Financial Freedom" (http://www.armchairmillionaire.com/fivesteps) is an interactive tool that can help you figure out how long it will take you to become a millionaire. By following the Armchair Millionaire's approach, you can learn to save and invest in your non-taxable accounts—401(k), IRA, or other retirement plans—as well as your taxable accounts.

You can also design your own portfolio to match the Armchair Millionaire's Model Portfolio (http://www.armchairmillionaire.com/portfolio). The founder of the Armchair Millionaire has invested his portfolio in stock market mutual funds (also known as index funds) using an asset allocation plan designed by a financial advisor. The site will show you how you can use their strategy in your own retirement accounts at any financial institution.

The Least You Need to Know

➤ There are many kinds of retirement plans. Your employer may offer a plan for its employees. You can also establish one yourself at a brokerage firm, bank, or mutual fund.

➤ The 401(k) plan offered by your employer might be the best way to save for retirement, especially if the company offers to match some of your contributions.

➤ You can sort through the IRA maze with the help of an online IRA calculator on the Web. You will be able to figure out whether a traditional IRA, a Roth IRA, or a nondeductible IRA is the best option for you.

➤ Social Security may provide part of your retirement income (but it's likely to be only a small part). You can request an estimate of your benefits from the Social Security Administration's Web site.

➤ A good plan can help you set and reach goals for your retirement savings. Online calculators can help you to understand how much you need to save and invest regularly to retire a millionaire. But the most important point to know is that you need to start planning for retirement now, no matter what your age.

Chapter 22

Paying for a College Education

In This Chapter

➤ Project how much a college education is likely to cost when your child is ready to enroll

➤ Navigate the array of options available to help you save for college

➤ Map your plan to save and invest for your child's college education

One of the most common fears of parents is how they will ever be able to pay for college for their children. And with the costs of a college education increasing faster than the rate of inflation, it's not likely to get any easier down the road.

The good news is that costs of a private-school education are not currently growing as fast as they had been in the past. In recent years, tuition has been rising about 3% to 5% a year at private schools, about half the rate it was 10 years ago. But now tuition at public colleges and universities is climbing between 6% and 10% a year.

In the 1996–1997 school year, according to the College Board, the average costs of a single

College Tuition Goes Up and Up and Up

In the 15 years prior to the 1995–1996 school year, tuition costs at private four-year colleges increased 90% (and that's after being adjusted for inflation). Median family income increased just 9% in the same period.

Source: The College Board

year at a private college or university came to $21,421. At a public institution, you could expect to shell out $10,069. These costs include tuition, fees, room and board, transportation, books, and supplies.

If these costs continue to grow, how much will a year of college cost when your child is ready to enroll? Turn to the College Cost Projector created by Mark Kantrowitz on his FinAid Web site, and you can get an idea of the range of how much you might need to fork over for your son's bachelor's degree in 2013 (`http://www.finaid.org/finaid/calculators/cost-projector.html`).

The College Cost Projector on the FinAid Web site can project the cost of four years of college when your child is ready to enroll.

College Cost Projector

College costs increase at about twice the inflation rate. Current increases have averaged from 6% to 7%. This **College Cost Projector** calculates an estimate of how much college will cost when you are ready to matriculate several years from now.

In the cost field, please enter the total cost of attendance, including tuition, fees, room and board, books, travel, and incidental expenses. According to the College Board, the 1995-96 average costs were $9,285 for public colleges and universities, and $19,762 for private colleges and universities.

```
Current One-Year Costs:  21421
Tuition Inflation Rate:  5%
Years to Enrollment:     15
```

```
   Calculate Projection        Reset Form
```

If you have your heart set on sending three-year-old Nelson to a private school, enter $21,421 as the Current One-Year Costs, enter a tuition inflation rate (perhaps 5%), and 15 years to enrollment. Click the Calculate Projection button.

The results of your projection might be a little overwhelming, at first. In this case, four years at a private college in 15 years are projected to cost $191,941.59.

You can go ahead and experiment with different rates of inflation, or try using the average costs of a public school. But you will have to face up to the fact that you've got some work to do! The most important thing to realize is that the time to start worrying about paying for your kid's college education is *not* when she's a senior in high school, but before she learns to walk! Just like with any investment, time can be your ally or your enemy.

```
College Cost Projector Results - Netscape                    _ 5 X
File  Edit  View  Go  Communicator  Help
 🔮 📷 🏠 🔍 📄 🖻 🔒 🔲                                        N
 Bookmarks  🔖 Location: http://www.finaid.org/finaid/calculators/finaid_calc.cgi   ▼

Financial Aid Information Page

College Cost Projector Results

Disclaimer: These values are estimates. Actual values may vary.

    Current One-Year Costs:        $21,421.00
    Tuition Inflation Rate:            5.00%
    Years to Enrollment:            15 years

    First Year Projected Costs:    $44,532.72
    Second Year Projected Costs:   $46,759.36
    Third Year Projected Costs:    $49,097.32
    Fourth Year Projected Costs:   $51,552.19
                                   -------------
    Total Projected Costs:        $191,941.59


FinAid Home | Table of Contents | What's New? | Mark's Picks | Index | Submissions |
Feedback

Service to students and their families is our highest priority.
```

How expensive could four years of college be in 15 years? Here's how you can find out.

Understanding Available Options

Saving and investing for college is different from saving for retirement or other goals. A number of special options are available just to help you save for college-related expenses. Most likely, however, you won't be able to rely on just a single college saving and investing plan to meet all your needs. Instead, you will need to use a combination of plans.

Your first step is to understand all the various options. After that, you can put together a strategy that works best for your particular situation.

Pay Your Tuition in Advance

One way to eliminate the worry of how to pay for a college education is to just pay the bill right now! At least 43 states now offer (or expect to soon offer) *prepaid tuition plans* or *college saving plans*.

Prepaid tuition programs enable parents to pay a child's college tuition years in advance. The state holds and invests the money you contribute to the plan, and eventually directs the proceeds toward the costs of your child's college expenses at a college or university in your state.

It's Always Better to Save

Some people think that they will be eligible for more financial aid if they don't save anything for college. In fact, your household's income is a much bigger factor when a financial aid package is determined. It's best to save, save, save!

Don't Forget the Other Costs of College

Prepaid plans cover tuition, but not other expenses such as housing. You will need to save separately for those costs.

States offer two types of prepaid tuition plans. The first is "unit-based," which enables you to buy units of future tuition at whatever pace and amount suits your budget. The second, "contract-based," requires you to commit to pay for two or four years of tuition, either in a lump sum or in monthly installments.

If you use a prepaid plan, you get to "lock in" today's tuition costs, protecting yourself from any future rapid increases in the price of a college education. On the other hand, you might be able to invest those funds yourself and get a greater return on your investment if tuition costs don't increase as rapidly in the future as they have in the past.

The biggest concern with prepaid tuition plans is, "What happens if Junior is admitted to Harvard?" Prepaid tuition plans generally cover the costs of tuition at a public college or university in your state. Most (but not all) prepaid plans will let you use the proceeds to cover a college tuition anywhere in the country, at a private or public institution. You need to make sure that your state's plan gives you the flexibility you need.

College Savings Plans

Some states offer an alternative to prepaid tuition plans that enables you save for college without locking in the future costs of tuition. A *savings account trust* enables you to save for college on a schedule that best suits you.

Because these plans are sponsored by a state, they can offer tax advantages, instead of guaranteeing that your savings will keep up with tuition inflation like a prepaid plan. That means you can delay paying federal taxes on the earnings in the college savings account until you withdraw the money to pay higher-education expenses—and then you pay taxes at the child's lower tax bracket. In most states, the earnings are exempt from state taxes altogether, as long as the money is used for tuition and other allowable expenses.

How do you choose between a prepaid tuition plan and a college savings account? You don't have much choice in the matter—it depends primarily where you live. States usually offer one type of plan or the other, and that determines which plan you will be eligible to use.

You can find out whether your state offers a prepaid tuition plan or a college savings account at the Web site of the College Savings Plans Network (http://www.collegesavings.org). State treasurers formed this organization to help their citizens to save for college. On this site, the "Information Clearinghouse" will tell you whether your state has a plan and what type of plan it offers.

The "States On-Line" section lists Web site or email addresses where you can get more information about a state's plan, or you look up the toll-free telephone number in the "Contact Your State" directory.

Although the choice between a prepaid tuition plan and a college savings plan comes down to what your state offers, the choice between a college savings plan and other plans may not be so clear cut.

Make Sure You Can Cover All the Costs of College

State-sponsored college savings accounts don't guarantee that the student's tuition will be paid in full. You have to make sure that you are saving enough to cover your future estimated expenses.

Usually, college savings plans offer a relatively fixed rate of return, similar to what you might receive in a savings account or from T-Bills. You should compare the rate of return you might be able to get in a mutual fund to the savings plan, as well as the potential tax savings you might get from a state-sponsored plan. Generally speaking, these plans are probably best suited for you if you are a "non-investor"—someone with no interest in managing a portfolio to help you meet all your financial goals.

Use this directory on the College Savings Plans Network Web site to find out whether your state offers a tuition prepayment or savings plan.

Education IRA

One of the latest additions to the college savings scene is the Education IRA, created by Congress in 1997. This account isn't really an "IRA," because it's not designed to help with your retirement; it does offer some tax savings like an IRA, however.

You Might Be Ineligible for an Education IRA

You can't contribute to an Education IRA if you have deposited money in a qualified state prepaid tuition program for the same child in the same tax year.

While the money is in the Education IRA, you don't have to pay taxes on the earnings. You can also withdraw the earnings tax-free if you are paying higher-education expenses, such as tuition, books, fees, supplies, or room and board. That's tax-free money!

You can open an Education IRA for each of your children or grandchildren (or any child under the age of 18) and contribute $500 per year to the account. Each child can have only one Education IRA, however, no matter who funds the account.

You can only fund an Education IRA if your income is below certain levels. To determine your eligibility, you have to use something called your *modified adjusted gross income*, or MAGI. Your MAGI is your AGI before any IRA deduction, foreign earned income exclusion, foreign housing exclusion or deduction, or exclusion of interest earned from Series EE Savings Bonds.

You Must Use the Proceeds from an Education IRA for Education Expenses

If you withdraw money from an Education IRA and don't use it for allowable higher education expenses, it will be taxed at the child's income tax rate, in addition to a 10% withdrawal penalty.

In 1998, you can contribute the maximum contribution of $500 to an Education IRA if you are a single filer with a MAGI below $95,000 or a joint filer with a MAGI below $150,000. Single filers with MAGIs between $95,000 and $110,000 and joint filers with MAGIs between $150,000 and $160,000 can contribute sharply reduced amounts to an Education IRA.

If you don't use the proceeds of an Education IRA for education costs, you can roll over an Education IRA into another account for another child younger than 22. Your child can keep an Education IRA open until he or she reaches the ripe old age of 30.

One advantage of an Education IRA is that the parent or guardian named on the account controls the Education IRA until all of its assets are withdrawn, even though the account is in the child's name.

Although the Education IRA has many advantages, its biggest drawback is that it just won't contribute a significant amount to your college savings.

Let's take a look. If tuition costs increase by just 4% a year (a conservative estimate based on the past), a private college that costs $18,000 a year today will cost you $154,846 for a four-year education in 18 years. So, if you invest $500 at the beginning of each year for 18 years and can achieve an annual return of 10%, you will end up with just over $25,000 in your Education IRA. That will make a slight dent in your $154,846 bill, but it's not nearly enough. Still, when you factor in the potential tax savings, you should definitely consider using an Education IRA before another option that doesn't have the tax advantages.

Ask Your Parents to Help Their Grandkids

If your MAGI is too high for you to make a contribution to an Education IRA for your kids, your own parents might be willing to make a gift to their grandchildren to fund the plan.

You can open an Education IRA at just about any brokerage firm or mutual fund company, and invest it in funds or stocks of your choice.

To explore more information on the Education IRA, Strong Funds sponsors a Web site devoted to this college savings plan (`http://www.educationira.com`). The site includes articles that can tell you more about the Education IRA and how it might fit into your overall college savings plan.

With Careful Planning, You Can Maximize the Benefits of Your College Savings

Because an Education IRA can limit your participation in other federal financial aid packages, such as the HOPE Scholarship Credit, you might consider ways of maximizing your benefits. You might spend all of your Education IRA savings in the first years of college, for instance, and then take the federal tax credits in later years.

The Education IRA Web site sponsored by Strong Funds can answer all your questions about this college savings plan.

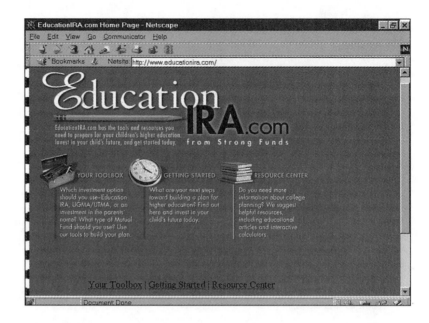

Roth IRA

One of the features of the Roth IRA is that you can take out the money you put into the account at any time and not have to worry about taxes or penalties. Besides being a retirement planning tool, however, a Roth IRA also has a provision that enables you to withdraw any earnings in your account and use them for higher-education expenses. There's no penalty for this early withdrawal, but you will have to pay taxes on the earnings, and you must use the money for tuition, fees, and other college-related expenses.

Here's an example. You and your spouse could contribute as much as $72,000 to your Roth IRA accounts in 18 years, all of which could be used for educational expenses without any tax worries. If you invest in mutual funds and can achieve a 10% average annual return, you would have an additional $19,000 that you could withdraw to use for allowable education costs (although you would have to pay taxes on that amount). To contribute to a Roth IRA, your income has to be below certain levels (see Chapter 17 for more on the Roth IRA). If your Roth IRA is a major part of your total retirement planning, it is not such a good idea to expect to take withdrawals for any reason before you retire.

If your overall retirement plan is in good shape, it makes more sense to look at the Roth IRA as a college-planning tool. You might also think of your Roth IRA as a "cushion" that you can tap into in case your other college saving strategies come up short.

U.S. Savings Bonds

Another way to save for education is to buy U.S. Savings Bonds through the Education Bond Program. There aren't any special "education bonds"; you just buy Savings Bonds at your bank and follow a few simple guidelines.

If you pay for higher-education expenses (or a prepaid tuition plan) for yourself, your spouse, or your dependents in the same year that you cash in savings bonds, you can skip the taxes on the interest you earned.

To qualify for the full tax exemption, you need to be at least 24 years old when you buy the bonds, and your adjusted gross income must be below $52,250 (if you are single) and $78,350 (if you are married, filing jointly). You get a partial exemption if your AGI is below $67,250 (single) or $108,350 (married).

Figure Out the Value of Those Savings Bonds on the Web

If you own U.S. Savings Bonds, it can be hard to know exactly how much they're worth at any time. The Federal Reserve Bank of New York makes it easier, with an online calculator that will tell you the current redemption value of any U.S. Savings Bond (http://www.ny.frb.org/pihome/svg_bnds).

Finally, the Savings Bonds must be purchased in the name of the parent or both parents to be eligible. Bonds registered in the name of a minor child aren't eligible.

If you use Series EE Savings Bonds in this way, you get the advantages of tax deferral for the life of the bond, and then you're exempt from paying taxes on the accumulated yield of the bond. But even with the tax savings, Savings Bonds are now paying only about 5%, making them best suited for non-investors. If you have any experience in the stock market at all, you will probably shun Education Bonds in favor of an investment account that will generate higher returns, at least for the bulk of your plan.

The Bureau of the Public Debt Saving Bonds can give you more information about Savings Bonds and the Education Bond program (http://www.publicdebt.treas.gov/sav/sav.htm).

Education Bonds Must Be Purchased in the Name of the Parents

If your child receives Savings Bonds as a gift, they can't be used for education expenses and receive the tax savings. If education savings is the goal, it's better if grandparents or others give cash to the parents, who can then purchase the Savings Bonds in the name of the parents.

HOPE Scholarship Credit

In 1997, President Bill Clinton signed into law the Hope and Opportunity for Postsecondary Education (HOPE) program to help parents and students with the cost of college. Known as the HOPE Scholarship Credit (after Clinton's hometown of Hope, Arkansas), taxpayers can now receive a tax credit of up to $1,500 on their tax returns when they pay college tuition and other certain fees. You can take this tax credit for yourself or your children in either of the first two years of college.

The Lifetime Learning Tax Credit is a related program that provides another one-time $1,000 tax credit for tuition expenses anytime *after* the first two years of college.

Because both of these are *tax credits*, they directly reduce your income taxes in the year that you take them. As usual, income limits determine whether you are eligible for the HOPE or Lifetime Learning tax credits. You are eligible if you are single and have a MAGI (modified adjusted gross income) of less than $40,000, or are married with a MAGI less than $80,000. You can take a reduced credit if your income exceeds those limits up to $50,000 (single) and $100,000 (married filing jointly).

If you're eligible, all you have to do is claim it on your federal income tax return. Instructions are included with the forms, or you can find more information from the Internal Revenue Service Web site (`http://www.irs.gov/prod/hot/not97-601.html`).

Custodial Account

Children younger than the age of 18 can't legally own stocks or mutual funds, but that doesn't mean that you can't invest on their behalf. A *custodial account* isn't a brokerage account for janitors—it's a special account that you can establish for your children with any bank or brokerage firm. The account is in the name of your minor children, but you manage all the assets as custodian until the kids reach adulthood, either 18 or 21 (depending on the state you live in).

Nothing Is Certain but Changes in the Tax Laws

Tax laws change, so who knows whether the HOPE Scholarship Credit will be around in another 15 years! If you're doing long-range college planning, it might be safer if you don't count on it.

If you want to get the most "bang for your buck" in your college saving plan, you will probably want to invest in stocks or mutual funds; custodial accounts enable you to do this for the direct benefit of your kids. Custodial accounts have an advantage when it comes to taxes, too. You don't have to pay any taxes on up to $650 of earnings if your child is under 14. The next $650 is taxed at 15%, and gains above $1,300 are taxed at the parent's rate. After your kid is 14, all earnings above $650 are taxed at the child's rate, usually 15%.

An individual can transfer up to $10,000 per year into a custodial account without facing federal gift taxes. You and your spouse could each make gifts of that amount each year.

But when you think about it, chances are that you will be investing in high-growth stocks and mutual funds before your child is 14 years old. That's when you will have the longest time before you need to tap into the fund for college expenses. Those stocks and funds won't have a lot of earnings or dividends on which you will be liable for taxes. As college looms nearer, you will probably start selling those growth stocks and investing in something a little less risky—and then you will be liable for taxes on capital gains. The tax advantages aren't all they're cracked up to be (although a 15% tax rate might be much better than your regular income tax rate).

Another potential problem with custodial accounts comes when you apply for financial aid. Assets held in your child's name are counted more heavily toward your family's expected contribution to college costs than assets held in your own name. Colleges expect that 35% of a child's assets will be used for college expenses, compared with just 5.6% of the parents' assets. This doesn't mean that you should avoid custodial accounts altogether, but it's probably not a good idea to put all your college savings eggs in this one basket.

Mutual Fund or Brokerage Account

After you have sorted through all the options for college savings, you're likely to find that you will probably have to do most of your college saving and investing in an account held in your own name at a brokerage firm or mutual fund company. If you rely exclusively on one or more of the other options, you are likely to come up short when it comes time to pay that first tuition bill.

You Will Eventually Have to Give Up Control of a Custodial Account

One potential problem with custodial accounts is that the custodian has control of the account only until the child reaches the legal age of adulthood. If your son wants to buy a red Corvette with the money instead of go on to college, there's nothing legally you can do to stop him!

There Are Two Forms of Custodial Accounts

Depending on the state where you live, you can open either a *Uniform Gift to Minors Act* (UGMA) account or a *Uniform Transfer to Minors Act* (UTMA) account. They are both custodial accounts, and have similar features.

The Money in a Custodial Account Can Only Be Used for Specific Purposes

If you're the custodian of a UGMA or UGTA account for your children, you can only withdraw funds for expenses that are "extras," and not the basics that parents must provide their children. Buying a computer is probably a legitimate reason to tap into a custodial account, but paying for groceries is definitely out.

Although There's No Need to Separate College Savings from Other Savings, It Might Help

There's no rule that says you have to have a separate "college" account. You might want to set up a separate account if you think you're prone to tapping into those funds for some other purpose.

Many mutual fund companies and brokers offer college savings plans to help you build up your portfolio. These plans have low minimums and encourage you to contribute regularly to meet your goal.

These accounts have none of the tax advantages of any of the other plans. So why save for college in a regular brokerage or mutual fund account? Consider the actual return of Education Bonds even after the tax savings.

If you invest $10,000 in Savings Bonds that will provide a 5% annual return for 15 years, you will end up with $20,789. If you're in the 28% tax bracket, the federal tax bill on the interest you earned on the bonds would come to $3,021. But because you're using this money for qualified education expenses, you're exempt from paying the $3,021 in taxes.

Now let's say you invest in a growth portfolio of stocks or mutual funds for those same 15 years. You probably won't have many dividends or other income to worry about, because this is a growth portfolio. You will be liable for capital gains at the long-term rate of 20%, however. If you can achieve average annual growth of just 7% in your portfolio, you will end up with $27,590. If you pay 20% of your profits in capital gains taxes, your total taxes paid will be $3,518, leaving you with $24,072. That's a few bucks ahead of where you would be if you had bought Education Bonds, even if you add in the tax savings. If you can do better than 7% in your portfolio, you will be even further ahead.

Prepaid tuition plans and state-sponsored college savings accounts are tied to tuition inflation, which has ranged in recent years from 3% to 10%. Depending on your investing ability and your risk tolerance level, a taxable brokerage or mutual fund account offers the opportunity to grow your savings faster.

Figuring Out How You Are Going to Pay for College

So how are you going to put all these plans together? Now that you know more about the options, you need to put together a plan. You will need to know when you need the money, which plans you will be able to use, how much you need to save, and whether you can tolerate the risk of investing the money or whether you would rather lock in a guaranteed (but lower) rate of return.

When it comes time to start saving and investing for college, just remember: It's more important that you start early, and save and invest regularly, no matter which savings plan you select.

Online Tools to Put Together Your Plan

Besides the College Cost Projector discussed earlier, other tools on the Web can help you map out your plan of attack.

The Office of Individual Investor Services of the National Association of Securities Dealers (NASD) hosts a college-planning calculator on their Web site (`http://investor.nasd.com/it5b.html`). This calculator will show you how much you need to save to pay for your kid's college education.

Let's say your son Nelson has just turned four years old. You've managed to save $3,000 in his college fund, and you would like to know how much more you need to set aside in the next 14 years.

To use the calculator, you need to answer a few questions. Do you expect Nelson to attend a private or public college? The amount of annual college costs will vary significantly depending on your choice. The NASD calculator suggest using $18,000 for a private college and $8,000 for a public institution. You have your hopes set on a private school, so you would enter $18,000.

Next, plug in how much have you already set aside for your child's education, $3,000, and the number of years (14) until Nelson starts college. You hope he will be on the four-year plan, so plug in 4 for the number of years you expect him to attend.

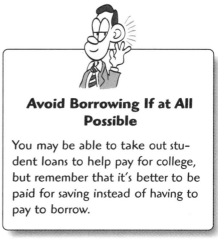

Avoid Borrowing If at All Possible

You may be able to take out student loans to help pay for college, but remember that it's better to be paid for saving instead of having to pay to borrow.

This College Calculator from the NASD's Office of Individual Investor Services requires that you answer just seven questions.

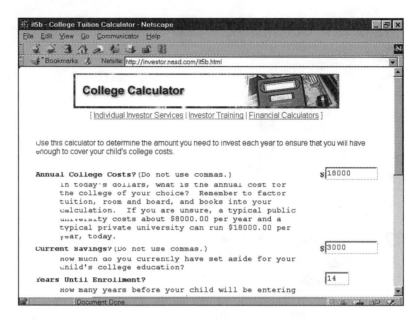

Use this calculator to determine the amount you need to invest each year to ensure that you will have enough to cover your child's college costs.

Annual College Costs? (Do not use commas.) $ 18000

In today's dollars, what is the annual cost for the college of your choice? Remember to factor tuition, room and board, and books into your calculation. If you are unsure, a typical public university costs about $8000.00 per year and a typical private university can run $18000.00 per year, today.

Current Savings? (Do not use commas.) $ 3000

How much do you currently have set aside for your child's college education?

Years Until Enrollment?   14

How many years before your child will be entering

A College Education Is Worth It

Are you wondering whether a college education is worth it after all? College graduates earn an average of $12,000 to $14,000 more per year than high school graduates do. The difference is even greater for those with a graduate or professional degree.

Source: U.S. Census Bureau

Now, estimate the annual return you can make on your college savings portfolio. Although you may be tempted to use a high rate of return, you should use a lower figure to be on the safe side. Because you expect to invest in the stock market, you are hoping for a return of about 11% annually over the long term.

Finally, you can enter an expected inflation rate over the course of your savings period. The calculator suggests 4%. You can also choose whether you wish to inflate your contributions as well. By selecting Yes, the amount you need to save each year will be increased by the inflation rate you selected.

Click the **Calculate** button and you will receive an outline of how much you must save each year from now until Nelson enrolls in college.

```
College Tuition Calculator - Results - Netscape                    _□×
File  Edit  View  Go  Communicator  Help
   ⟲  ↻  ⟳  ⌂  ⟐  ⤓  ⬇  ⛫  ▣                                      N
   Bookmarks  ⚓  Netsite: http://investor.nasd.com/cgi-bin/fin_calc.pl        ▼
College Tuition Calculator                                              ▲
▬▬▬▬▬▬▬▬▬▬▬▬▬▬▬▬▬▬▬▬▬▬▬▬▬▬▬▬▬▬▬▬▬▬▬▬▬▬▬▬▬▬▬▬▬▬▬▬▬▬▬

    Annual College Costs:           $18,000.00
    Years Until Enrollment:         14
    Number of Years Enrolled:       4
    Current College Savings:        $3,000.00
    Annual Yield:                   11.000%
    Predicted Inflation:            4.000%
    Annual Contribution             $2,362.60

    The tuition column below shows what the tuition costs are
    likely to be by the time your child enters college.  This
    supposes that the annual tuition will increase each year
    at a rate matching the inflation rate.

    Year        Deposit        Tuition        Balance
    ----        -------        -------        ----------
    Now           0.00           0.00           3,000.00
    1998       2,362.60          0.00           5,692.60
    1999       2,457.10          0.00           8,775.89
    2000       2,555.39          0.00          12,296.63       ▼
 Document: Done                               ▣ ▧ ⬚ ⬛ ✎
```

The College Tuition Calculator tells you how much you need to save and invest each year to cover your child's college costs.

In this example, in 14 years the cost of one year of Nelson's college would be $31,170.22. You need to save $2362.60 a year to be able to pay for the entire bill, increasing that amount by 4% each year to keep up with inflation.

If you spread that $2,362.60 evenly throughout the year, you have to save $45.44 a week and get a return of 11% on your portfolio.

You can experiment with various rates of return, inflation, and costs to see different scenarios. If you have more than one child, you will have to run each projection separately and then do some addition to figure out how much you need to save. After you know how much you need to save, however, the final step is to get started.

Your College Fund Will Influence Your College Selection

The larger your college fund, the greater the choices your children will have when it's time for them to select a school.

The Least You Need to Know

➤ College tuition, fees, and other expenses are likely to increase at a rate faster than inflation. You can use a calculator on the Web to see just how high costs may be when your child is ready to enroll in college.

➤ Many plans are available to help you save for college, from state-sponsored prepaid tuition plans to the new Education IRA. You will probably need to use several of these plans and accounts to reach your college savings goal. Some plans are better suited for "non-investors"; others are more appropriate for those willing to tolerate the risks of investing.

➤ You can build a plan using a tool on the Web that will demonstrate how much you need to save and invest regularly to reach your goal. Investing in the stock market, either in stocks or mutual funds, will probably need to be part of your plan.

Planning to Take Care of the "I Wants"

In This Chapter

➤ Build a plan to meet short-term goals

➤ Learn why the stock market is not suited for goals that don't have a long-term horizon

➤ Find the best products for your short-term savings

Funding your retirement and saving for a college education are two goals that are (or at least should be) essential components of your overall financial plan. Chances are that you have some other goals in life besides helping your kids through college and making a comfortable retirement plan for yourself. Maybe you have your eye on an 18-foot sailboat, or you want to throw a big wedding bash for your daughter (or daughters).

You can include these other nonessential goals in your saving and investing plan, too, but you need to approach them somewhat differently than your long-term savings. The following sections introduce you to some Web tools that can help you create the best plan for your short-term goals.

Planning for a Home, Boat, or Dream Vacation

No matter what goal you're saving for, you will still need a roadmap to get you there. You need to figure out the amount of money you will require, how much you will need to save, how much you can earn on your savings, and how you will put together all these components.

Inflation Means That You Will Need to Save More to Meet Your Goal

Even when planning for short-term goals, you can't completely ignore the impact of inflation. It's a good idea to build in a little bit extra when you're estimating the total cost of whatever goal you're trying to reach. That way you will help ensure that you won't come up short.

A good place to start is the savings calculators at FinanCenter.com (`http://www.financenter.com/savings.htm`). It offers several "ClickCalcs," interactive calculators that do all the math based on a few figures you provide.

Select the calculator titled "What will it take to save for a car, home, etc.?" Let's say you would like to save $10,000 to buy a new car over the next five years, and you have already got $1,000 in the bank. In the appropriate places on the calculator, fill in the amounts requested: the total amount you need ($10,000) and the amount of your current savings you can invest right now ($1,000).

Next, you need to estimate how much you can put away each month—let's say $100—and the number of months until you need the money, 60 (5 years times 12 months in a year equals 60 months).

Then, estimate the rate of return you can achieve on your savings. You should probably start with about 5%. (You will learn later in this chapter how to get the best returns for your short-term savings.)

Use FinanCenter.com's savings calculator to figure out how much you will need to save regularly to meet your goal.

![Netscape browser window showing the FinanCenter savings calculator titled "What will it take to save for a car, home, etc.?" with input fields: Total Amount You Need $10000, Amount You Can Invest Now $1000, Amount You Can Save Monthly $100, Months You Wish to Save 60, Return You Can Earn 5%, Your Federal Tax Rate 28%, Your State Tax Rate 8%]

Finally, enter your federal and state tax rates. This will give you an idea of how much you will have to pay in taxes on your earnings each year. You can enter zeroes in these fields if you like, if you're not worried about the effect of taxes on your savings, or if you aren't going to be paying any taxes out of those funds. (Some people make a point not to touch any of the money they have set aside for a specific purpose, not even to pay taxes.) In this example, a federal tax rate of 28% and a state rate of 8% were entered.

After you have entered all these variables, click the small arrow in the bottom-right corner of the screen. You will be presented with the results of your plan—including any shortfalls you might be facing—and some suggested courses of action.

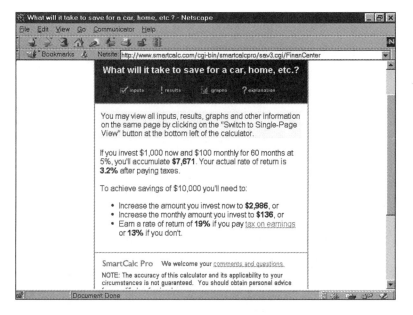

The FinanCenter.com savings calculator will project any shortfall you may face in meeting your goal and provide suggestions for getting back on track.

In this example, your $100 a month won't get you to your goal in five years. If you increase your monthly savings to $136, or increase your initial investment to $2,986, however, you will score a bullseye!

You can try different scenarios, perhaps trying to reach your goal in three years rather than five, or saving much more on a monthly basis. Just don't use the Back button in your browser to try a new situation—you will lose all the data you have already entered. Instead, click the Inputs link at the top of the calculator, and you will go to a screen where you can make adjustments.

For more in-depth planning, Quicken.com has a section called "Life Events" (http://www.quicken.com/life_events) that provides tools for budgeting and saving for the big milestones of life. Paying for a big wedding can be quite a drain on your bank account unless you plan ahead. And ask any proud new parent about the costs of having a baby, and you're likely to be deluged with awe-inspiring tales. Quicken.com's resources can help you create a plan and keep your finances under control.

Where to Save and Invest for Your Short-Term Goals

After you have figured out how much you need to save, you can turn your attention to finding the best places to stash the cash. Obviously, with a short-term goal, you want the highest return for the least amount of risk. Where do you turn?

Before you begin your online search, stop for a moment to take this quick quiz. Let's say you just won the lottery at the county fair, and are driving home in your Ford F150 pickup with a picnic basket filled with $5,000 in ones, fives, and tens. Do you

A. Stuff the cash under your mattress?

B. Stuff the cash in your cookie jar?

C. Bury the cash in a Mason jar in the backyard?

D. Put it in the bank?

The answer should be fairly obvious, but just in case, the right answer is *D*. The problem with answer *A* is that lumpy mattresses make for a bad night's sleep, even neglecting the fact that U.S. currency is notoriously combustible in the event of a fire. *B* can't be right; where do you think the burglars will look first when they rob your house (or at least second, after they look under your mattress)? And you need to remember the specific location of choice *C*, particularly when the man with the backhoe is about to dig the new hole to relocate your septic tank.

You have to face all sorts of risks like these whenever you're dealing with your savings. You may have other dreams you would like to fulfill, but you need to tackle them with a somewhat different strategy.

Here's why. When it comes to investing in the stock market, you must have a long-term approach. You need to have at least five years for your investment in stocks or mutual funds to really pay off and to weather any occasional storms the markets may provide.

As a result, if you need access to your savings in less than five years, you probably shouldn't be putting your money into the stock market. There's just too much risk involved, and it might not sit too well with

Don't Shoot Yourself in the Foot with Your Long-Term Savings

Don't make the mistake of thinking that putting all your money in the bank is enough of a plan to help you reach your financial goals. Investors who won't need to touch their money for 10 to 20 years, and who are too conservative, are shooting themselves in the feet. They are likely to fall far short when retirement arrives. For short-term goals, however, a bank might be just the place.

your family if you have to postpone moving to a bigger home because the stock market declined 30% and you no longer have enough for a down payment.

You Need Time for Your Savings to Really Grow

Way back in Chapter 2, you learned about compound interest and how it works. Here's a refresher: When you invest for many, many years, most of what you end up with in your portfolio will have come from the profits that you earned over the years (and the profits earned on those profits). On the other hand, when you have your money working for only a few years, the biggest part of your account will come from your own contributions, the money you socked away. The conclusion? A heavy-duty savings plan is required when you have short-term goals. It's the only way you will get there.

For short-term goals, you will have to put your money to work in some other way. Besides a savings account at your neighborhood bank, you might consider purchasing a bank CD with a great rate that you found offered on the Internet.

Although those CDs you listen to in your stereo or use in your computer may be more fun, bank CDs can make you money! Of course, these CDs are Certificates of Deposit, financial instruments sold by banks with a specific term (typically from 6 months to 10 years) and a fixed interest rate.

The main advantage of CDs is that you can lock in an interest rate and know exactly what your return will be while you hold the CD. But that's also the disadvantage—if interest rates should increase while you hold your CD, you will miss out on that higher rate of return.

CDs have termination fees if you close out the CD before maturity, penalizing you for your bad manners. These penalties can wipe out much of your gains, so be sure that you're willing to lock in to a fixed-term CD before you buy.

Although many individuals are content dealing with their personal bank when they're in the market for a CD, it might pay you to shop around in your community for the best deal you can get. Or you can search for rates from institutions across the country using the Web. One of the most useful things you can do on the Web, in fact, is to comparison shop for the best rates for your short-term savings from banks all over the country.

How to Tell Whether a Bank Is Legitimate

More and more banks are offering products on the Internet. Without the ability to visit a branch, however, how can you tell whether a bank is legitimate or an outright fraud? One way is to verify that the bank has a legitimate charter (a license to do business from the state or federal government), and that it is a member of the Federal Deposit Insurance Corporation (FDIC). The FDIC provides a database on its Web site (`http://www.fdic.gov/consumer/suspicious`) that enables you to search for any bank and determine whether it is properly authorized to do business. The site also includes other helpful tips about how to avoid suspicious Internet banks.

At least one organization tracks the interest rates and other savings rates offered by banks all over the United States, for both Certificates of Deposit and regular savings accounts. Bank Rate Monitor (`http://www.bankrate.com`) will provide a list of banks that offer savings products with the best return.

Search for the best CD rates from banks all across the country at the Bank Rate Monitor's Web site.

Select **Savings** from the menu on the site, and review the 100 highest yields from banks nationwide. If you prefer to do business with a bank in your area, enter your state and community, the product you're interested in (CD, checking, savings, or money markets), and the length of time you're willing to invest. You will see a list of banks and rates that meet your criteria.

Besides CDs, another option for your short-term savings might get you a slightly higher return: buying shares in a special kind of mutual fund called a *money market fund*. Of course, the downside is that you won't get a guaranteed rate like you would with a CD.

Would you buy a mutual fund with a share price that never changes? That's what money market funds are—mutual funds with a share price of $1 that invest in short-term, high-quality securities in an effort to generate current income for investors.

Money markets are great for investors looking for a safe place to park some cash. You can redeem your shares at any time, and many money market funds offer investors check-writing privileges. And you can generally get a higher yield than you can with a regular bank account.

Let Your Broker Sweep Up for You

Usually, brokerage firms automatically invest any cash in their clients' accounts into shares of money market funds. Many will "sweep" any cash into these funds on a daily basis, ensuring that your money is always working for you.

There are two types of money funds: taxable and tax-free. Taxable funds invest in Treasuries and other nongovernment short-term debt obligations. Tax-free funds invest in municipal and state short-term debt obligations, and offer lower yields than taxable funds as a result. Usually, investors with very high incomes would choose tax-free funds to avoid the extra tax bite at their higher tax rates.

IBC Financial Data (http://www.ibcdata.com) is a terrific resource for unearthing the best current money market rates. The site's Money Fund Selector walks you through the process of finding the best money market funds, whether your primary concern is safety, tax savings, or yield. Select from the Top Money Funds, or browse the funds by category in the Money Funds Listing section. The site also provides more information on money funds than you ever thought possible!

Money Market Funds Are Growing in Popularity with Investors

The first money market fund, The Reserve Fund, began in 1972. Today you can choose from more than 1,300 money market funds, which hold total assets of over $1 trillion dollars.

Source: IBC Financial Data

IBC Financial Data can tell you all you need to know about money market funds—including finding the best rates.

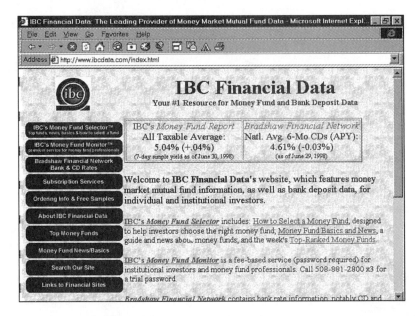

The Least You Need to Know

➤ You need to determine your saving goals, and then build a plan to help you get there. Use a calculator on the Web to figure out how much you need to save on a regular basis.

➤ Decide where to invest your savings. You will probably want to buy a Certificate of Deposit or money market mutual fund. You can find the best returns by searching on the Internet.

➤ No matter how you plan to reach your short-term goals, the key to success is the ability to save money on a regular basis and put it away where you won't touch it.

Chapter 24

More Investments to Consider

In This Chapter

➤ The hard, cold truth about options and commodities, and why you should avoid them

➤ Where to begin to search for information about bonds on the Web

➤ Questions you should ask before you invest

You can find thousands and thousands of investment-related sites on the Web, each one vying for your dollars. So how do you make sense of everything that's out there? It's not easy, but here are some tips to help you ferret out the truth—whether it's an opportunity to invest in commodities, options, or bonds, or some other exotic offer you may come across on the Web.

How to Lose a Bundle Fast in Commodities

In recent years, a whole new category of outrageous sports has become popular, from street luge to skysurfing to downhill inline skating. These sports make pro football look downright tame in comparison. These events are known as *extreme sports* because the risks involved go way beyond the traditional sporting life.

In the same way, it's probably a good idea to put commodities and options into the category of *extreme investing*. Some of the material in this chapter could be so hazardous to your long-term financial plan that it ought to carry a warning label, something like this:

Caution! Investing in commodities and futures can result in really, *really* big losses of money.

We're operating under a yellow caution flag right now for a couple of reasons.

First, on the Complete Idiot's Guide Investing Risk Scale, commodities and options jump off the top of the charts. In general, investing in derivatives is risky business. How risky? Consider this: When you purchase a stock or mutual fund, the maximum amount that you can lose is the amount that you have invested. A stock can fall in price until it's worth just a few pennies; as a common stockholder, however, you have no obligation to invest any more of your money in a bankrupt business.

When you invest in commodities and options, however, it's possible that you could lose *more* than the total of your investment. *Remember* this point, especially if you find an attractive Web site that seems to lay out a clear plan for you to make a lot of money trading commodities.

Second, any Web site that suggests that beginners can make a fortune trading options or commodities should be viewed with suspicion. It's certainly possible that you could be a profitable commodities trader, but it's also possible that you could win the lottery or wake up to find Ed McMahon and Dick Clark on your doorstep with a juicy check made out in your name. It's possible, all right, but it's sure not very likely.

If you decide to investigate commodity trading, even after these warnings, you need to understand a lot about how they work. You need to understand the different commodities that are traded on futures exchanges all across the United States (and the world). Each exchange specializes in one or more commodities, including contracts on black tiger shrimp, butter, cheddar cheese, cocoa, coffee, corn, fresh pork bellies, and platinum (to name a few). Just about any raw material can be sold as a commodity, as long as a formalized market is established on a futures exchange.

Commodity exchanges (and the entire commodity trading business) are regulated by the federal government's U.S. Commodity Futures Trading Commission. The agency protects market participants against manipulation, abusive trade practices, and fraud.

The Commission's Web site (http://www.cftc.gov) is a good place to start if you want to learn more about commodity futures trading. The site contains educational articles and brochures, including "Futures and Options: What You Should Know Before You Trade" and "Glossary: The Language of the Futures Industry," as well as notices of enforcement actions against misbehaving market players.

The National Futures Association (http://www.nfa.futures.org) was authorized by the CFTC and is a self-regulatory organization for the commodity futures industry. All commodity brokers and dealers must be NFA members, and the Association makes sure that all members follow high standards of conduct. The group publishes a number of free booklets that you can request from its site. You can also learn at its clearinghouse of disciplinary information about the firms and individuals involved in the futures industry, and how you can check out a broker or firm before you do business with them.

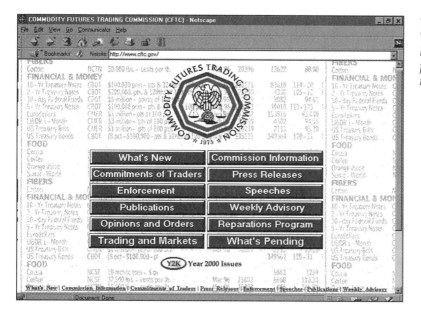

The Commodity Futures Trading Commission regulates the commodity futures and options market.

Are Options a Choice for You?

Options are first cousins to commodity futures, in that both exist only on paper. Options provide the holder with the right, but not the obligation, to buy or sell a certain security (usually stock, index, bond, or a currency) at a specific price within a specific period.

A stock option contract represents 100 shares of the underlying stock (an index option's value is determined by multiplying the index by $100). When you buy or sell an option, the price you pay for the right to eventually buy or sell the underlying shares is called the *premium*.

Unlike commodity futures, the extent of your potential losses when trading in options is the amount of the premium you paid. Commodity futures are an obligation to buy or sell the underlying asset; options are a right that you can exercise or not—it's your option! If the price of the stock or index didn't move in the direction that you predicted, you merely ignore the option when it expires.

One thing you will notice when you get interested in options is that you will see the same warning label popping up all over the place. The companies in the industry have all agreed to make sure that individual investors understand the risks involved with options trading. The notice reads like this:

Options involve risks and are not suitable for all investors. Prior to buying or selling an option, a person must receive a copy of "Characteristics and Risks of Standardized Options." Copies of this document may be obtained from your broker or from any of the exchanges listed above. A prospectus, which discusses the role of the Options Clearing Corporation, is also available without charge on request. Send your request to the Options Clearing Corporation, 440 S. LaSalle St., Suite 2400, Chicago, IL 60605, or to any exchange on which options are traded.

The Difference Between Employee Stock Options and Exchange-Traded Options

Don't confuse employee stock options, such as those that your company might issue to you, with stock options that trade on an exchange. Employee stock options generally can't be sold, and so they are only valuable to you (and you only) when you cash them in, and as long as the stock price exceeds the exercise price (but you wouldn't cash them in if the price were lower than the exercise price).

You can visit the Options Clearing Corporation's Web site at http://www.optionsclearing.com and read or download a copy of this booklet. It's required reading. While you're at the OCC's Web site, be sure to read another of its publications, "Understanding Stock Options."

The Options Industry Council is another Web site you should review (http://www.optionscentral.com) if you're interested in options. This industry group wants to help you learn about options, and will even send you a free videotape, software, and guide on request. Click **Resource Center** to explore all the information on the Council's Web site.

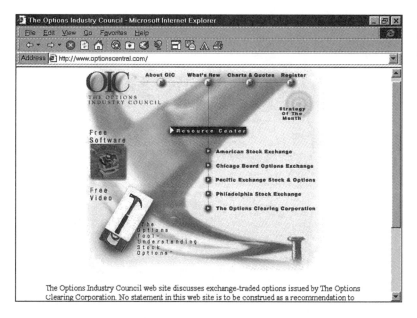

The Options Industry Council can help you learn more about options.

The Options Industry Council web site discusses exchange-traded options issued by The Options Clearing Corporation. No statement in this web site is to be construed as a recommendation to

Blessed Be the Bonds That Yield

Bonds are another security that you might like to invest in at some point in your lifetime. When you get right down to it, a bond is really nothing more an IOU. When you buy a bond, you are lending money to a corporation or government agency, or to a local or state government, or perhaps even to Uncle Sam! In return, the borrower agrees to repay the loan to you with interest.

Although the basic idea about bonds is pretty simple, there are thousands of variations on this idea. Bonds that are offered for sale to the public can have quite different features. These differences stem from such factors as who is offering the bond for sale (a corporation, a municipal government, or the federal government, for instance), the terms for paying interest (each month or all at once at the end of the bond's life), and many other factors.

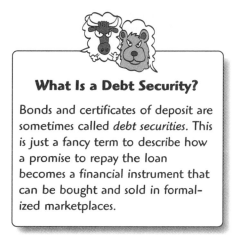

What Is a Debt Security?

Bonds and certificates of deposit are sometimes called *debt securities*. This is just a fancy term to describe how a promise to repay the loan becomes a financial instrument that can be bought and sold in formalized marketplaces.

If you would like to learn more about bonds and the countless varieties, or about how bonds might fit in your portfolio, the Bond Market Association stands ready to help (http://www.investinginbonds.com). The Association is a trade industry group for banks and securities firms involved in underwriting and selling bonds. They publish guides to bond investing, both on their site and in booklet form, that answer just about every question you could have about bonds.

313

The Bond Market Association can help you learn about investing in bonds.

The Bond Market Association's Web site is outstanding, and is filled with information. But its site is really unusual when it comes to researching bonds online. Compared to the plentiful amount of information available on the Web about stocks, mutual funds, commodities, and options, only a handful of sites are devoted to bonds. Are bonds that boring?

Not really, but a couple of reasons conspire to limit the amount of information you can find on the Internet about bonds.

The first is that you can determine what a bond is worth with a fair degree of certainty. The prices of stocks, on the other hand, rise and fall due to a multitude of factors. After you know when a bond comes due (its maturity date), the interest rate it pays, and its face value, most experts will agree pretty closely on the value of that bond.

Without a lot of differing opinions about the prices of stocks, you won't find people who are interested in arguing about bonds in the same way. And you won't find many quote servers that offer prices of bonds on the Web.

The U.S. Bond Market Is Enormous!

The bond market in the United States is the world's largest securities market. It's even bigger than the U.S. stock market! The total value of the U.S. bond market in 1996 was more than $11.0 trillion, compared to $8.9 trillion for the stock market.

Source: The Bond Market Association

Another reason for the lack of information about bonds is that, in most cases, you need to work with a broker if you want to include bonds in your portfolio. Sure, you can buy Savings Bonds or Treasury Bonds directly from the government, but if you want to buy municipal bonds or corporate bonds, you need to employ the services of a full-service broker. And full-service brokers have been slow to provide any kind of research on their Web sites—and that includes information about bonds.

Discount brokers are not much better when it comes to bond information. You can get current prices of corporate bonds from the Charles Schwab Web site (`http://www.schwab.com`) if you are a client of that discount broker. DLJ Direct (`http://www.dljdirect.com`) allows clients to purchase Treasury Bonds directly on its Web site.

One fairly new entry into the Web investing world is an online brokerage firm devoted to bonds, TaxFreeBond.com (`http://www.taxfreebond.com`). The company manages a searchable database of bonds on its Web site, so you can peruse the available bonds to find potential candidates for your portfolio.

Another way you can use the Web if you are a bond investor is to learn more about the Treasury Direct program of the U.S. government.

A Crash Course in Treasury Debt Obligations

The United States government issues several different kinds of "debt obligations," including Bonds, Bills, and Notes. They are classified according to their maturities:

Treasury Bills have maturities of one year or less.

Treasury Notes have maturities of 2 to 10 years.

Treasury Bonds have maturities greater than 10 years (and as much as 30 years).

Treasury Bonds, Bills, and Notes are all issued in face values of $1,000, although each type of security has different purchase minimums. Investors often shorten the word *Treasury* to just the letter *T* when referring to these bonds. Therefore, Treasury Bonds are known as T-Bonds, Treasury Notes are called T-Notes, and Treasury Bills are T-Bills. Treasury Bills are issued in three maturities.

Administered by the Bureau of the Public Debt (`http://www.publicdebt.treas.gov`), Treasury Direct is a way for independent individual investors to buy Treasury Bonds, Bills, and Notes directly from the Department of the Treasury in their regular auctions.

The Bureau's Web site is a complete repository of information about bonds issued by the U.S. Treasury. You can also review the results of recent auctions that are posted on the site, along with the schedule of future auctions.

Everything you always wanted to know about Treasury debt obligations, Savings Bonds, and the Treasury Direct program is available from the Bureau of the Public Debt.

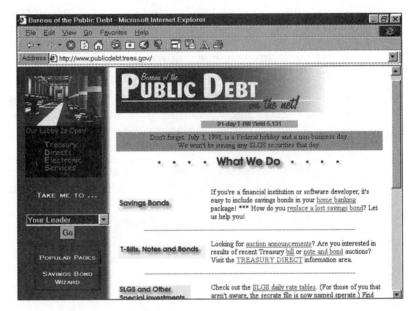

Ten Things to Consider *Before* You Invest in Anything!

Now that you're nearly finished reading this book, does that prepare you to tackle any potential investment and wrench the profit from it? Unfortunately, no. For every legitimate investment that you will find on the Web, there are dozens of shady deals, overly complex schemes, and probably inappropriate "opportunities" that you should avoid like poison ivy.

At some point in your investing career, you may be offered the chance to "invest" in tax-lien certificates, eel farms, ostrich farms, or time-share real estate. You may be offered a surefire method of investing in "rolling stocks" or a "guaranteed" program to profit from seasonal commodity trading. Some investors may find these schemes to be profitable, or even lucrative. But chances are just as good that you will see your investment move right down the drain.

Most investors do just fine sticking to stocks, bonds, mutual funds, or perhaps real estate. But if you're ever tempted by some flashy opportunity to "make money fast," here are some final words to help you protect yourself. Answer these questions honestly, and if you find yourself trying hard to justify the answers, you should recognize that as a sign of trouble:

1. Is this an investment or a gamble? If you find yourself saying, "Oh, what the heck!" as you write out a check, you're probably throwing good money out the window. Investing isn't a game of chance, and when you invest with a sound long-term strategy, the odds are overwhelmingly in your favor. If you sense the odds tipping against you, think twice. And if you want to gamble, book a trip to Las Vegas and get it out of your system!

2. How does this opportunity fit into your investment plan? Is it part of your retirement strategy, to help you reach your college savings goal, or are you just "taking a flier" with your hard-earned cash?

3. Do you have reasonable expectations for a return on your investment? Greed is a powerful force, and sometimes your greed can make you think that an out-landish promise of profits is reasonable. Remember that you can't "make money fast" without facing up to a whole lot of risk.

4. Who regulates the market in this security or opportunity? Most investments in the United States are regulated by a federal or state government agency. That means that you can verify the legitimacy of any offer with the appropriate authorities. Find out who regulates a particular investment and check it out.

5. Who is the individual or organization selling this investment? What are their credentials? Do they need to be licensed or registered with the state or federal government or other regulatory agency? Are they properly registered or licensed?

6. What happens if you change your mind? It's a simple question, but find out what happens after you write the check if you decide to pull out. Can you get your investment back? Is there a penalty? Or are you locked in for a specific period of time?

7. What happens if you need to sell your investment? Is there a market where this investment is regularly bought and sold by other investors? Maybe you can make a bundle by investing in an ostrich farm (although that's dubious); but if you need to sell your investment, where are you going to go to find potential buyers? Are you going to have to find a buyer on your own?

8. Does this opportunity require you to sell anything to other people? *Multilevel marketing* is the term used to describe businesses that are built on individuals who sell to others, and then move up the pyramid to become distributors. Amway is the best known example of a multilevel marketing firm. You shouldn't confuse these with investing, however. Anytime you're required to sell to others to realize a profit should be taken as a sign that you should take a rain check.

9. What did your lawyer say about the paperwork that you were asked to sign? You did have a lawyer look it over, didn't you? Don't sign anything without having an attorney review the documents first.

10. Is it okay if you "sleep on it" for a day or a week? There's no opportunity so great that it won't wait for you—and there will be plenty of others down the road, too. If anyone tries to use high-pressure tactics to get you to act right away, it's time to beat a hasty retreat and think about it, starting with question #1!

If any of these questions start to bring on "reasonable doubt" about the "investment" that you're considering, that's a good enough sign that you should probably move on. There is plenty to learn about investing in stocks and mutual funds—enough to keep you busy and occupied for a lifetime! After you have mastered stocks and funds, then (and only then) should you consider alternative investments.

The Least You Need to Know

➤ Commodity and options trading are risky and probably not suitable for beginners. Period.

➤ The Internet is not home to an abundance of information about bonds, although you can learn about the Treasury Direct program on the Web. Some brokers are beginning to make it easier for investors to access information or purchase bonds online.

➤ Most investors will never have a need to invest in anything other than stocks, bonds, or mutual funds. If you have an urge to expand the repertoire of your portfolio, you should ask some important questions—*before* you invest.

Index